Social Psychology an Consumer Culture

MW00773622

Social Psychology and Theories of Consumer Culture: A Political Economy Perspective presents a critical analysis of the leading positions in social psychology from the perspective of classical and contemporary theories of consumer culture. The analysis seeks to expand social psychological theory by focusing on the interface between modern Western culture (consumer culture) and social behaviour.

McDonald and Wearing argue that if social psychology is to play a meaningful role in solving some of society's most pressing problems – such as global warming, obesity, addiction, alienation and exclusion – then it needs to incorporate a more comprehensive understanding and analysis of consumer culture.

Wide-ranging and challenging, the book offers a fresh insight into critical social psychology appropriate for upper undergraduate and postgraduate courses in personality, social psychology, critical and applied psychology. It will also appeal to those working in clinical, counselling, abnormal, and environmental psychology and anyone with an interest in the integration of social psychology and theories of consumer culture.

Matthew McDonald is a visiting research fellow in the Graduate School of Psychology, Assumption University, Bangkok, and a chartered member of the British Psychological Society. He is the author and co-author of a number of books, the most recent including *Critical Social Psychology: An Introduction* (2nd edition; with Brendan Gough and Marjella McFadden) and *Epiphanies: An Existential Philosophical and Psychological Inquiry*.

Stephen Wearing is an associate professor in the Management Discipline Group at the University of Technology, Sydney. He is the author, co-author and editor of a number of books, including *Tourist Cultures: Identity, Place and the Traveller* (with Deborah Stevenson and Tamara Young) and *Journeys of Discovery* (with Kevin Lyons).

Social Psychology and Theories of Consumer Culture

A Political Economy Perspective

Matthew McDonald and Stephen Wearing

LONDON AND NEW YORK

First published 2013
by Routledge
27 Church Road, Hove, East Sussex BN3 2FA

Simultaneously published in the USA and Canada
by Routledge
711 Third Avenue, New York, NY 10017

Routledge is an imprint of the Taylor & Francis Group, an informa business

British Library Cataloguing in Publication Data
A catalogue record for this book is available from the British Library

Library of Congress Cataloging in Publication Data
McDonald, Matthew.
Social psychology and theories of consumer culture : a political economy
perspective / Matthew McDonald & Stephen Wearing.
    p. cm.
    Includes bibliographical references.
    1. Consumption (Economics) – Social aspects. 2. Social psychology
    I. Wearing, Stephen. II. Title.
    HC79.C6M386 2013
    306.3–dc23   2012036636

ISBN: 978-0-415-56003-0 (hbk)
ISBN: 978-0-415-81203-0 (pbk)
ISBN: 978-0-203-06803-8 (ebk)

Typeset in Times New Roman
by HWA Text and Data Management, London

Printed and bound by CPI Group (UK) Ltd, Croydon, CR0 4YY

Contents

Preface

The idea for this book came to me (Matthew McDonald) after lecturing my first semester of undergraduate social psychology at Roehampton University, London, in 2006. Having taken a course in undergraduate social psychology as a student ten years previously, I felt the subject matter failed to engage with contemporary social forces and the implications of these for understanding social behaviour in all of its complexity. I wanted to know how social behaviour was influenced by political and economic forces like neoliberalism, cultural values and globalisation, as well as understanding what role social psychology might play in solving some of the world's most pressing problems such as climate change, obesity, mental illness, alienation and urban/suburban planning. Unfortunately, my experience as a lecturer of social psychology mirrored my experience as a student. However, as a lecturer I had more freedom to set the syllabus and was therefore in a position to raise some of the issues that are the basis of this book. Yet I was still constrained by a disciplinary framework that rarely ventured into these vital topics and so I found myself turning to other social science disciplines such as political economy, sociology, media studies, geography and history in order to fill in the gaps for my students.

For both Stephen and me, one of the most fascinating contemporary social forces and the one with which modern Western societies have become synonymous is consumer culture. In our combined years of reading, teaching and research in the social sciences we have always believed that consumer culture has never been given the significance it deserves by social psychologists (despite some of the links which exist between social psychology and consumer psychology). Our book views consumer culture from the perspective of political economy, so those readers hoping for an inquiry into social psychology's empirical and theoretical influence on the cognitive, affective and behavioural responses to products and services, and to their marketing and advertising, will find little to satisfy them here. So what is meant by a political economy perspective? Simply that we seek to explore consumer culture and its links with aspects of politics and economics in contemporary Western society, and how these influence and shape social behaviour at the individual and group level.

Our inquiry is also heavily based in theory. We assume from the outset that all social science is theory in one way or another and that a critical evaluation of any body of knowledge is only truly 'critical' if it sets out to question the underpinning assumptions (its theories and philosophies) upon which it rests. This includes a field's theory of knowledge, ontology, language, culture, power, politics and ethics. Yet we have tried to avoid where we can focusing exclusively on abstract theoretical and philosophical analysis, so we have attempted throughout the book to use examples to support our arguments. While our inquiry explores a range of concepts and theories from various perspectives, it is designed to assist social psychologists to better understand consumer culture, how it intersects with and is critical of the leading positions in the subdiscipline, and how an understanding and greater incorporation of consumer culture into its leading theories would enable social psychology to once again contribute to understanding and helping to solve some of humanity's most pressing problems.

Matthew McDonald and Stephen Wearing

Acknowledgements

We are grateful to many people whose support and assistance made this book possible. In particular we wish to thank Dave Peters for his research assistance on Chapter 6, Simon Walbrook for introducing us to the documentary film-maker and writer Adam Curtis, Michael Wearing for his comments on Chapter 2, and Desley Deacon for her comments on our interpretation of feminist theory.

Most especially I (Matthew McDonald) wish to thank my wife Susmita Das, who provided invaluable editorial assistance, for her love and support every step of the way. Without her this book would not have been possible.

1 Introduction

Social psychology and consumer culture

The purpose of this book is to critically analyse and expand the leading positions in social psychology from the perspective of classical and contemporary theories of consumer culture. We argue that a more comprehensive understanding of consumer culture would enable social psychology to once again play a meaningful role in solving some of the dilemmas that modern Western discourses, institutions and practices pose for individuals, groups and society at large, such as climate change, obesity, mental illness, alienation and urban/suburban planning.

We use the term social psychology in our inquiry to refer to 'psychological social psychology' as distinct from 'sociological social psychology'. The other important distinction we make when using the term social psychology is that we are implicitly referring to 'mainstream' social psychology as opposed to 'critical social psychology' (e.g. Gough and McFadden, 2001; Hepburn, 2003; Ibanez and Iniguez, 1997; Tuffin, 2004). Much of our inquiry critiques mainstream social psychology; as such we frequently draw on insights from the critical social psychology literature, which provides an alternative perspective that supports our thesis.

The discipline of psychology, and by extension social psychology, has typically focused most of its attention on *production* (Moscovici, 1972), whereas *consumption* and its culture has often been trivialised (Kasser and Kanner, 2004). One reason for this is that production in the form of work, commerce and industry is emphasised by governments, policy-makers and academics, through legislation, public policy, research and its funding. In contrast, consumption is seen as an inconsequential activity engaged in during one's leisure time.[1] In the Protestant tradition consumption and leisure are seen as indulgent, decadent, feminine pursuits not worthy of serious intellectual analysis (Mackay, 1997; Ritzer *et al.*, 2001; Scanlon, 2000b).

The activity of consumption has not been completely ignored by psychology. However, its research and theory on this topic is narrow in scope, focusing on the cognitive, affective and behavioural responses to products and services, and to their marketing and advertising – topics that collectively make up the field of 'consumer psychology' (Jacoby, 2001). Consumer psychology takes a 'micro perspective' on questions of consumption, producing a set of micro-theories on phenomena such as memory, perception, attitudes and decision-making. Topics of study include consumer preferences for colour combinations, whether an overweight waitress makes you eat more and the success of hybrids involving dissimilar products.

In contrast, the inquiry presented in this book takes a 'macro perspective' by focusing on the *culture* of consumption and its links with political economy.[2] Our focus on political economy is related more specifically to the role that neoliberal economics has played and currently plays in the maintenance of consumer culture in the West – a topic we will explore in more detail later in this chapter. Our focus on the broader political and economic structures of consumer culture will lead us into discussions on globalisation, commodification, lifestyle choice, the mass media, advertising, urban/suburban planning and alienation.

Research on economics and consumption in psychology generally falls within the remit of social psychology (Lunt, 1995). However, the uninitiated student of social psychology, whether at high school, college or university, would be hard pressed to find any reference to consumer culture in an introductory social psychology textbook. As Kasser and Kanner comment:

> the discipline of psychology has been largely reticent about consumer culture . . . issues of consumerism, commercialization, and materialism have generally not entered the science or practice of psychology as key variables to be understood.
>
> (2004: 4)

Kasser and Kanner argue there are three main reasons for this. The first is that psychology has been slow to focus on variables outside the individual person, focusing on intra-psychic processes instead[3] (Kasser and Kanner, 2004: 4). This is reflected in social psychology's emphasis on 'social cognition' (Reicher and Wetherell, 1999). Social cognition analyses social behaviour through individual cognitive processes such as perception, memory, thinking and feeling. The emphasis on social cognition is complemented by a narrowly conceived methodological approach which stipulates that research incorporate experimental designs, the carrying out of multiple study packages and the prioritisation of mediational analysis through the use of secondary measures (Cialdini, 2009). Social psychology's focus on these elements and modes of research has led to the production of knowledge that rarely asks and answers socially relevant questions.

Social psychology's current obsession with social cognition is a departure from its traditional mission. It started out analysing and seeking to provide solutions to some of the most pressing social issues of the early to mid-twentieth century. Some of these included the Great Depression, immigration and political ideologies such as communism, fascism and democracy (Greenwood, 2004a; Pancer, 1997). Kurt Lewin, a pioneering social psychologist, favoured an applied focus, seeking to conduct research and generate theory that would influence public and social policy for the betterment and welfare of society (Moscovici, 1972;

Pancer, 1997). However, during the 1950s and 1960s there was a move away from an applied focus in social psychology as it came to be seen as atheoretical and unscientific.[4] The response to this seeming problem was to test theory under more rigorous conditions, by conducting laboratory experiments, which were viewed as more 'scientific' because variables could be controlled and observed under greater scrutiny. This change in emphasis was criticised by a number of social psychologists (a criticism that continues to the present day) who argued the subdiscipline has become less relevant to social behaviour in real-world settings owing to this change in direction (Armistead, 1974; Brewster-Smith, 1983; Cialdini, 2009; Greenwood, 2004b; Oishi *et al.*, 2009; Pancer, 1997; Parker, 1989; Ring, 1967; Silverman, 1977). Moscovici notes:

> social class structure, the phenomenon of language, the influence of ideas about society, all appear critically important and claim priority in the analysis of 'collective' conduct though they hardly make an appearance in contemporary social psychology..
>
> (1972: 20)

As a consequence, social psychology has lost touch with everyday life. Buunk (2006: 84) writes that 'when people do understand what social psychology is, they are usually interested in precisely those issues that today's social psychologists often shun'. Argyle (1992: p. xi) made a similar criticism when he wrote that social psychology lacked an applied focus, which had made it boring, abstract, and remote from real life.

The second point raised by Kasser and Kanner (2004: 4–5) is that psychology has tended to collude with consumerism[5] by testing and developing theories designed to market products and services, communications and advertising, without questioning its benefits for individuals, families and society at large. Bowlby points out:

> There is an intimate connection, institutionally and intellectually, between psychology and marketing during the first forty years of this century and beyond. As psychology became separated off from philosophy on the one hand and neurology on the other as an independent discipline, the primary questions with which it was concerned were often identical to those that preoccupied advertisers . . . psychologists at the time were laying out areas of investigation which overlap to a striking extent with those that concerned advertisers from a pragmatic point of view; and the developing institutional fields known as 'consumer psychology' or the 'psychology of selling'.
>
> (1993: 96)

This intimate connection that Bowlby refers to can be traced back to psychology's early days. For example, the psychologist Walter Dill Scott wrote two books at the turn of the twentieth century applying psychological theory to advertising: *The Theory and Practice of Advertising* published in 1903 and *The Psychology of Advertising* published in 1908. Both of Scott's books and the science of psychology generally, were 'instrumental in professionalising the industry of sales and selling' (Hansen *et al.*, 2003: 48; see also Lynch, 1968: 152). John Watson was a similar example. Watson pioneered the school of *behaviourism*, which came to dominate the science of psychology in the early part of the twentieth century.[6] In 1921 Watson, who had been a previous president of the American Psychological Association, left his academic post at John Hopkins University to join the J. Walter Thompson advertising agency where he eventually became Vice President. Watson was a major advocate of Thompson's corporate mission, which sought to replace traditional needs with modern consumer needs and desires (Cushman, 1995: 154–6; Ewen, 1976/2001: 84–5; Thorne and Henley, 2005: 343–5). Ewen states:

> Advertising directed some of its messages directly at children, preferring their 'blank slate' characters to those of their parents whose prejudices might be developed. J. B. Watson, the psychologist/ad man, had given underpinning to such a strategy. If the children were indoctrinated in the 'behavioristic freedom' which characterized the modern industrial world, he argued, business might be able to intervene in the values and definitions of culture.
>
> (1976/2001: 143–4)

Like Scott and Watson, Edward Bernays (nephew of Sigmund Freud), pioneered techniques in public relations, advertising and marketing in order to influence public opinion in support of consumer lifestyles (Curtis, 2002; Ewen, 1976/2001: 83). Bernays used theories and research in social psychology (crowd psychology, persuasion) and psychoanalysis (the unconscious) to further corporate and political aims of mass persuasion. Like Gustav Le Bon, Bernays believed that individuals under the social influence of crowds have the potential to regress to more primitive, irresponsible and infantile states of mind, leading to violence and other forms of animalistic behaviour (Graumann, 2001: 11–13). The US government of the time was afraid of this danger within its growing urban population. Bernays, along with his colleague Walter Lippman, assisted the US government in managing this threat by setting in motion a series of programmes designed to 'manufacture the consent' of its urban population. In effect, these programmes used the latest thinking in persuasive communication techniques to link consumer products and services with unconscious desires, in an attempt to keep the urban population happy, quiet and docile (Curtis, 2002; Ewen, 1996; Hansen *et al.*, 2003). Cushman adds:

> The use of psychology in advertising was a development of major economic and cultural importance. It reflected a trend that had begun with mesmerism, had grown stronger with positive thinking and abundance theory, and shifted and finally co-opted psychoanalysis: the combination of liberation theory and the psychoanalytic unconscious, used in the service of corporate interests such as the management of labor and the manipulation of the consumer.
>
> (1995: 154–5)

Psychology's long-running and intimate relationship with consumerism was summed up in a recent article published in *The Psychologist* (the monthly publication of the British Psychological Society) on the psychology of advertising, which noted that: 'Psychology and the advertising industry have always had a close "personal" relationship' (Florance *et al.*, 2011: 462). This special relationship can be seen in the role that psychology has played in the development of advertising strategies and techniques throughout the twentieth century, which linked people's desires, passions, hopes and anxieties, with material comfort, pleasure and therapy (Cushman, 1995; McDonald *et al.*, 2008; Miller and Rose, 1997). This collusion with consumer culture is rarely questioned by psychologists, because of their belief, some might argue illusion, that psychology is a politically neutral science. This apolitical stance has blinded social psychologists to the potentially pernicious effects of the mass media and advertising, and the internalisation of consumerist values.

There is also the issue of studying consumption at the level of cognition, which has narrowed psychology's analysis in this sphere, so that its research and theories typically focus on issues of 'consumer choice' and the preferences that determine these (Bowlby, 1993). This particular approach to understanding consumption fails to connect with much useful work carried out in other areas of social science that go beyond an individual's cognition by seeking to understand the ways in which consumption is linked to broader social and cultural forces (e.g. neoliberalism, the mass media, advertising, globalisation) in Western society, whose influence on social behaviour is profound. Moreover, there is a need to engage with fundamental debates in the wider social sciences about the benefits and drawbacks of consumerism. Moscovici notes:

> It is only the exploration of new realities that will enable social psychology to progress and will take it out of the restricted framework of commercial and industrial activities within which it is confined at present.
>
> (1972: 65)

Kasser and Kanner's (2004: 5) third point is that psychology has generally taken an ambivalent attitude towards social policy and social criticism. While some movements and schools in psychology have shown a preparedness to engage in these activities (e.g. critical psychology, humanistic psychology, community psychology and discursive psychology), the science of psychology as a whole has not sought to precipitate or influence social policy or social change. Since the Second World War psychopathology and the study of its treatment (abnormal and clinical psychology) has become one of the largest areas of research in the psychological sciences in terms of research funding and scientific publication. While abnormal and clinical psychology acknowledges historical, social, cultural, political and economic factors that contribute to mental distress, they rarely discuss these in depth or seek to influence political or policy processes that may create conditions for their change (Fox *et al.*, 2009). The problem here as Fromm notes is that social psychologists want us to believe that:

contemporary Western society and more especially, the 'American way of life' corresponds to the deepest needs of human nature and that adjustment to this way of life means mental health and maturity, social psychology, instead of being a tool for the criticism of society, thus becomes the apologist for the status quo.

(1956/1991: 71)

Kasser and Kanner (2004: 5) argue that psychology's unwillingness to analyse the broader political and economic aspects of consumer culture is a good example of its general attitude towards social policy debates and social criticism in general. The authors evidence this with an anecdote about a journal article they submitted to a psychology journal on materialism that was rejected, in part, because one of the reviewers along with the journal editor felt the findings were anti-capitalistic, and that their research was the sort that the conservative right in the United States frequently points to when it wants to cut research funding. In many ways this anecdote sums up the current state of play with regards to social psychology's attitude towards the political and economic aspects of consumer culture.

So what is consumer culture? What influence does it play in our everyday lives, and how has it been conceptualised? In the following section we will introduce the concept of consumer culture by discussing its prominence in our day-to-day lives. We will then conduct a brief definitional review of the concept, as an entrée to a deeper more extended review of the theories of consumer culture to be presented in Chapter 2.

Consumer culture

Consumption and everyday life

It has to be made clear from the outset that consumption is an active form of relationship (not only to objects, but also to society and to the world), a mode of systematic activity and global response which founds our entire cultural system.

(Baudrillard, 1968/1996: 217)

The purchase of a consumer product or service has become such a common and unremarkable aspect of everyday life that most of us barely think about it. Yet consumption and its culture has become an integral facet of social life in modern Western society and the central means by which individuals communicate self-identity. It is often invoked by politicians as a means to express citizenship, patriotism and national pride during periods of crisis. The quantity and quality of our acquisitions are often used to measure our success or otherwise in life. Consumer products and services function as a basis for social groupings and as a means to acquire membership to them. They stimulate imagination, envy and desire, and contribute to psychological distress as much as they provide pleasure, satisfaction and the means to pursue freedom through choice. Last but not least, consumer culture has come to determine the design and organisation of our urban and suburban landscapes. Lunt and Livingstone note:

> involvement with material culture is such that mass consumption infiltrates everyday life not only at the levels of economic processes, social activities and household structures, but also at the level of meaningful psychological experience – affecting the construction of identities, the formation of relationships, the framing of events.
>
> (1992: 24)

Evidence of consumer culture's significance can be seen in the amount of time and money spent each year on products and services. The average person in the United Kingdom now spends more time watching television (and its concomitant advertising) and shopping than any other leisure activity (Office of National Statistics, 2010). In 2005 the United States Census Bureau found that American households spent $425 billion at restaurants, $400 billion on vehicle purchases, $250 billion on clothing, $200 billion on furniture and appliances, $150 billion on entertainment, $100 billion on electronics, $100 billion gambling at casinos and $60 billion on alcohol (Quinn, 2008). When taken together, household consumer spending adds up to a staggering sum of money. In order to entice consumers to buy their products and services, business also spends billions of pounds each year, marketing and advertising their products and services, communicating messages that self-identity, love, beauty, friendships and the ideal lifestyle[7] can all be purchased. Our urban and suburban landscapes are designed to make consumption as convenient and safe as possible. Shopping strips, malls and arcades are centrally located, well serviced by public transport and/or provide the opportunity to easily and safely park cars. Urban spaces are emblazoned with advertising messages and images which can be seen on road- and rail-side billboards, the inside and outside of public transport, rail and bus stations, shop windows, shopping malls, buildings and sporting stadiums. Away from the public sphere we find our private lives are similarly infiltrated with advertising messages and images beamed to us through the television, radio, letter box, the internet and telephone.

Governments, universities, labour unions, the mass media and banks tell us that 'consumer confidence' is the single most important measure of the health and wellbeing of our societies. In times of economic crisis, recession and depression our politicians speak of 'consumer led' recoveries and often set public policies designed to stimulate consumer spending.

Out of the pain and misery of the Great Depression and then the Second World War, Western governments wanted to ensure a prosperous peacetime. They did this by calling on business to make new products, create new markets and encourage the populace to take up consumption-based lifestyles. It was during this period that consumption became not only a personal indulgence but a civic responsibility designed to improve the living standards of everyone (Cohen, 2003; Curtis, 2002).

It is therefore no surprise that prominent social theorists have come to agree that modern Western culture is a *consumer culture* (e.g. Baudrillard, 1970/1998;

Bauman, 2005; Giddens, 1991; Gorz, 1989; Harvey, 1989; Riesman, 1961a; Ritzer, 1998b); that is a culture 'organised around the consumption (of goods and leisure), rather than the production of materials and services' (Marshall, 1998: 112–13). As a consequence consumer culture influences and shapes our thinking, behaviours, habits, customs, language, dress and our social interactions and relations. Ritzer notes:

> Most generally, consumer culture means that a large number of people, perhaps most or all of society, have come to *value* consumption. That is, consumption is not just about acquiring the basics that people need in order to survive. Rather, people collectively come to see consuming, as well as the goods and services obtained, as important and valuable in their own right.
>
> (2007: 164)

Ritzer here points to the ways in which consumer products and services have a meaning that transcend their purely physical characteristics. They have become prized cultural symbols that are used as a form of communication in social interactions and relations and in the formation of self-identity (Douglas and Isherwood, 1982; Lury, 1996: 12; McCracken, 1988: 71; Trifonas and Balomenos, 2003: 7). These are issues we will now explore.

Consumer culture: some conceptual definitions

The concept of consumption, Ritzer *et al.* (2001) proposes, covers four main topic areas. We will specifically focus on three in our inquiry. They include: (1) objects of consumption, (2) subjects of consumption and (3) sites of consumption. The 'objects of consumption' are the actual products and services that consumers purchase, such as cars, mobile phones, toasters, fridges, clothing, computer games, jewellery, holidays, shoes and eating out at restaurants. Early theorists of consumption such as Karl Marx and Adam Smith viewed consumer objects as a means to satisfy basic human needs, serving an essentially utilitarian purpose. This has now radically changed as the majority of products and services purchased today are not necessary to basic survival. More recent scholars of consumption propose that products and services are largely aesthetic in nature, acting as *signs* and *symbols* that signify social meaning (to be discussed in more detail Chapter 2) (Baudrillard, 1970/1998; Lury, 1996; Miller, 1987).

The 'subject of consumption' refers to the individuals and groups who purchase products and services. In the consumer culture literature the subject of consumption is variously celebrated and maligned. The consumer *champion* is seen as a rational economic maximiser, expressing their rights and freedoms in the marketplace (and in society more widely), fulfilling basic and other higher order needs. In contrast, the consumer *dupe* is a forlorn figure, manipulated and controlled by the corporate marketing and advertising machine. They are viewed as unthinking automatons swayed by the fickle superficial dictates of fashion, forever comparing themselves to others in the race to fulfil manufactured needs, surrounding their lives with superfluous material items and leading a largely meaningless life because of it.

These contrasting modes of subjectivity reflect two basic approaches to analysing the thinking and behaviour of people in consumer cultures. The first, the *cultural studies* approach, focuses on the meanings and dynamics of consumption in everyday life and the way in which people play with and manipulate consumer signs and symbols for the purpose of impression management, creating links and associations with others in the social milieu, and lending an element of stylisation to the project of life. This is a micro-level interpretation of the phenomenon that is often depoliticised (Schor, 2007). The *critical* approach is more judgemental, linking consumer culture to artificial social relations, political repression, the destruction of social and natural environments, alienation and ultimately despair, dissatisfaction and psychological distress. This macro-level approach has been criticised for theorising consumers as passive subjects lacking agency. However, the critical approach Schor (2007) argues has become relevant once again due to the emergence of globalisation and the catastrophic environmental degradation it has added to. The inquiry presented in this book draws on both approaches to understanding consumer culture. However, we tend to lean more towards the critical approach as it accords with our previous research on consumer culture (e.g. McDonald *et al.*, 2008; Wearing *et al.*, in press; Wearing and Wearing, 1992; Wearing and Wearing, 2000).

Despite the differences between these two approaches, both cultural and critical theories of consumer culture view it as central to the formation of self-identity in contemporary Western society. Both approaches highlight the shift from a relatively fixed self-identity rooted in traditional institutions, such as family, church, community, trade unions and other political/community affiliations, to a more fluid entity rooted in reflexive individualism, impression management and the commodification of human interactions and relations (Bauman, 1988, 1992, 2000; Elliott, 2008; Elliott and Lemert, 2009; Featherstone, 2007; Fromm, 1956/1991; Giddens, 1991; Lasch, 1979; Sussman, 1984).

'Sites of consumption' refer to the spaces and places where consumer products and services are bought and sold. In modern Western towns and cities these sites include shopping malls, shopping arcades, shopping precincts, boutique stores, supermarkets and franchised outlets, as well as entertainment and hospitality venues such as cinema complexes, casinos, bars, clubs, theatres, theme parks, cruise ships, restaurants, fast-food chains, cafés, hotels, holiday resorts, sporting stadiums and airports. Many of these sites are used by consumers as spaces in which to congregate in comfort and safety,[8] socialise and experiment with different self-identities (Kowinski, 1985). Sites of consumption create and fuel desire by offering fantasies, spectacles and dream worlds that inspire the consumer's imagination (Ritzer *et al.*, 2001: 422). The marketplace has always played an important role in human settlements, however, modern sites of consumption, those that came into existence after the Second World War, have transformed the urban/suburban landscape.

Referred to by Ritzer (2009) as 'cathedrals of consumption' these sites represent a shift in the way people consume products and services affecting every aspect of social life. Their quasi-religious nature is designed to enchant through the use of spectacle, extravaganza and simulations.[9] The focus on spectacle has transformed the traditional marketplace, and the towns and cities we now live in. Prior to the advent of modern sites of consumption, shopping typically involved entering a small specialised store or open-air market place, where purchases had generally been decided on beforehand. In the modern era shopping has become a highly popular leisure activity that involves 'wandering through displays of objects trying on goods (or trying on fantasies) (which) need not include an actual purchase' (Ritzer *et al.*, 2001: 423). As sites of consumption have come to increasingly dominate urban/suburban landscapes around the Western world, they have become significant spaces for social interaction and self-identity experimentation, and therefore a phenomenon of interest to social psychology, one that has yet to be fully explored in detail.

In a similar vein to Ritzer *et al.* (2001), Featherstone proposes that consumer culture is *the culture* of consumer society,[10] indicating 'that the representation (signs and images) and values of contemporary societies revolve around consumption: the purchase and enjoyment of goods for the construction of lifestyle' (2001: 2662). The advent of mass production – increased efficiencies in production, the advent of scientific management and assembly lines – required a new era of mass consumption in order to absorb the greatly increased output of consumer products and services, ensuring the economies of the West continued to grow economically. The traditional Protestant aesthetic of individual sacrifice, hard work, thrift, delayed gratification and reinvestment of profits eventually gave way to the new ideology of consumerism (Ewen, 1976/2001; Featherstone, 1991; Laermans, 1993; Smart, 2010). As de Grazia (1996: 3) notes, 'there was nothing natural or inevitable about the development of modern consumption practices'. The citizen had to be taught to become a consumer by learning how to express and satisfy long-suppressed desires, to seek out new pleasures, to spend now and save later. This process was facilitated in the early part of the twentieth century by the US government in conjunction with high-profile psychologists such as Edward Bernays, and some of the country's largest corporations. Workers were to be looked upon not simply as producers, but as consumers as well. This required they be paid more money and work less hours so they had more discretionary income and time to buy products and services (Ewen, 1996: 222). This stimulated economic growth and prosperity. The second major element in turning people from producers into consumers was the development of the mass media and advertising.

> In the 1920s the foundation of a consumer culture became established with the new media of motion pictures, tabloid press, mass circulation magazines and radio extolling the leisure lifestyle, and publicising new norms and standards of behaviour. Advertising became the guardian of the new morality enticing individuals to participate in the consumption of commodities and experiences once restricted to the upper classes . . . Images of youth, beauty, luxury, and opulence became loosely associated with goods awakening long-suppressed desires, as well as reminding the individual that he/she has room for self-improvement in all aspects of his/her life.
>
> (Featherstone, 1991: 172)

Even accounting for the significant increases in production output that occurred in the late nineteenth and early twentieth centuries, production mechanisms since this time have made quantum leaps in efficiencies, rationality and subsequent output. This has fuelled a constant stream of new and value-added products and services, providing an extensive 'repertoire of resources for the construction and renewal of identities and presentation of the self' (Featherstone, 2001: 2664). In consumer cultures, products and services form the basis of social identity by providing a measure of distinction, bringing individuals together, building bonds and friendships, while separating groups based on taste and the choice of particular objects and the differing lifestyles they signify.

Featherstone (1991, 2001, 2007), like Ritzer *et al.* (2001), argues that an important characteristic of consumer cultures has been the redesign of urban and suburban spaces to accommodate shopping malls, shopping precincts and other consumer/entertainment complexes. These sites are designed to make shopping a pleasurable leisure experience. They are viewed by many as a form of entertainment in their own right, or providing some form of entertainment, as much as they are places in which to purchase products and services. Sites of consumption are geared particularly towards women, providing a space where they can move freely in security, engaging and experimenting with lifestyles, and conducting social interactions and relations in safe comfortable surroundings (Featherstone, 2001: 2665).

Consumer culture is constructed around products and services drawing on a wide range of imagery, sign play and narratives, a process Featherstone (2001: 2666) refers to as *aestheticisation*. Corporations compete with each other by employing marketing and advertising specialists to undertake sophisticated analysis into their current and future market of customers and to develop and mobilise advertising campaigns in order to elevate their products and services in the minds and imaginations of consumers. Drawing on the work of artists and intellectuals, this group of specialists (dubbed 'para-intellectuals' by Featherstone) act as *cultural intermediaries* in consumer societies.

> These groups, which include those members of the new middle classes working in media, fashion, design, advertising, marketing, and the culture industries, are those who design the consumer culture representations, the informational aspects of consumer goods, and the experiential dimension of consumer sites.
>
> (Featherstone, 2001: 2667)

In his final topic Featherstone (2001: 2667–8) discusses globalisation and the limits to consumer culture. Western consumer lifestyles depend on the extraction and manipulation of a wide range of natural resources, many of which are depleting at an ever accelerating rate. At the same time as depletion is occurring, the exploitation of natural resources such as oil and coal is producing toxic waste and pollution on an unprecedented scale, the most catastrophic of which are CO_2 gases that are contributing to climate change. The creation of modern consumer cultures has led to a new set of modern risks that have become global in scope. In response pressure groups have sought to raise public consciousness, change political and economic orthodoxy, challenge environmental exploitation such as the development and use of modern technologies (e.g. genetically modified food, nuclear power, car use) and to promote greater equality between rich and poor nations.

Capitalism, free markets and consumer culture

Toward a free market economy

Consumer cultures, like other cultural phenomena, gained widespread acceptance through the mobilisation of various ideologies,[11] in this case the 'free market'. As Moscovici (1972: 58) notes, 'our market economy forces us all to become buyers and sellers of goods and services'. The expansion of the market economy into virtually every aspect of modern life has had the effect of discrediting traditional norms predominantly through the influence of the mass media and advertising, which have become the 'central purveyors of the new consumer culture values' (Featherstone, 1991: 173). These values include the eschewing of social solidarity in favour of 'individualism, private property, personal responsibility, and family values' (Harvey, 2005: 23).

The first vestige of a consumer culture has been traced back to the sixteenth century (McKendrick *et al.*, 1983; Slater, 1997) and in some cases even earlier. Consumption in the form of the 'acquisition and display of luxurious and fashionable goods and clothes can easily be traced back to antiquity, yet for much of history the right to them has been restricted to all but the small elite' (Featherstone, 1983: 4). This situation has now radically altered so that every citizen of modern Western society has become a consumer of one type or another, and that consumption has become the underpinning principle of our economy and culture, as opposed to an epiphenomenal characteristic as it was in previous historical eras (Corrigan, 1997: 1). Evidence of the centrality of consumption can be seen in the role that consumer spending plays in fuelling the modern economic system, without which it would collapse. In the aftermath of the Second World War, Western governments began to exhort their citizens to embrace consumer lifestyles in order to stimulate and rebuild their economies and countries. Consumer spending not only facilitated the fulfilment of desires, it also became a duty carried out on behalf of one's country, an expression and practice of national pride, citizenship, patriotism and civic responsibility (Aldridge, 2003; Cohen, 2003; Daunton and Hilton, 2001; Trentmann, 2007).

> [T]oday's economy is based not on the restriction of consumption, but on its fullest development. Our economy would face a severe crisis if people – the working and middle classes – were not to spend most of their income on consumption, rather then to save it. Consuming has become not only the passionate aim of life for most people, but it has also become a virtue.
>
> (Fromm, 1962/2009: 63)

The basis of Western society's current economic system and in particular the 'Anglo' countries of the world (United Kingdom, United States, Ireland, Canada, Australia and New Zealand) stemmed from a set of theories developed by two highly influential economists of the twentieth century, John Maynard Keynes and Frederick von Hayek. Initially colleagues at Cambridge University during the 1940s, Keynes and von Hayek developed ideas on economics and social theory that took diverging paths (McCormick, 1992). Yet both of their approaches to economic theory became ideologies in their own right during the twentieth and twenty-first centuries.

For Keynes the Great Depression of the 1930s was the result of unfettered free markets and the greed of wealthy industrialists and stock market gamblers who presided over them. The remedy, Keynes proposed, was greater government planning and regulation of the economy in order to provide a stabilising influence over the excesses of the market. In the aftermath of the Second World War Keynesian economics became electorally successful in many Western countries as they recovered from the shattering experience of world war. Keynes's ideas tapped into a growing desire for societies that pooled their resources and regulated the market in order to create greater equity and stability via universal access to education, healthcare and welfare for those in need. To achieve this end government would need to take greater control in planning the economy, in order to tame the volatility of the market, avoiding the pain and suffering inflicted by the Great Depression (Yergin and Stanislaw, 2002).

In contrast von Hayek rejected Keynesian macro-economics. In his books *The Road to Serfdom* and later *Individualism and Economic Order* he critiqued 'the welfare state, the mixed economy, and collectivism from a purely libertarian perspective' (Yergin and Stanislaw, 2002: 81). Von Hayek believed that central planning of the economy focused too much power in the hands of government, which led to the erosion of personal freedoms, social justice and equality. He illustrated his arguments with a historical analysis of Nazi Germany and the Soviet Union (Yergin and Stanislaw, 2002).

Von Hayek's ideas were largely ignored during the late 1940s at the time his books were published. It was not until many years later that life was breathed into his ideas by Keith Joseph and Margaret Thatcher through their respective associations with the Institute of Economic Affairs based in London (Yergin and Stanislaw, 2002). Thatcher had read *The Road to Serfdom* as an undergraduate at Oxford University, and later as a government minister. She was greatly inspired by von Hayek's ideas on market economics and the 'price system' – a mechanism where prices for products and services are determined by the market, so that buyers and sellers set prices in mutual consent (Tomlinson, 1990; Yergin and Stanislaw, 2002). These and other ideas she believed were a cure for the ills that had beset the British economy in the 1970s. These included escalating inflation and difficulties in trying to finance budget deficits as a result of welfare provision. Clarke notes:

> Neoliberalism emerged as an ideological response to the crisis of the 'Keynesian welfare state', which was precipitated by the generalised capitalist

crisis associated with the end of the post-war reconstruction boom and was brought to a head by the escalating cost of the US war against Vietnam at the beginning of the 1970s.

(2005: 58)

When Thatcher became Prime Minister of Great Britain in 1979 she enacted a raft of new economic policies that had a profound effect on the country's social and cultural landscape. These included the deregulation of financial institutions, the privatisation of government/national enterprises, or the introduction of 'market mechanisms' and corporate management strategies into government services such as welfare, healthcare and education, along with a reduction in government funding, the reduction of direct taxation on both households and business, and the undermining of collective labour movements and other forms of social solidarity (Harvey, 2005). Few British institutions emerged unscathed (Campbell, 2004). It was Thatcher's belief that free (unregulated) markets would increase individual freedoms, lead to greater participation in democracy and rein in inflation (Yergin and Stanislaw, 2002). Her programme of reforms was based on a conflation of neoclassical economics with the philosophy of liberalism, celebrating the rational individual seeking to maximise their personal needs.

Thatcher's ideas jumped across the Atlantic where they were taken up by Ronald Reagan, supported by the influential academic economist Milton Friedman from the University of Chicago. Friedman had long been critical of government intervention in the economy which he argued led to 'excessive public sector growth, over-administration, bureaucracy and rigidity, which in turn create new economic distortions leading to a new cycle of intervention' (Dean, 2010: 71; see also Harvey, 2005: 65). Reagan, like Thatcher, sought to liberalise the US economy by employing a set of principles not unlike those applied in the UK. These included the freeing up of the domestic market, enhancing consumer choice in order to increase individual freedoms and limiting the state's role in society. Successive US governments, from Reagan onwards, have been instrumental also in liberalising global trade relations by impelling countries to open up their markets to greater competition. These policies were enshrined in what became known as the Washington Consensus, a set of ten economic policy prescriptions developed by the International Monetary Fund (IMF), the World Bank and the US Treasury Department as part of a reform package for developing countries faced with economic crisis. These policy prescriptions have now become a global economic standard and the ideal against which most Western governments construct their own economic policy (Chomsky, 1999; MacEwan, 1999; Sim, 2004). These policies were supported by elements of the British and US ruling classes (e.g. politicians, pro-business intellectuals and lobbies, corporate executives and media owners) who popularised the idea that government interference, public enterprise, bureaucrats, red tape, regulatory agencies, unions, co-operatives and welfare dependency stymied the economy and reduced individual freedoms (Connell, 2010: 27). The free market was promoted as a superior mechanism for resolving social and economic problems, as well as increasing individual freedoms and economic prosperity (Harvey, 2005; Lemke, 2001).

Neoliberalism

Economic and financial globalisation and the free market economic policies that enable it to function fostered the rebirth of *liberalism*, to become what is now termed *neoliberalism*. Neoliberalism is based on a 'set of value judgements about the superiority of market forces over bureaucratic decision making' (Snooks, 2000: 114). It asserts liberalism from an economic standpoint, and is rooted in the thinking of Adam Smith and the Enlightenment project. Harvey adds:

> Neoliberalism is in the first instance a theory of political economic practices that proposes that human well-being can best be advanced by liberating individual entrepreneurial freedoms and skills within an institutional framework characterized by private property rights, free markets, and free trade.
>
> (2005: 2)

Free markets it asserts, is the essence of democracy because it increases personal freedoms via consumer sovereignty, emphasises rationality and enables the individual to give expression and style to their personal life through consumer choice (Kotz, 2002). Frank explains:

> Since we all participate in markets – buying stock, choosing between brands of shaving cream, going to movie X instead of Y – markets are an expression of the vox populi. Markets give us what we want; markets overthrow the old regime; markets empower the little guy. And since markets are just the people working things out in their own inscrutable way, any attempt to regulate or otherwise interfere with markets is, by definition, nothing but arrogance.
>
> (2000: 42)

By emphasising consumer sovereignty and choice in public and economic policy, people are given the freedom to buy and sell and to set prices based on market indicators. According to neoliberal theory when consumer choice is properly exercised it results in prosperity for all (Gergen, 1991: 240; Smart, 2010: 31–4). Since its introduction in the 1980s neoliberalism has redefined citizenship, so that politicians view citizens primarily as consumers as opposed to producers (Ritzer and Slater, 2001); their private desires are seen as sacrosanct and beyond the judgement of social analysts or political actors (Slater, 2005: 139).

> In a consumer culture, then, key social values, identities and processes are negotiated through the figure of 'the consumer' (as opposed to, say, the worker, the citizen or the devotee); central modern values such as freedom, rationality and progress are enacted and assessed through consumerist criteria (range of choice, price, calculations and rising affluence, respectively); and the cultural landscape seems to be dominated by commercial signs (advertising, portrayals of 'lifestyle' choices through the media, obsessive concern with the changing meaning of things).
>
> (Ritzer and Slater, 2001: 6)

Markets and consumer culture have come to dominate daily life as supporters of neoliberalism seek to expand markets in places where they exist, and to initiate them in places where they do not. This has taken neoliberalism into a strategy of stimulating an endless commodification of social and cultural life (Connell, 2010: 23). In order to support the expansion of markets around the world trade barriers have progressively come down (forced down in many cases) in order to allow for an ever increasing stream of new products and services to inhabit the global marketplace. The freeing up of the market has allowed consumer culture to dominate many aspects of globalisation (Harvey, 2005). This has led to a corresponding rise in the stock of cultural symbols now available for consumption. Free market forces enable everyone, not just elites, access to a variety of cultural symbols, which are packaged and sold as part of an array of competing lifestyles that consumers are free to choose from. Giddens notes:

> in conditions of high modernity, we all not only follow lifestyles, but in an important sense are forced to do so – we have no choice but to choose. A lifestyle can be defined as a more or less integrated set of practices which an individual embraces, not only because such practices fulfil utilitarian needs, but because they give material form to a particular narrative of self-identity.
>
> (1991: 81)

Neoliberalism views human nature through the prism of economics, based on the guiding assumption that human beings act primarily out of self-interest (Steger and Roy, 2010: 12; see also Hahnel, 2002). Deregulation and the increase in marketplace choice and competition through the price mechanism are designed to empower the consumer so that producers are forced to respond to their expressed preferences. In effect consumers are given sovereignty over their needs, desires, wants and identities through greater purchasing power (Slater, 1997: 34–8; Slater and Tonkiss, 2001: 67). They are also set free from government interference to compete in the marketplace in order to maximise their own material gain and wellbeing. In the process of deregulation a new social contract was struck. Governments reduced regulation and interference in the market, while emphasising consumer sovereignty, with the expectation that each citizen would take greater control and responsibility for their lives. Consumerism is therefore the behavioural response to a market-meditated mode of life (Bauman, 2004: 304). Neoliberalism functions through the institution of techniques and programmes that shift the regulatory competence of the state onto responsible, rational, enterprising individuals (Lemke, 2001: 101–2; Rose, 1996: 150–68). This new social contract signalled a shift in social policy away from external government toward *self-government* as the ideology of collective social provision gave way to individualism.

The policy of self-government and its emphasis on individualism is vividly illustrated in a number of areas of contemporary modern life. Welfare or social security for example, is now based on policies of mutual obligation requiring welfare recipients to enter into contracts to become more responsible, productive and competitive individuals (Dean, 2010: 200–3). Under such a system personal failure is attributed to personal failings, 'and the victim is all too often blamed' (Harvey, 2005: 76). Social risks such as illness, unemployment and poverty, once viewed (in part) the responsibility of government, are increasingly seen as individual concerns. The workplace and the modern-day corporation is another example where self-governance and individualism have come to signal the spirit of the times. Collective associations in the form of labour unions have declined in most modern corporatised workplaces where the relationship between employer and employee is based on individual wage bargaining, the establishment of individual performance objectives, individual performance evaluations, individual salary increases or granting of bonuses as a function of competence, and of individual merit and individualised career paths (Bourdieu, 1998). Self-governance has come to greatly influence corporate organisational culture and is used as a means to increase productivity and profits by emphasising employee aggression, competitiveness, rivalry, independence, enterprise, entrepreneurship, dynamism, productivity and flexibility (Birch and Paul, 2003; Bourdieu, 1998; Casey, 2002; Deery and Walsh, 1999; Hughes, 2005; Rose, 1996; Schor, 1991; Sennett, 1998). Much of the corporate culture we see today is driven by an increase in global competition stimulated by deregulation, which organisations have responded to by instituting their own internal policies of economic rationalisation (Chomsky, 1999; Ritzer, 2000).

However, the events of September and October 2008 placed a significant question mark over the neoliberal model of economics. Triggered by the sub-prime mortgage crisis in the US, a number of leading North American and European financial institutions declared insolvency, precipitating a credit crisis and major declines in stock indexes around the world. CEOs of the world's largest investment banks and insurers in the US and UK, who for years had been railing against government regulation and interference in the market, found themselves turning to those very same governments to rescue them from bankruptcy and losing the savings and pensions of millions of people.

Much of the blame for the global financial crisis of 2008 has been placed on the risk-taking behaviour of large global investment banks, and the lack of government regulation and oversight of the finance sector more broadly. These same commentators and even some previous and current heads of government are now on the record stating that neoliberal economic policies are defunct and that greater regulation of the financial sector is required in order to avoid economic catastrophe in the future.[12] Public policy responses in the US and UK to the global financial crisis sought to restore confidence in the market and to promote lending, credit and consumer spending once again. This call by governments to the banks to continue lending money and for private citizens to continue spending, particularly on products and services produced nationally, is reminiscent of the late 1940s and early 1950s when consumer spending was linked to national pride and citizenship in the aftermath of the Second World War (Cohen, 2003).

Although neoliberalism found itself out of favour during and shortly after the 2008 global financial crisis, it has returned to fill the void in economic policy (Couch, 2011; Warde, 2011). While there have been a number of significant macro-economic interventions by governments, such as stimulus spending packages, the neoliberal economic model continues to underpin micro-economic activity in the majority of Western countries today (Steger and Roy, 2010; Couch, 2011; Warde, 2011). Couch (2011) argues that neoliberalism has been able to weather the global financial crisis and the huge fall out that ensued because of the influence that large multinational corporations have been able to command over public life and their desire to see the political and economic status quo remain firmly in place. Their influence is exerted in a number of ways, which is significant given the extraordinary levels of wealth that are concentrated in some multinational corporations. The most visible of these are the large donations they make to political parties and their intense lobbying of law-makers in order to influence public policy that upholds their interests. This is coupled with their many advertising and public relations exercises, as well as their purchasing and controlling of large sections of the mass media, which they use to persuade the public to support neoliberal economic policies which are claimed to be the most effective method for ensuring growing prosperity and freedom (Harvey, 2005: 39–63).

The effect of the 2008 global financial crisis on consumption was to merely slow it down, as Humphery notes:

> The notable feature of the financial market crash of 2008, and the subsequent end of the long consumer boom, was that the overconsumption of goods and resources in the West did not somehow miraculously cease; it has merely been scaled down for a time.
>
> (2010: viii)

The most recent global recession of 2008, and those that preceded it in 1929, 1973, 1980 and 1990, underscore the profound role that political economy plays in everyday life. By ignoring the politics and economics of contemporary society and the profound influence it has on social behaviour at both the individual and group level, social psychology has made itself irrelevant (Cushman, 1995; Greenwood, 2004b; Lemke, 2001; Pancer, 1997; Parker, 2007; Rose, 1996, 2008; Sampson, 1989). This is evident in its focus on intra-psychic variables at the expense of research on wider economic and political factors, such as consumer culture. Moscovici (1972: 54–5) notes: 'Society has its own structure which is not definable in terms of the characteristics of individuals; this structure is determined by the process of production and consumption, by rituals, symbols, institutions, norms and values.'

Outline of the book

As stated at the outset, the aim of this book is to critically analyse and expand the leading positions in social psychology from the perspective of classical and contemporary theories of consumer culture. Theory and research on consumer culture is scattered across a variety of disciplines in the social sciences. As such, this book covers an eclectic range of concepts, theorists, and topics that span the consumer culture literature. By covering a range of theories, along with some of their empirical examples, we will illustrate the various ways in which consumer culture challenges and can potentially expand existing social psychological theory, research and the topics that dominate it. Given the disparate nature of the consumer culture literature and the various social science disciplines that comprise it, differences in ontology and epistemology between the various perspectives are a common feature. However, the scope of this book is not to explore these philosophical differences in depth, as there are other books that do justice to these issues.

In Chapter 2 we will review various theories of consumer culture related to social psychology. These include self-identity, emotional and behavioural problems, and geographic space. A number of theoretical perspectives and theorists are covered including 'historical precursors', 'poststructuralism', 'social theories' and 'feminism'. This review will provide the theoretical and philosophical basis from which to critique and expand existing social psychological theory in the following chapters.

Self-identity, that is the individual's experience and internal representation of him/herself and their world, has become a central concept of inquiry in social psychological theory. Chapter 3 begins by reviewing the most popular social psychological theories of self-identity, which include social cognition and social identity theory. The chapter then highlights the limitations of these theories by illustrating the influence that consumer culture exerts over the formation and maintenance of self-identity in modern Western society. These include the commodification of self-identity, narcissism as it relates to individualism, the manner in which consumer products and services are used to signal distinction and status, the reproduction of gender, and the way in which consumer culture undermines attempts at constructing a stable self-identity.

Chapter 4 explores the link between emotional and behavioural problems and consumer culture. The chapter begins with a discussion on the influence of social psychological theory on abnormal and clinical psychology. Social psychological theories that have crossed over into abnormal and clinical psychology are briefly reviewed. This is then followed by a critical analysis of these theories with a focus on the influence of the mass media and advertising, alienation and exclusion, and consumer culture's obsession with the body.

Chapter 5 analyses the relationship between consumer culture and geographic space. The chapter begins with a discussion on the influence of social psychological theory on environmental psychology. Social psychological theories that have crossed over into environmental psychology are briefly reviewed. The second part of the chapter applies spatial concepts developed in the consumer culture literature to social-environmental psychological theories. The chapter begins with an analysis of the commodification of social interactions and relations in consumer and urban/suburban spaces. The last section of this chapter analyses the ways in which social behaviour is governed through the planning, design, organisation and management of consumer and urban/suburban spaces.

In the concluding chapter we analyse the environmental limits of consumer culture and the role that social psychology may potentially play in leading the West towards more sustainable forms of consumption. The chapter then ends with a summary of the main points raised in our inquiry of consumer culture, highlighting the challenges this poses to social psychology in its attempt to move out of the shadows of its self-imposed irrelevance.

2 Theories of consumer culture

Introduction

The purpose of this chapter is to review elements of the consumer culture literature which will form the theoretical and philosophical basis for critiquing and expanding social psychological theory in later chapters. The following review will focus on three main topic areas relevant to social psychology and consumer culture: self-identity, emotional and behavioural problems, and geographic space. Even with this topical narrowing, theories of consumer culture are sprawling, fragmented and multidisciplinary in scope. Theories of consumer culture can be found in disciplines as diverse as anthropology, sociology, cultural studies, media studies, marketing and human geography. As theories of consumer culture have emerged from a number of academic disciplines and theoretical perspectives the chapter has been arranged to reflect this. It begins with an outline of the 'historical precursors' briefly reviewing the work of Karl Marx, Thorstein Veblen, Georg Simmel and Erich Fromm. This is then followed by a review of theories under three headings: poststructuralism, social theories and feminist theories.

Historical precursors

It was not until the mid-nineteenth century that scholars began to systematically analyse consumption and its culture. It was during this period that cultural values in the West began to shift, precipitated by the movement from a social life based on production towards a social life based on consumption (Ewen, 1976/2001). Karl Marx was really the first scholar of note to inquire into consumer culture, although it is important to point out that the main thrust of his work was an analysis of nineteenth-century production and the struggle between the different social classes that inhabited Europe during that period of time. According to Marx this struggle took place predominantly between the ruling classes or the bourgeoisie (the owners of capital) and the working classes or the proletariat (labour). Marx along with his fellow German co-author Friedrich Engels saw this class struggle as part of the evolution of capitalism towards a more equitable system of politics and economics based on communism.

Marx asserted that much of what we think about ourselves and others is influenced by ideology. That is, our thinking is patterned by the ideas that a particular society develops, and these ideas are 'determined by the particular structure and mode of functioning of the society' (Fromm, 1962/2009: 9). If the particular structure of a society runs counter to healthy social interactions and relations then the people that comprise it are likely to experience estrangement (alienation). In the case of capitalism, Marx argued that it denies the potential to actualise because capitalist modes of production lead to the estrangement of the individual from themselves, others and society.

As noted so far, Marx focused much of his theoretical analysis on production and conflict between social classes. However, his analysis also provides a number of valuable insights into consumption and its culture (Bocock, 1993: 42; Smart, 2003: 9–11). Where production has the potential to stimulate healthy social relations, in a capitalist economy it is subordinated to the owners of capital who return products and services back to the workers who produced them as commodities for purchase. It is through the practice of consumption in capitalist economies that culture is reproduced and ritualised. These insights led Marx to believe that it was 'economic life' (in the nineteenth century) as opposed to 'religion', that was the primary cause of alienation. The subjective experience of life had been reduced to a mere effect of political and economic conditions (Henry, 1999: 118).

What set Marx apart from his economic contemporaries of the time was his unique approach to theorising the value of commodities. The classical economist Adam Smith established a measure of a commodity's value by drawing a distinction between its 'natural price' – that is, the labour, land, and its production costs – and its 'market price', which is influenced by supply and demand. Marx however believed that too little importance was attributed to the intrinsic use-value of the product itself, and the labour that was used to create it. He drew a distinction between what he termed 'use-value' and 'exchange-value', arguing that products and services were of value because of the use they provide. In pre-capitalist societies a product or service derived its value from the labour, know-how, and ingenuity that went into it; it was understood and valued because of the social relations invested in it. In capitalism social relations are ignored, so that use-value is usurped by exchange-value – a value that is understood in relation to other commodities only and the market forces that determine its monetary worth (Marx, 1867/2004). In the capitalist mode of production labour is also turned into a commodity:

> Labor produces not only commodities: it produces itself and the worker as a *commodity* – and this in the same general proportion in which it produces commodities. This fact expresses merely that the object which labor produces – labor's product – confronts it as *something alien*, as a *power independent* of the producer. The product of labor is labor which has been embodied in an object, which has become material: it is the *objectification* of labor.
>
> (Marx, 1844/1973: 107–8)

'Commodity fetishism' is the term that Marx used to describe this process, in which a product's social relations are hidden or obscured from view for both the worker and the consumer, who come to value (to fetishise) the commodity for its inherent characteristics (Paterson, 2006: 16–18). This concept has been extended to the idea of 'commodification', which is defined as the transformation of an object, service, time, ritual or even a person into a commodity, which is not by nature a commercial entity.[1] Commodity fetishism and commodification have come to pervade every aspect of modern life in Western society, a state of affairs that Marx viewed as highly problematic because it has the effect of trivialising the intrinsic worth of a product or service and the human relations invested in it.

A classic example of commodification in modern times is the celebration of Christmas, which for a minority of people in the West is looked upon as an important holy day marking the birth of Jesus Christ. For the majority, Christmas is associated with shopping, gift-giving, eating, drinking and time away from work. Its commodification has transformed its intrinsic worth as a celebration of a significant event into a commodity for the purpose of making profit. In another example we can see how leisure (that is, time free from work) is valued for its rest, recreation and potential for self-enhancement. Its commodification – its manipulation by the market with a focus on profit – has resulted in a leisure that has come to largely comprise passive vicarious amusements and entertainments that disengage the individual from themselves and others (Wearing and McDonald, 2004; see also Wearing and Wearing, 1992).

Life in capitalist economies creates what Friedrich Engels termed 'false consciousness'.[2] Social psychological theory is based on the assumption that human beings are free thinking, free acting agents whose behaviour stems from their own subjective will, whereas Marx and Engels argued that it is largely determined by historical, political and economic forces (Fromm, 1962/2009: 82). For example, most people accept the transformation of a commodity's use-value into exchange-value, which alienates the individual from the creation of their own labour, other workers and society at large. It betrays social relations whose value is usurped by money and the pursuit of capital accumulation. This degrading of social interactions and relations is falsely conceived as a 'natural law' which prescribes that individuals and groups are always in competition with one another for scarce resources, a circumstance which is antithetical to the concept of society (Augoustinos, 1999). Competition is beneficial most of all to capital, and the owners of capital, whose ideas of natural order and social organisation exert a hegemony over the working classes. In this way the owners of capital subordinate the wider population to internalise and accept their moral, political, economic and cultural values. The working classes are dominated through a mixture of coercion and spontaneous consent, reinforcing their own servitude (Gramsci, 1971). People living on the lower rungs of society are misled into thinking that their station in life is determined by their own moral lacking or resolve, which blinds them to their own servitude in providing labour for the capital-owning classes (Augoustinos, 1999).

This set of circumstances leads to what Marx referred to as *alienation*, or estranged labour (Marx, 1844/1973). The causes of alienation include the increasing technological means of production, the increase in wealth for the owners of capital at the expense of workers (referred to by Marx as 'surplus value'), the control of labour in fewer hands and the increasing division of labour.

> Alienation (or 'estrangement') means, for Marx, that man does *not* experience himself as the acting agent in his grasp of the world, but that the world (nature, others, and he himself) remain alien to him. They stand above and against him as objects, even though they may be objects of his own creation. Alienation is essentially experiencing the world and oneself passively, receptively, as the subject separated from the object.
>
> (Fromm, 1961/2004: 37)

Contrary to popular belief, Marx's criticism of capitalism aimed to effect a spiritual emancipation through liberation from economic determinism. He believed that capitalist modes of production deny human and social potential, turning people into impotent commodities for the purpose of serving 'virile machines' (Fromm, 1961/2004: 2). Instead of experiencing oneself as a socially engaged and creative being, people come to experience themselves through the worship of commodities. The objects (and services) of people's work become alien beings, eventually ruling over them, becoming powerfully independent of the producer (Fromm, 1961/2004: 40). 'This commodity-man knows only one way of relating himself to the world outside, by having it and by consuming (using) it' (Fromm, 1962/2009: 40).

Like Marx, Georg Simmel was a scholar with an interest in politics and economics and its effects on social life. He concluded, in much the same way that Marx did, that capitalist economics did more to isolate people than to bring them together. This is what he had to say about its impact on personality:

> In the Middle Ages a person was a member bound to a community or an estate, to a feudal association or a guild. His personality was merged with real or local interest groups, and the latter in turn drew their character from the people who directly supported them . . . This interdependence of personality and material relationship which is typical of the barter economy, is dissolved by the money economy . . . It fosters a distance between personality and property by mediating between the two . . . In this way, money produces both a previously unknown impersonality in all economic ownership and an equally enhanced independence and autonomy of the personality.
>
> (Simmel, 1991a: 17–18)

Simmel observed that consumer culture at the turn of the twentieth century had become a replacement for religion in that it cultivated tastes, provided a basis for the construction of self-identity and a sense of one's place in society, just as the practice of religion had done so successfully for many centuries prior (Beck, 2001: 265). At the heart of consumer culture is the 'money economy', which has come to mediate virtually every aspect of social exchange (Simmel, 1907/1990).

The clinical nature of these exchanges positioned people in ways that generated 'a series of instrumental practices and rational dispositions' (Allen, 2000: 60–1).

> Money offers us the only opportunity to date for a unity which eliminates everything personal and specific, a form of unification that we take completely for granted today, but which represents one of the most enormous changes and advances of culture . . . economic activity of a person and his individual colouration, his actual ego, which now completely retreats from those external relationships and in that way concentrates more than ever on its inmost strata . . . The streams of modern culture rush in two seemingly opposing directions: on the one hand, toward levelling, equalization, the production of more and more comprehensive social circles through connection of the remotest things under equal conditions; on the other hand, towards the elaboration of the most individual matters, the independence of the person, the autonomy of its development.
>
> (Simmel, 1991a: 20–1)

Simmel observed this in the growth of urbanisation across the Western world, which he argued is designed to serve the needs of the money economy, prioritising 'modes of interaction through exchange' (Miles, 2010: 17). The city dweller encounters innumerable persons in the course of the day, the majority of whom are strangers (Simmel, 1950a). This anonymity creates a desire for recognition and distinction as city dwellers seek to assert their individuality through fashion. Simmel (1991b) labelled this phenomenon 'status competition', which is driven by the problem of how to construct a unique self-identity in the face of an overwhelming anonymity (see also Bocock, 1993: 16).

While consumer culture may well provide a replacement for religion, its intimate links with the money economy is a destabilising force for many people. The reason for this is that money acquires its meaning by being 'given away' or 'circulating'. This in turn speeds up all related activities, making them continuous[3] (Simmel, 1907/1990). The effects of the money economy, particularly the increase in credit has meant that people are much more likely to spend to excess, leading to unsustainable levels of debt. The 'rapid circulation of money induces habits of spending and acquisition; it makes a specific quantity of money psychologically less significant and valuable' (Simmel, 1907/1990: 199). This has had a profound effect on the pace and rhythm of modern life, social interactions and relations, and the experience of time and space (Allen, 2000: 65).

As Western society began to move towards a culture of consumption, consumption items themselves began to take on a significance of their own in distinguishing social class (an idea that has firmly established itself in the work of the majority of contemporary consumer culture theorists). Thorstein Veblen, the American economist and sociologist, wrote about these changes in his book *The Theory of the Leisure Class* (1899/1994). In it Veblen coined the term 'conspicuous consumption' to describe the particular behaviour of both rich and poor in gaining advantage and favour through displays of wealth. These social behaviours were designed to communicate standing and status, and had become an increasingly common ritual in urban American society at the turn of the twentieth century (Ritzer *et al.*, 2001: 414). Veblen observed that one of the ways in which wealth was displayed was through the 'voluntary abnegation of pecuniary labour' (Rojek, 2000: 1). However, there has been an almost complete turnaround in this state of affairs in modern Western society. Research carried out by Rojek (2000) on the lives of wealthy elites such as Bill Gates, Warren Buffet and Richard Branson found they typically work longer hours than the average (the issue of longer working hours and its relationship with consumption will be discussed in more detail in Chapter 4).

While there is an ongoing debate over whether working hours have increased or decreased in Western countries over the last fifty years, a number of social theorists have come to agree that, despite the continued emphasis on work and production, Western society has become synonymous with consumption (Baudrillard, 1970/1998; Bauman, 2005; Cook, 2007; Cross, 1993; Lury, 1996; Miles, 2000; Sassatelli, 2007).

Writing during the period 1940–70 Erich Fromm was one of the first social psychologists to analyse consumer culture in any depth. While Fromm is referred to here as a social psychologist he certainly never inhabited the mainstream of the subdiscipline, which he felt was an apologist for the capitalist status quo. In his introduction to *The Sane Society* David Ingleby argues that Fromm is markedly different from most other social psychologists in that he wanted to say something important about human life and he was prepared to study beyond the limits of the subdiscipline in order to get it right. The problem that Fromm faced in working within the bounds of social psychology is that most social psychologists are happy to moralise without admitting it, and 'without straying from a banal and socially uncritical standpoint' (Ingleby, 1991/2002: p. lii).

Fromm's work is a rich amalgam of theoretical perspectives that include humanism, existentialism, psychoanalysis and Marxism. Fromm's commentaries on consumer culture are most fully explored in his two books *To Have, or to Be* (1947/2003) and *The Sane Society* (1956/1991). In the first book Fromm outlines two forms of existence, the 'having mode', a life based on material possessions, money and power, and the 'being mode', a life based on love, sharing and productive activity. In his second book (*The Sane Society*) Fromm outlines the process by which mass conformity to capitalist values and ideals is achieved, and the process by which a work and consumer ethic is internalised, which he links to new forms of psychological distress and isolation.

According to Fromm (1956/1991: 61) the demise of traditional institutions and the security afforded by an uncontested place in society has meant that people have become compelled to construct a uniquely personal self-identity in order to survive. Like religion in the premodern era, capitalism is transmitted in early childhood. The family functions as an agent of economic and social ideology, imparting desirable characteristics, so that children and adolescents become pre-adapted to its requirements. Children are socialised into the world of work and consumption by internalising an ethic of discipline, 'particularly orderliness and punctuality to a degree unknown in most other cultures'. Children learn to relate to themselves and others as commodities through their relations with family, peers, schooling and the mass media. Western capitalist society produces a social character in which these strivings become inherent (Fromm, 1956/1991: 78).

> Success depends largely on how well a person sells himself on the market, how well he gets his personality across, how nice a 'package' he is; whether he is 'cheerful', 'sound', 'aggressive', 'reliable', 'ambitious'.
>
> (Fromm, 1947/2003: 51)

Human qualities, like friendliness, courtesy, kindness and an ability to get on with others, are transformed into commodities. They become features of an individual's 'personality package' which is bought and sold in the marketplace (Fromm, 1956/1991: 138). Self-identity becomes a kind of cultural resource, asset or possession (Lury, 1996: 8).

As a practising psychoanalyst, Fromm was greatly interested in the causes of psychological distress and the role that capitalism played in its causes:

> [M]ental health cannot be defined in terms of the adjustment of the individual to his society, but, on the contrary, that it must be defined in terms of the adjustment of society to the needs of man, of its role in furthering or hindering the development of mental health.
>
> (Fromm, 1956/1991: 70)

According to Fromm the main threat to psychological health and wellbeing in the West is capitalist economic theory because it is based on the assumption that human nature is naturally competitive, aggressive, greedy and self-interested, making capitalism appear to be the system that most closely corresponds to human nature, placing it beyond the reach of criticism (Fromm, 1956/1991: 74). This problem begins with the widely accepted view that everything in the world can be equated with a price. Cars, cigars, clothing, watches and even people are described and understood in monetary terms, ceasing to have value for their usefulness; their primary quality becomes one of exchange-value only. This focus on abstract monetary dimensions precludes any kind of concrete experience. 'There is no frame of reference left which is manageable, observable, which is adapted to *human dimensions*' (Fromm, 1956/1991: 116).

The sense of control that individuals and groups have over their life has decreased in modern society according to Fromm. Human life has come to be increasingly filled with abstractions and the need to keep pace with the circulation of capital and changing technology.

> [M]an does not experience himself as the active bearer of his own powers and richness, but as an impoverished 'thing', dependent on powers outside of himself, onto whom he has projected his living substance.
>
> (Fromm, 1956/1991: 121)

As a consequence, alienation has come to inhabit everyday life. Alienation – which Fromm views as a sickness of the self – has become key to understanding psychological distress in modern Western society. Alienation represents a failure to fully experience one's self which may be characterised by one or more desires (e.g. money, power, status, sex and sex appeal), which becomes 'dominant and separated from the total personality, thus becoming the ruler of the person' (Fromm, 1962/2009: 41–3). The act of consumption should be a concrete act that is felt as a meaningful and productive experience. Instead it has become a pursuit that merely satisfies artificially stimulated desires which are impossible to fulfil (Fromm, 1956/1991: 130). Most of life now occurs outside the individual's control and purview, mental distress is often characterised by the experience of nothingness. People are increasingly absorbed in seeking and experiencing pleasure, relating to themselves as a system of desires and satisfactions. 'I have to work in order to fulfil my desires – and these very desires are constantly stimulated and directed by the economic machine' (Fromm, 1956/1991: 161).

Poststructural theories of consumer culture

From a poststructural perspective consumer culture is seen as a 'process governed by the *play of symbols*, not the satisfaction of material needs' (Bocock, 1993: 75; see also Miller, 1987). Its other main area of contribution has been its emphasis on discourse and the ways in which consciousness is governed or subjected to particular modes of thinking and behaviour by dominant social and cultural institutions; ideas which reached their apotheosis in the work of Michel Foucault.

In an interview prior to his death Foucault (1983: 208) stated that the goal of his work had been to 'create a history of the different modes by which, in our culture, human beings are made subjects'. Foucault theorised subjectivity in his ideas on governmentality, and its related concepts of discipline and power/knowledge, which he illustrated through various historical periods, such as the construction of madness as a disease (Foucault, 1961), and the development of the Western system of prisons (Foucault, 1975).

Foucault also applied his theory of governmentality to the history of modern Western neoliberal democracies (Dean, 2010: 175–204; Lemke, 2001). As previously noted in Chapter 1, conceptually neoliberalism links freedom with consumer sovereignty and choice; the individual in this system is empowered to maximise their personal economic and individual fulfilment. The basis of neoliberalism is a reduction in government services (or government interference) in the private lives of its citizens, with a concomitant expectation that each individual will take control of their own lives. In order for this ideal to function, governments institute techniques and programmes that shift the regulatory competence of the state onto responsible, rational, enterprising and productive individuals (Dean, 2010: 180–204; Lemke, 2001: 101–2; Rose, 1996: 150–68).

According to Foucault government in neoliberal democracies functions at both the macro level of state politics (e.g. international relations, border protection and setting macro-economic policy) and at the micro level of the individual (e.g.

schooling, healthcare, policing, employment and consumption) (Lemke, 2001). As Dean (2010: 20) notes, the government of the prison, the economy and the unemployed also governs 'our own bodies, personalities and inclinations', which 'entails an attempt to affect and shape in some way who and what individuals and collectives are and should be'. Read (2009: 3) makes a similar point when he states that neoliberalism is not just a method for governing states and economics 'but is intimately tied to the government of the individual, to a particular manner of living'. One of the goals of neoliberalism is to foster a population of individuals who will play an active role in their own 'self-governance' by interacting with the market and consumption through calculated acts and investments (Rose and Miller, 1992).

Techniques and programmes of governance are mobilised through various discourses and power/knowledge (Foucault, 1975), such as social science disciplines like psychology (Rose, 1996). From a Foucauldian perspective, discourses are not simply linguistic systems or text, 'but relatively well-bounded areas of social knowledge' (McHoul and Grace, 1993: 31). These bodies of knowledge comprise sets of rules and conditions which are established between institutions, economic and social practices, and patterns of behaviour (Foucault, 1969, 1991). They generally function outside of conscious awareness and they habitually influence social behaviour. Examples of dominant consumer culture discourses include the political linking of consumer sovereignty and choice with freedom (Smart, 2010), the linking of citizenship and national pride with consumption (Cohen, 2003; Ewen and Ewen, 1992; Munck, 2005; Smart, 2010), the work and spend treadmill that many people choose to pursue (Cross, 1993; Schor, 1991, 1999), the commercialisation of childhood and adolescence (Barber, 2007; Cook, 2004; Schor, 2004; Seiter, 1993), and the celebration of consumer values through the mass media and advertising (Ewen, 1976/2001; Ewen and Ewen, 1992; Hackley, 2002; Wickham, 1997). These phenomena are occasionally resisted by various interest groups, however, they have come to represent socially accepted practices and 'ways of being' in modern Western society (Smart, 2010).

An important aspect of Foucault's work was his linking of spatial organisation with different forms of governmentality (Elden, 2001). Foucault's (1961, 1975) illustration of the historical process of 'Othering' documented how out-groups were pushed to the periphery of society, both metaphorically and geographically. His analyses have revealed how space is used as a 'disciplinary' mechanism for policing and controlling certain elements of the population (Foucault, 1986). According to Voyce (2006) and Edensor (1998) these kinds of spaces are epitomised by shopping malls, shopping precincts, theme parks and popular tourist sites which are geared towards the promotion of consumption, where consumers are actively monitored and marginalised groups (those without the means to consume) are excluded. These commercially created spaces of consumption, which are not subject to borders, boundaries or particular geographic regions, reflect a placeless interpretation of a discursively constructed set of symbols and sets of rules designed to maximise consumption in that space.

The second key poststructuralist to have made a significant contribution to the understanding of consumer culture is Jean Baudrillard, whose most singular analysis of the phenomenon is presented in his book *The Consumer Society: Myths and Structures* (1970/1998). The main thrust of Baudrillard's analysis of consumer culture is his contention that its primary mode of function is the manipulation of *signs* and *symbols* (Ritzer, 1998a). Consumer products and services, such as cars, home furnishings, clothing and travel, convey social meaning; their symbolism represents cultural markers of taste, social hierarchy, lifestyle choice, values, group memberships and self-identity. The consumer is rendered passive in such a system in which 'the hyperreality of consumption codes, simulates and replaces the social in its entirety'[4] (Slater, 2005: 141). The superficial nature of this hyperreality is countered by the marketing, mass media and advertising industries which attempt to convince consumers that products and services are 'real'; thus the obsession with genuineness and authenticity in much advertising.

Consumer signs and symbols are imbued with social and cultural value by what they signify, and what they signify is defined by their relationship and place within the entire system of commodities and signs. These are played, manipulated and experimented with in order to fashion a self-identity. 'Sign fetishism' Baudrillard (1970/1998) argues has replaced commodity fetishism, and 'sign value' has replaced use-value and exchange-value. Use-value is subsumed by the floating signifier effect, so that social meaning can potentially be attached to any cultural product or service (Featherstone, 1991: 174). Hierarchy and social status are defined by product or services signs, as opposed to the products and services themselves. The importance placed on 'branding' by many of world's largest corporations is a vivid example of this.

Consumer culture is therefore a process in which the purchaser is actively engaged in trying to create and maintain a sense of self-identity through the display of purchased products and services and the signs and symbols they communicate to others (Baudrillard, 1970/1998).

Like other consumer culture theorists, Baudrillard argues that modern Western society is increasingly organised around the satisfaction of *desires* as opposed to *needs* (Baudrillard, 1970/1998: 10). Desire is limitless, whereas needs are not:

> If consumption appears irrepressible, this is because it is total idealist practice which has no longer anything to do (beyond a certain point) with the satisfaction of needs, nor with the reality principle . . . Hence the desire to 'moderate consumption', or to establish a normalizing network of needs, is naïve and absurd moralism.
>
> (Baudrillard, 1970/1998: 24–5)

Baudrillard (1970/1998: 129) also emphasised the human body in his analysis of consumer culture. He proposed that citizens of consumer cultures are encouraged to rediscover their bodies by liberating them from puritanical ideologies, so that the body becomes an 'object of salvation'. As a consequence, self-identity has become an increasingly embodied entity, once located in biology, and now transformed where it becomes a construction of consumer discourse. 'Our conceptions of our bodies, their parts and functions, are produced by cultural notions and components of culture, such as rituals, costumes, ways of eating and ways of living our bodies' (Bocock, 1993: 88). These discourses are communicated through the mass media and advertising which attempt to persuade audiences to invest in their bodies (which has become an extension of self-identity) in order to form them into smoother, more dynamic, more perfect, more functional objects for the outside world (Baudrillard, 1970/1998: 131). The reward for ascetic body work is not spiritual salvation, or much vaunted good health, 'but an enhanced appearance and more marketable self' (Featherstone, 1991: 171). The commercial obsession and commodification of the body and self-identity has become a staple feature of consumer culture, where it is viewed as the most precious of all exchange materials (Baudrillard, 1970/1998: 135). Ritzer notes:

> What concerns Baudrillard . . . is the role played by sexuality in the consumer society. Not only does sexuality tinge everything that is offered for consumption, but sexuality is itself offered for consumption.
>
> (1998a: 14)

A sexualised body, sociability and compatibility become personal assets in a consumer culture. The ability to be able to relate to others, to direct and stimulate interpersonal exchange, becomes a mark of 'personality' (Baudrillard, 1970/1998: 170). The inability to successfully master these skills is to have 'no personality', which is fatal to the individual's potential for success in a consumer culture. As a consequence children in the West are socialised into a system based on the 'commodity logic' which acts as a form of social control. 'Social control takes place by linking emancipation with repression and thus controlling needs by hanging them on the partial satisfactions provided by consumer goods and services' (Genosko, 2005: 32). One aspect of this socialisation process can be seen in the falling away of the 'heroes of production' – the self-made 'men', corporate founders, pioneers, explorers and colonisers – to the 'heroes of consumption' – film, music, and sporting stars – whose excessive expenditure, luxurious lifestyles and narcissism is exalted in the pages of magazines and television programmes (Baudrillard, 1970/1998: 45–6).

Consumption also socialises people in the ways it reproduces the class system, which it maintains in two main ways. First, from an economic perspective in terms of individual and family income; this determines purchasing power and consumer choice. Secondly, and more deeply, there is discrimination between those who achieve consumer mastery of aesthetic forms of knowledge and cultural accomplishment, compared to those who do not. The upper classes advertise their superiority through their displays of cultural understanding exerting power through cultural knowledge in the consumer choices they make (Baudrillard, 1970/1998: 59–60). In this way many of Baudrillard's ideas have come to resonate in the work of Pierre Bourdieu, to whom we will now turn.

Bourdieu's most significant work on consumer culture is outlined in his book *Distinction: A Social Critique of the Judgement of Taste* (1982). In it he argues that consumption is a social and cultural practice for establishing difference, at both the individual and group level, where demarcations are expressed through *taste* and choice of lifestyle, so that the presentation and eating of food, for example, is used as a means to signal lifestyle, knowledge and taste (Bourdieu, 1982: 61). Taste plays a key role here as Bourdieu (1982: 56) notes: 'Taste is the basis of all that one has – people and things – and all that one is for others, whereby one classifies oneself and is classified by others.'

That lifestyle is a marker of social class is not a new idea in social and cultural theory. Nevertheless, Bourdieu's (1982) contribution is significant because he was able to illustrate the ways in which taste determines social status. Individuals and groups paint a picture of themselves, to themselves and to others through the expression of taste. Taste therefore becomes a means for reproducing social class and status.

An individual's taste stems in part from what Bourdieu (1982) referred to as 'habitus'. A person's habitus resides largely in the unconscious, where it is shaped by historical, social and cultural factors that structure dispositional tendencies and practices that persist over time and across varying situations. In Bourdieu's own words:

> The conditionings associated with a particular class of conditions of existence produce *habitus*, systems of durable, transposable dispositions, structured structures predisposed to function as structuring structures, that is, as principles which generate and organize practices and representations that can be objectively adapted to their outcomes without presupposing a conscious aiming at ends or an express mastery of the operations necessary to attain them. Objectively 'regulated' and 'regular' without [being] in any way the product of obedience to rules, they can be collectively orchestrated without being the product of the organizing action of the conductor.
>
> (1990: 53)

These acquired competencies or abilities also function on a conscious level, reflecting an understanding of 'cultural fields' which form ways of thinking, perceiving and behaving. However, habitus is more than just a set of competencies and abilities for it is inscribed onto the body and can be observed in an individual's body shape, posture, movement, gesture, accent, tone of voice, degree of self-esteem and sense of ease in varying situations (Featherstone, 1987: 64). It is shaped in childhood through family, schooling, peer group and social class. Slater notes:

> Extended to consumer lifestyles, every object chosen and every consumer ritual can be related back to fine and realistic calculations of possible social moves and constraints, an inner sense of appropriate aspiration and how to act on it.
>
> (1997: 163)

The psychological literature tends to use the term habit in a much more limited way when compared to Bourdieu's usage as illustrated here in his theory of habitus. In psychology, habit usually refers to the model of conditioned reflexes advocated by the behaviourist wing of discipline (Camic, 1986, cited in Crossely, 2005: 104). Also a social psychologist would likely view habitus as another term for 'personality', however, there are important differences between social psychological definitions of personality and Bourdieu's concept of habitus; most notably, habitus is both unconscious and conscious, it is inscribed on the body for others to see, and it is heavily influenced by social and cultural conditions. Whereas personality, from a social psychological perspective, is predominantly viewed as a combination of inherited traits.

The term 'field' (or cultural fields) is used by Bourdieu and Wacquant (1992) to refer to the different elements of social life and practice such as family, economy, religion, media, sport, education, politics, art and science. Each of these fields has its own institutions, hierarchies, discourses and rules. Fields and the rules that govern them emerge through conflict and the exercise of power as different groups compete with one another to legitimise their values and interests; they are dynamic and exist in a constant state of flux. Individuals and groups also compete with one another to attain (in the case of consumer culture) 'cultural capital' through their knowledge and choice of consumer products and services. Harker *et al.* state:

> the definition of capital is very wide for Bourdieu and includes material things (which can have symbolic value), as well as 'untouchable' but culturally significant attributes such as prestige, status and authority (referred to as symbolic capital), along with cultural capital (defined as culturally-valued taste and consumption patterns) . . . For Bourdieu, capital acts as a social relation within a system of exchange, and the term is extended to all the goods, material and symbolic, without distinction, that present themselves as rare and worthy of being sought after in a particular social formation.
>
> (1990: 1)

Social theories of consumer culture

As a grouping, social theorists have been the most active scholars to theorise and empirically investigate consumer culture. The most prominent of these include Anthony Giddens, Ulrich Beck, Zygmunt Bauman, George Ritzer and Henri Lefebvre, along with others such as Chris Lasch and Mike Featherstone (for a more detailed review of Featherstone's work see Chapter 1 and for Lasch Chapter 3).

Much of Giddens's, Beck's and Bauman's work has focused on the change in social life that has occurred over the last 150 years, and the emergence of a more fluid self-identity stemming from the social, cultural, economic and political globalisation that has come to dominate the late twentieth and early twenty-first centuries. All three authors are in agreement that social life has altered due to greater uncertainty and the demise of relatively stable (traditional) institutions. In the pre- and early-industrial phases self-identity was determined by one's station at birth, family, community, religious observances and social class. Individuals and groups were embedded in a wider web of meaning through stories, seasonal rituals and well-defined cultural frames of reference (Bauman, 1996; Beck *et al.*, 1994; Giddens, 1991). Kellner notes:

> in traditional societies, one's identity was fixed, solid, and stable. Identity was a function of predefined social roles and a traditional system of myths which provided orientation and religious sanctions to one's place in the world, while rigorously circumscribing the realm of thought and behaviour. One was born and died a member of one's tribe or group with one's life trajectory fixed in advance. In pre-modern societies, identity was un-problematic and not subject to reflection or discussion. Individuals did not undergo identity crises, or radically modify their identity . . . In modernity, identity becomes more mobile, multiple, personal, self-reflexive, and subject to change and innovation.
>
> (1992: 141)

The conditions in which this shift in social life occurred have been variously referred to as 'late modern', 'postindustrial', 'posttraditional', 'postfordist' or 'postmodern'.[5] All of these terms point to the pluralised nature of contemporary Western society, which offers multiple identities, images and diverse lifestyles from which to choose and which are filtered through abstract systems and commodification (Bauman, 1988, 2000; Beck, 1992; Giddens, 1991). Slater comments:

> Consumer culture is therefore something like a permanent identity crisis, with a constant state of anxiety and risk attached and little possibility of establishing what is right or correct consumption because there is constant change and competition of lifestyles.
>
> (2005: 144)

In *Modernity and Self-Identity* Giddens (1991) argues that self-identity has now become a task that is continuously shaped and reflected upon. The once fairly static nature of self-identity has become a dynamic entity that Giddens and other social theorists have labelled 'reflexive'. This reflexivity is played out and expressed in the choice of lifestyle, which has become particularly significant in the formation and maintenance of self-identity. As Giddens (1991) notes, the more that traditional institutions lose their hold, the more that day-to-day life is reconstituted by the interplay between the local and the global, the more individuals are forced to negotiate lifestyle choices among a diversity of options. 'Of course, there are standardising influences too – most notably, in the form of commodification, since capitalistic production and distribution form core components of modernity's institutions' (Giddens, 1991: 5). Giddens also identified the body as playing a key role in the reflexive maintenance of self-identity, which many people feel compelled to vigorously work on and transform in their development and choice of lifestyle (Giddens, 1991: 7; see also Shilling, 2003).

Like Simmel, Giddens points to the problems that have arisen from the increased freedoms and uncertainty that have taken place as a consequence of the demise of traditional institutions and the sense of security they once afforded. This demise provokes new anxieties and problems which Giddens (1991) refers to as 'ontological insecurity'. Ontological insecurity is a state of precariousness where a person lacks the basic assurances from which to negotiate the various existential conditions of life – freedom, choice, responsibility, meaning, anxiety, and death – which are now commonly solved through consumer/lifestyle choices (Chaney, 1996; Cushman, 1990). Giddens notes:

> The project of the self becomes translated into one of the possession of desired goods and the pursuit of artificially framed styles of life . . . The consumption of ever-novel goods becomes in some part a substitute for the genuine development of the self.
>
> (1991: 198)

A person's sense of self-identity has become intimately connected to consumer culture, which has come to structure many aspects of everyday life (Giddens, 2003), and which some social theorists argue has led to pathological forms of individualism, feelings of isolation and alienation, addiction and unsustainable levels of debt (to be discussed in more detail in Chapter 4). For example, Chris Lasch (1979) argues that an increasingly 'narcissistic personality' has emerged over the course of the twentieth century in the wake of the decline in traditional institutions. As links to more traditional institutions and roles become disconnected, commodity purchasing and mass media consumption come to the fore.

> The American economy, having reached the point where its technology was capable of satisfying basic material needs, now relied on the creation of new consumer demands – on convincing people to buy goods for which they are unaware of any need until the 'need' is forcibly brought to their attention by the mass media.
>
> (Lasch, 1979: 72)

Despite the potential problems that arise with the demise of traditional institutions, Giddens (2003) argues that the new freedoms associated with late modernity are important because they provide opportunities to question life and the nature of society. In this respect Giddens disagrees with Foucault's thesis on governmentality that hidden power/knowledge compels people to unconsciously consume. Instead, he argues that most consumers are active, reflexive, knowing agents; he does concede however that some people still become lost in consumer-driven lifestyles:

> it can be the case that you get embedded in a life-style that drives you in a certain direction, and that can be a substitute for a cogent sense of who you are and what your life should be.
>
> (Giddens, 2003: 392)

Featherstone (1991: 175) makes a similar appraisal, stating the loss of traditional values such as social solidarity needs to be weighed against the greater influence individuals now have over the direction of their life. Beck (2001) cautions however, arguing that reflexivity 'does not mean that people today lead a more conscious life. On the contrary, reflexive signifies not an increase of mastery and consciousness, but a heightened awareness that mastery is impossible' (Beck, 2001: 267).

Like Giddens, Bauman (2005: 24) argues that late modern Western society engages its citizens primarily as consumers. This differs from its predecessor, the 'producer society', which engaged its members primarily as producers. The shift from a producer to a consumer society, Bauman argues, requires a rethink in the ways that people now experience life. This includes the relationship between state and market, social solidarity, community memberships, social, structural and hierarchical distinctions, and self-identity.

The shift from a production- to a consumption-based society has led to social relations that are less like Foucault's panopticon where the dominant motif of the world was that of the 'factory', to one that is based on aesthetic consumption where the dominant motif of the world has become the 'shopping mall'[6] (Bauman, 2005). Panoptical institutions were designed to discipline docile bodies through training regimes, guidelines and routines. These institutions were suitable for producing producers; however they do not adequately train consumers who need to be encouraged to tap into their deepest desires, and who must learn to choose from a myriad of products and services in order to fulfil these (Bauman, 2005). Quoting Mark C. Taylor and Esa Saarinen, Bauman (2005: 25) notes 'desire does not desire satisfaction. To the contrary, desire desires desire.' The practice of consumption is therefore no longer instrumental; instead it has become 'autotelic', that is, pursued for its own sake (Bauman, 2004: 294). In the eighteenth and nineteenth centuries consumption functioned largely as a means to satisfy basic living and material needs (e.g. food, shelter, clothing and warmth). In the twentieth and twenty-first centuries, with the advent of the mass media, marketing and advertising industries, consumption based on satisfying needs has become a constraint. Basic needs are now much more easily satisfied in the West where production and supply chain mechanisms have become highly rational and efficient; however, with 'desire' a person's needs become limitless. 'The passage from satisfying needs to gratifying desires was obviously a revolutionary step for consumption and its place in the individual's life-in-society' (Bauman, 2004: 298).

Unleashing desire instituted a new force in the stimulation of economic growth, which had hitherto been shackled by the modest forces of material need. Foucault's conceptualisation of power/knowledge as a disciplining force is also challenged by Bauman (1992) who argues that power in consumer society is exercised as a seductive force stimulated by desire (an idea echoed in the work of Jean Baudrillard). Ideally the consumer is never totally satisfied. They are placed in a position where they exist in a constant state of flux, oscillating between the seduction and temptation of new products and services. Normative regulation is therefore viewed as dysfunctional, freedom of choice reigns supreme. 'The consumer must be guided by aesthetic interests, not ethical norms' (Bauman, 2005: 31).

This ties in closely with the principles of neoliberalism which is designed to allow consumers to choose between a myriad of products and services (Bauman, 2005: 58). It is for this reason that it is more accurate to speak of self-identity in the plural: 'the life itinerary of most individuals is likely to be strewn with discarded and lost identities' (Bauman, 2005: 28), on account of the choices that a globalised world now offers. And yet choice can be a morally hazardous exercise, becoming a highly individualised concern reflecting a person's competencies and skills. The underclass in consumer cultures, therefore, become 'the aggregate product of wrong individual choices; proof of the "choice incompetence of its members"' (Bauman, 2005: 76). Consumer choice also has the potential to create an inexhaustible source of insecurity. Overwhelmed, consumers are often happy to hand over the responsibility of choosing to others such as the mass media and advertising.

> Hapless consumers are grateful to whoever offers to take over and carry the burden of choice that they would otherwise find unbearable. Manipulators are welcome as liberators from chores of exercising private responsibility, not as invaders of privacy; as friendly guides, rather than bossy impostors.
>
> (Bauman, 2004: 303)

Having now briefly reviewed some the social theories of consumer culture related to self-identity and emotional and behavioural problems, we now turn to social theoretical conceptions of consumer space. Henri Lefebvre along with Anthony Giddens and Michel Foucault are prominent thinkers in this area of inquiry, and their ideas will form much of the theoretical basis for our critique of social and environmental psychology in Chapter 5.

Lefebvre (1974/1991a, 1947/1991b) was inspired mainly by the works of Karl Marx, which he applied to his theorising of human geography. Lefebvre highlighted the relationship between space and social life and the shift from manufacturing- to service-based economies in the West, coupled with the development of global information technology networks, which have facilitated new forms of spatial organisation and existence (Zieleniec, 2007: 60). Lefebvre (1976b) conceptualised space as active and dynamic, something that is continuously produced, reproduced and contested; a site in which power relationships evolve and play out. Like Harvey (1973: 14), Lefebvre argued that space is not an empty container in which things are placed and happen. Instead space is socially produced, representing distinctive human practices and cultures. 'In other words, a person's understanding of their social reality conditions their usage of space in respect of how they interact with others in specific places for particular reasons (i.e. for work, leisure, consumption, etc.)' (Zieleniec, 2007: 73). This view stands in contrast to the physical or natural scientific view of space as an object devoid of ideology and politics (Lefebvre, 1976b), one that is commonly invoked in the social and environmental psychology literature.

In capitalist economies space is always owned by someone; it therefore has the potential to be used as a means for excluding the Other, and to act as a force for injustice (Shields, 2004). Zukin (1991), like Lefebvre, also places power at the centre of her conceptualisation of space (or 'landscapes' in Zukin's terminology) which go beyond simple physical surroundings to encompass material and social practices and their symbolic representation. In this view, spaces and the pathologies associated with them (exclusion, prejudice, injustice and violence) are socially produced. Capitalism has transformed space into a commodity, reproducing capitalist modes of production and consumption, which shape the nature of social interactions and relations that occur in them (Lefebvre, 1974/1991a, 1987). This is particularly so for cities in the West, which have devolved into commercially produced spaces, commodified spectacles and opportunities for shopping and other consumption-based leisure activities. Under capitalist modes of production and consumption space becomes homogenised and hegemonic, as social interactions and relations are commodified (Lefebvre, 1974/1991a). Consumer spaces with their shared symbolic features, attractions and images reflect the ideologies of the powerful. They reproduce societal norms and values, capitalist modes of production and consumption such as orderliness, punctuality, the conquest of nature and commodification (Lefebvre, 1974/1991a, 1976a; see also Fromm, 1956/1991 and Baudrillard, 1970/1998).

Feminist theories of consumer culture

One of the most striking features of consumption and its culture is the clear demarcation that it draws between the genders. Despite the greater participation of women in the workforce in the late twentieth century, and other areas of life where they have experienced a degree of liberation, women are still held to be largely responsible for work inside and associated with the home (e.g. cooking, cleaning, food shopping and child rearing) (Hochschild, 1989; Lachance-Grzela and Bouchard, 2010). Capitalism, Bocock (1993: 95) argues, continues to function from a binary relation of production and consumption: production (work) for men which is treated as serious and important, consumption for women (house work, shopping) which is treated as playful and unimportant.

The reproduction of gender identities and stereotypes in consumer cultures is driven predominantly through representations in the mass media and advertising (Bordo, 1993, 2000; Cowan, 1983; Fischer and Arnold, 1990; Hochschild, 2003; Lury, 1996; Matthews, 1987; Sassatelli, 2007; Scanlon, 2000a). Gender identities are also constructed around consumer products and services, which are conceived, designed and marketed along gendered lines (Sassatelli, 2007: 28). Evidence for this can be seen in television advertising (Coltrane and Messineo, 2000), television programming (Seiter, 1993; Stole, 2003), and in the gendering of children's toys and clothing (Rogers, 1999). The average person in the West is annually bombarded with thousands of 'gender defining' messages and images through the mass media and advertising. And it is still the case that women are represented as most suited to homemaking and nurturing, which ties in with their seemingly greater knowledge and expertise as consumers. Men on the other hand are typically represented as reluctant consumers (this is now beginning to change as we will see in Chapter 3) who are enticed to consume the images of women's bodies, suggesting that the conquest of sexual relations can be achieved through the purchase of the right kinds of products and services (Scanlon, 2000a). Therefore, as a gendered process, consumption and its culture is a site of power relations (Sassatelli, 2007: 28). Roberts notes:

> If we were to adopt Michel Foucault's notion of power relations, we could say as well that commodities constitute a set of forms of cultural domination through which power is exercised and social organization constituted.
>
> (1998: 841)

Of course the construction of gender in the mass media and advertising does not accurately convey the diverse nature of gender roles in contemporary Western society, which have become much more ambiguous and fluid. Nevertheless, the pressures exerted on girls and women to conform to particular idealised representations in consumer cultures tends to be much greater than it is for boys and men (Jagger, 2001). This treatment instils in girls and women ambivalence towards their bodies. Highly sexualised media images and messages warn women to simultaneously be afraid of their bodies (of becoming fat, emitting unpleasant odours and bleeding), while at the same time they are encouraged to celebrate their bodies, to view them as a passport to happiness; it is through the body that a woman is able to entice a man, which should be their main objective in life (Ussher, 1989: 38). Featherstone notes:

> Women are of course most clearly trapped in the narcissistic, self-surveillance world of images, for apart from being accorded the major responsibility in organising the purchase and consumption of commodities their bodies are used symbolically in advertisements.
>
> (1991: 178–9)

As previously noted, the body is emphasised and celebrated in consumer cultures. Karl Marx played a crucial role here by reimagining the body in his theory as a historical and not merely a biological arena, an arena shaped by the political and economic organisation of social life (Bordo, 1993: 33). In consumer culture the body is linked to a plethora of idealised images of youth, health, fitness, beauty and sex appeal. This has the effect of increasing behaviours related to 'body maintenance' and 'the performing self'. When compared to men, women spend much more of their time on activities associated with body maintenance in the form of exercise, shopping for clothing and cosmetics, hair appointments, bathing, grooming and in the application of makeup (Featherstone, 1991: 182). The embodied emphasis on the self has led to the emergence of what Featherstone (1991: 187–93) refers to as the 'performing self', which 'places a greater emphasis upon appearance, display and the management of impression'. The density of interpersonal interactions makes it difficult to stand out in any meaningful way; to do so impressions need to be managed with style, panache and careful bodily presentation (Featherstone, 1991: 191).

Summary and conclusion

A range of different theories on consumer culture with a focus on self-identity, emotional and behavioural problems and geographic space have been reviewed for the purpose of critiquing and expanding social psychological theory in later chapters. It was identified that Western society has shifted from an economy based on 'production' to an economy based on 'consumption'. This has had far-reaching effects on the formation of self-identity and social behaviour. In pre- and early-industrial phases in the West self-identity was fixed by predefined roles and a social structure that was rigid and unchanging. In the industrial and post-industrial period self-identity is now viewed as a problem requiring resolution; it has become a reflexive entity concerned with making choices between competing identities and lifestyles. In the productivist phase self-identity was anchored to the realms of work, family and community bonds. As this realm has become more unstable, insecure and fluid, consumption has come to fill the void. This can be seen in the nature of human interactions and relations which are now increasingly commodified, in the replacement of needs with desires, in the linking of distinction and status with access to consumer symbols and the learning of skills to manipulate and master these, and in the construction of gender identities by the mass media and advertising.

In taking account of the formation of self-identity in consumer cultures, various problems were identified. The first of these was the spectre of alienation (isolation) stemming from the decline in genuine social relations, which are being replaced with instrumental (economic) relations between people, and relations between people and commodities. Key to this separation is the aggression and competition that neoliberalism encourages between people and organisations, which is viewed as a natural state of affairs. The exercise of power, once achieved through the training of docile bodies for the purpose of production, is now exercised through seduction, for the purpose of consumption. Desire has come to replace fulfilment, and consumer discourses and ideologies are internalised by the forces of neoliberal governmentality. These discourses and ideologies have led to the increasing embodiment of self-identity, which can be seen in the pressure placed on girls and women to simultaneously celebrate the emancipation of their bodies, and to apply a high degree of disciplinary surveillance over its imperfections and failings.

Theories concerning the changing design and organisation of urban/suburban spaces in consumer cultures were also outlined. These changes have led to a growth in urbanisation and greater feelings of anonymity as the population of towns and cities has significantly expanded. It was also argued that geographic space is not merely a backdrop or empty container in which social behaviour occurs. Instead the planning, design and organisation of space in the West are guided by capitalist/neoliberal ideologies and discourses. Space is designed to speed up the flow of capital (or at least not hinder its movement), and this produces corresponding social interactions and relations. In order to maintain the flow of capital, specifically consumer spending, consumer and urban/suburban spaces prejudice and exclude undesirables who potentially threaten this process.

3   Self-identity in consumer culture

Introduction

The purpose of this chapter is to review the leading theories of self-identity in social psychology and then to critically analyse and expand on these as they relate to elements of consumer culture. The concept of self-identity in social psychology has established itself as a central construct of inquiry. Its most popular theory – social identity theory – contains a number of integrated conceptual components. These include social comparison, self-esteem and self-enhancement. These and other related theories will be reviewed in the first part of this chapter. This is then followed by a critical analysis of these theories within the consumer culture literature. This analysis highlights a number of social forces exerted by consumer culture that significantly influence and shape self-identity. The topics to be covered here include commodification, narcissism, distinction, gender and discourse.

Before entering into this analysis it is important to note that, in the following outline and in subsequent chapters, we are not claiming to offer an exhaustive review of social psychological concepts and theories. Instead we seek to highlight their most salient points and how these intersect with our reading of the consumer culture literature reviewed in Chapter 2.

Self-identity in social psychology

History

In many senses this now classic quote taken from the anthropologist Clifford Geertz sums up the challenge that social psychological conceptions of self-identity must contend.

> The Western conception of the person as a bounded, unique, more or less integrated motivational and cognitive universe, a dynamic centre of awareness, emotion, judgement and action, organized into a distinctive whole and set against a background of other such whole and against a social and natural background, is, however incorrigible it may seem to us, a rather peculiar idea within the context of the world's cultures.
>
> (Geertz, 1975: 48)

As Geertz notes, the Western concept of self-identity is a product of its unique historical, cultural, social, economic and political context. As previously discussed in Chapter 2, the experience of self-identity has altered as a consequence of the demise of traditional institutions such as work, family, community bonds and religious observance in Western society. What has emerged in their place is an individualised subject influenced and shaped by consumer culture.

Social psychology's initial forays into theorising self-identity drew on a number of perspectives including structuralism (Wilhelm Wundt), psychoanalysis (Sigmund Freud), sociology (Durkheim, Weber) and symbolic interactionism (William James, George Herbert Mead, Charles Cooley) (Thorne and Henley, 2005: 506–8). Each of these perspectives emphasised the 'social' nature of self-identity, which was influenced and shaped via interactions and relations with societal institutions, groups and other individuals. In these interactions self-identity assimilates external persons, objects, ideologies and institutions, a process summarised as 'society shapes self, shapes social behaviour' (Stryker and Burke, 2000: 284). Contemporary social psychology texts make brief mention of these theoretical perspectives as a part of the subdiscipline's historical antecedents. Yet research and theorising conducted over the last forty years has tended to ignore these theoretical traditions and their recent interpretations and applications, in favour of a predominantly individualised cognitive approach to understanding self-identity (Hollway, 2007).

In the 1930s American social psychology took what Greenwood has labelled an individualistic asocial turn that began with the work of Floyd and Gordon Allport.

> Allport is often represented as having established that social psychological phenomena are nothing more than aggregations of individual psychological explanation, amenable to the experimental methods of individual psychology.
> (Greenwood, 2004a: 136)

In 1935, Gordon Allport proposed what has become the most popular definition of social psychology today: 'the scientific investigation of how the thoughts, feelings, and behaviours of individuals are influenced by the actual, imagined or implied presence of others' (Allport, 1954: 5). In 1924 Gordon Allport's brother, Floyd, published *Social Psychology*, which went on to become a seminal text in the subdiscipline, solidifying its adherence to an individualistic ontology. As an example: 'There is no psychology of groups which is not essentially and entirely a psychology of individuals' (Allport, 1924, cited in Hogg and Vaughan, 2005: 116). It was claimed that (Floyd) Allport's approach to social psychology led to 'experimental precision to an area that had been a loose amalgamation of sociology, instinct psychology, and evolutionary theory' (Post, 1980: 369). The cultural politics of the time influenced a movement away from an emphasis upon character, self-sacrifice, hard work and sobriety, towards an emphasis on personality, which Gordon Allport reflected in his work (Nicholson, 2002).

Social cognition

From the late 1940s to the 1970s some of the most iconic research in social psychology was carried out. The majority of this research employed either experimental designs conducted in laboratories or quasi-experimental designs conducted in the field. These included studies by Muzafer Sherif, Leon Festinger, Solomon Asch and Stanley Milgram. By the early 1970s the 'cognitive approach' to psychology had emerged, eventually dominating the discipline, particularly in the US. Social psychology adapted the cognitive approach to suit its own methods and topics, where it morphed into 'social cognition':

> Social cognition was the dominant topic of conferences in the late 1970s, and of edited collections in the early 1980s. Fiske and Taylor's definitive text *Social Cognition* came out in 1982. In the early 1980s the journal *Social Cognition* was instituted, along with the 'Attitudes and Social Cognition' section of the *Journal of Personality and Social Psychology*.
>
> (Greenwood, 2004a: 239)

During this period social psychologists referred to the 'sovereignty' of social cognition as the subdiscipline became synonymous with cognitive psychology: 'reaffirming that social psychology is just a branch of individual psychology' (Greenwood, 2004a: 239; see also Oishi *et al.*, 2009). This is reflected in the philosophical assumptions that underpin social cognition, which states that social behaviour stems from individual cognition in social situations. Much of social psychology's focus during this time was directed towards understanding the processing, storing and retrieval of information and the effect of this on perceptions, memories, thoughts and feelings. This has endured to the present day where social cognition continues to be the dominant theoretical approach. Hogg and Vaughan note:

> It (social cognition) has taught us much about how we process and store information about people, and how this affects the way we perceive and interact with people. It has also taught us new methods and techniques for conducting social psychological research – methods and techniques borrowed from cognitive psychology and then refined for social psychology.
>
> (2005: 42)

Studies on self-identity that use a social cognitive perspective typically focus on how knowledge related to the self is processed and stored. One of the earliest studies to employ a social cognitive approach to conceptualise self-identity was carried out by Bem (1972). According to Bem, evaluations of self-identity are formed from internal attributions, which he referred to as 'self-perception theory'. Self-perception theory proposes that we evaluate our thinking and feeling and make judgements about self-identity based on this information. In more ambiguous situations, we observe our overt behaviour and the circumstances in which this occurs in order to develop a clearer picture of who we are.

Thus, to the extent that internal cues are weak, ambiguous, or un-interpretable, the individual is functionally in the same position as an outside observer, an observer who must necessarily rely upon those same external cues to infer the individual's inner state.

(Bem, 1972: 2)

Taking some of these ideas further Markus (1977) developed the concept of self-schemas. Self-schemas are knowledge structures or mental categories that influence the way we recognise and store information related to self-identity. Self-schemas function by confirming our existing self-concept. People are either schematic or aschematic with respect to various traits or characteristics such as independent/dependent, outgoing/dull, leader/follower. If an individual is schematic for 'independence' then they will have memories of previous behaviours that indicate this. The source of self-schemas is thought to be cognitive carriers of dispositions indicating a biological basis.

In a confirmatory study Rogers *et al.* (1977) investigated information processing functions related to self-identity; specifically how self-related information is encoded. The authors found that participants had a heightened sensitivity to words that were salient to their self-schemas. Schematic words were stored for longer periods in the participants' memories than those words that were less salient or aschematic.

In a later study Markus and Nurius (1986) introduced the theory of 'possible selves'. Possible selves are cognitive representations of what we would like to become, or indeed, not become, as the case may be. Possible or future selves not only serve to organize information, they are a powerful motivational influence, directing us to become what we desire. In a related study Higgins (1987) investigated the potential discrepancies that arise when we compare our 'actual self' (how we currently are) with our 'ideal self' (how we would like to be), and 'ought self' (how we think we should be).

Failure to resolve the actual–ideal discrepancy produces dejection-related emotions (e.g. disappointment, dissatisfaction, sadness), whereas failure to resolve the actual–ought discrepancy produces agitation-related emotions.

(Hogg and Vaughan, 2005: 121)

The major problem that arises from cognitive interpretations of self-identity is the lack of understanding of what might shape self-schemas or possible selves in the first place. That is, what are the *origins* of self-schemas and possible selves, apart from the commonly cited claim they arise from dispositional tendencies? For example, Markus and Nurius (1986: 954) begin their article by suggesting the pool of possible selves stem from particular sociocultural and historical contexts, and 'from the models, images, and symbols provided by the media and by the individual's social experiences'. This however is as far as the authors go in analysing this important idea. It begs the question where these models, images and symbols come from, and the process by which they are internalised by the individual. As well as exploring the sociocultural context and role played by the mass media in shaping self-schemas and possible selves, there is also a need to investigate more deeply the ideologies and discourses that are particular to each society and historical period and the manner in which these open up and limit one's knowledge about self-identity.

Social identity theory

Social cognitive concepts (e.g. self-perception theory, self-schemas, possible selves) along with social identity theory have become the most popular theoretical perspectives used to interpret self-identity by social psychologists. Social identity theory informs a number of social psychological projects/topics including attitudes, conformity, attributions, stereotypes and organisational behaviour. Social identity theory proposes that self-identity is defined by one's 'personal identity' or personality (our perception of self and its unique or idiosyncratic combination of traits), and a 'social identity' which is defined by our membership of social groups (Hogg, 2003).

Social identity theory stemmed initially from the work of Henri Tajfel, a Polish-born British social psychologist, who studied the process of social categorisation and inter-group relations. Tajfel (1970) conducted a series of laboratory experiments that employed the 'minimal group paradigm', a technique used to establish groups on an insignificant and artificial (i.e. minimal) basis in order create discrimination between them. From these and subsequent studies, he and his colleagues proposed that social group membership (e.g. membership of a profession, sporting team, family, school, subculture and/or nationality) provides the basis by which individuals categorise themselves in society (Tafjel *et al.*, 1971; Tajfel, 1974). Membership of social groups and their shared categorisations form the basis of self-identity (e.g. attitudes, perceptions, beliefs, and values) and social behaviour. 'It is not simply a group one is objectively in, but one which is subjectively important in determining one's actions' (Turner *et al.*, 1987: 2). The individual evaluates their in-group(s) (the groups to which they belong), contrasting these with out-group(s) (other groups to which they do not belong) (Tafjel and Turner, 1986). This contrast forms the basis for understanding one's own distinctiveness and difference.

> The basic idea is that social category (e.g. nationality, political affiliation, sports team) into which one feels one belongs, provides a definition of who one is in terms of the defining characteristics of the category – a self-definition that is a part of the self-concept.
>
> (Hogg *et al.*, 1995: 259)

Social psychologists understand social identity as a 'cognitive *tool* that individuals use to partition, categorize, and order their social environment and their own place in it' (Owens, 2003: 224).

Self-esteem, that is, the individual's evaluation of the self, is determined in part by one's in-group memberships, which regulate how we feel about ourselves. In our pursuit of self-esteem we favour in-group norms, characteristics, attitudes, and beliefs over those of out-groups. This inherent bias enhances the prestige of one's in-groups and one's sense of self-identity, enabling a positive view of oneself. Hogg *et al.* note:

> It is assumed that people have a basic need to see themselves in a positive light in relation to relevant others (i.e. to have an evaluatively positive self-concept), and that self-enhancement can be achieved in groups by making comparisons between the in-group and relevant out-groups in ways that favour the in-group.
>
> (1995: 260)

Regardless of the group's material status (measured by income, occupation, education, position in a cultural or class hierarchy, or choice of lifestyle), even the most disadvantaged groups in society use this inherent bias to view themselves in a favourable light. People who belong to poorer backgrounds with little status for example may see themselves as more genuine, grounded and authentic; looking upon wealthier groups with more status as shallow and superficial (Gough and McFadden, 2001: 201–2). However, inquiries of this nature are strangely absent from the social psychology literature. As is a willingness to ask deeper questions about the ways in which historical, cultural, social, economic and political forces shape group memberships and how this influences an individual's thinking and behaviour.

The basic need to see oneself and one's group memberships in a positive light is linked with other social psychological theories including 'self-enhancement', 'self-affirmation' and 'impression management'. As social beings we are motivated to 'enhance the positivity or decrease the negativity of the self-concept' (Sedikides and Strube, 1995: 1330). A number of experimental studies testing these concepts, predominantly on undergraduate students, indicates a propensity for people to view themselves in a positive light, despite information or actual material conditions indicating otherwise, and in more favourable terms than other individuals and groups (e.g. Brown and Gallagher, 1992; Joseph *et al.*, 1992; Kruegar, 1998). Similarly, self-affirmation proposes that people are motivated to protect their image of self-identity from attacks on its integrity (Steele, 1988).

As well as protecting our favourable concept of self-identity, we also engage in various strategies and behaviours in an effort to convince others to view us in a positive light. This is referred to as 'impression management' (Hogg and Vaughan, 2005: 139–41). Impression management behaviours stem from an ongoing concern with how others perceive and evaluate us (Leary, 1995). Leary's account of impression management grew out of research initially conducted by Erving Goffman (1959). Goffman invoked the theory of 'dramaturgy' to interpret social behaviour. Dramaturgy uses the stage or theatre as a metaphor, the idea being that society is a stage, and the people who inhabit it are its players (Marshall, 1998: 171). Upon this stage we each seek to play that part of ourselves and to display our most favourable characteristics that we want others to see in us. Others' impressions of us are often tightly controlled and stage-managed where possible.

In summary, despite invoking the term 'social', social psychological theories of self-identity are underpinned by an individualistic ontology, which separates the individual from their social and cultural context (Gergen, 2012; Henriques *et al.*, 1984; Hollway, 2007). Its singular emphasis on individual cognitive processes has led to a narrow and impoverished theory of self-identity, which locates the social inside the mind of the individual (Moscovici, 1972), effectively delegitimising the historical, cultural, social, economic and political forces that influence and shape the construction of self-identity. Jenkins argues:

> despite Tajfel's original ambitions, 'social identity theory' remains an individualist perspective: groups are, at best, taken for granted as simplified and reified features of the human landscape, actual interaction is largely ignored, and identification appears to take place solely 'inside people heads'.
>
> (2008: 115)

Self-identity in consumer culture

The commodified self

Self-identity (or personality) is commodified in consumer cultures. In other words it is transformed into a commodity, where it is packaged, presented and sold, like any other commodity. Commodification is a pervasive feature of consumer culture influencing social behaviour in myriad ways. The mass media and advertising encourages people to unleash their inner most acquisitive desires so that, along with personal indulgence, the individual is trained to desire success in every sphere of life, but most importantly in career,[1] particularly in the US.

> American society is marked by a central stress upon personal achievement, especially secular occupational achievement. The 'success story' and the respect accorded to the self-made man are distinctly American if anything is.
>
> (Williams, 1970: 454)

Success in consumer culture has become associated with a set of particular personality traits that include flexibility, entrepreneurial, independent, productive, competitive, aggressive and extraverted (Boltanski and Chiapello, 2006; Cushman, 1995: 149; Fromm, 1956/1991; Lasch, 1979; McDonald *et al.*, 2008; Sennet, 1998, 2006; Simmel, 1991a). Personality in consumer cultures refers to one's ability to be attractive and charming to others, to stand out in the crowd, to be unique and distinctive. These qualities Cushman states are best learnt during one's leisure:

> Personality, since it made one attractive to others, led to business success as well as personal success. Success in business was predicated on the ability to sell – not only goods, but oneself as well. Social performance, not hard work, became the key to wealth and power.
>
> (1995: 65)

That these traits and behaviours correspond with capitalist/neoliberal principles of self-governance is no coincidence. Success in consumer culture is built upon an individual's reflexive understanding and expression of self-identity as a cultural resource or asset that is packaged and presented in the marketplace for the purpose of gaining influence and favour (Baudrillard, 1970/1998: 131; Bauman, 2007: 6; Fromm, 1956/1991: 138; Lasch, 1979: 57–8; Lury, 1996: 8).

The development of information communication technologies such as the internet has turned out to be particularly well suited to the commodification of self-identity. This can be seen in the growing popularity of internet dating and romance services where prospective partners are coached on how best to sell themselves by posting flattering photographs, developing appealing headlines and writing profiles that accentuate their most unique and desirable characteristics – a process not dissimilar to the marketing and advertising of a car or piece of furniture. In 2011 it was estimated that five million people in the United States became paid users of internet dating services, representing an industry worth approximately US$1.9 billion.[2]

The other major self-commodifying internet phenomenon to have gained worldwide prominence is Facebook.[3] Touted as a 'social networking site' Facebook allows its users to create an appealing image of one's self-identity. Users post photographs of themselves and their friends, as well as a running commentary on the details of their day-to-day exploits. Facebook is designed to give its users the impression that the outside world is interested in their life, not unlike that of a celebrity, and that such details contain a form of currency or value in the contemporary world. Proof of this can be seen in the massive popularity of reality television programmes, which trade on the day-to-day exploits of 'non-celebrities'. For users of Facebook, one's status is determined by the number of 'friends' one has, so that quantity carries greater value than quality, providing evidence of one's popularity. In many ways Facebook provides a stage for its users to perform like actors in front of an audience of 500 million other registered users. In both of these examples we see how self-identity and social interactions and relations in consumer culture are subsumed under the process of commodification and its corresponding system of impression management.

Internet dating and Facebook illustrate the importance of developing the right personality in order to successfully sell oneself, and the manner in which market forces act as a mediating role in its construction and maintenance. The internalisation of market ideologies is evidenced by the Western societal valuing of individualism, competition, aggression, enterprise, innovation, self-absorption and consumerism (Cushman, 1995; Lasch, 1979; Lemke, 2001; Munck, 2005; Smart, 2003, 2010; Steger and Roy, 2010; Twenge and Campbell, 2010). Despite the obvious flaws in its experimental research design the social psychology literature has observed (in a limited manner) the changing experience in self-identity that these social forces have wrought. These include a striving for increased self-esteem, or at least avoiding low self-esteem, engaging in competition with other individuals and groups, constant evaluation of self-identity by comparing it with others, a desire for narcissistic enhancement in all spheres of life (physical, mental and spiritual[4]) and engagement in impression management (e.g. Hogg, 2000; Hogg and Abrams, 2003; Rosenfeld *et al.*, 1995; Sedikides and Gregg, 2003; Snyder, 1974). The problem with these studies and others like it is that they view these social behaviours as timeless universal features of human conduct. This is not surprising when you consider that many social psychological studies are conducted in laboratories using experimental methods with university students as their research participants. As Moscovici (1972: 56) notes, social behaviours are the product of particular societal ideologies. A good example of this narrowing of analysis in social psychology can be seen in a study conducted by Buffardi and Campbell (2008) that linked narcissistic tendencies with the use of social networking sites. Buffardi and Campbell concluded that narcissists were more likely to actively participate in social networking sites such as Facebook and their personal pages were more likely to contain self-promoting material. While such a study is to be applauded for investigating a contemporary everyday social phenomenon (a rare thing in the social psychological literature), it fails to ask some important questions. For example, what are the historical, social and cultural origins of these behaviours? Do these behaviours represent an increasing trend in self-commodification, and if so, is it a phenomenon that we can link to the rise of consumer culture and the ideologies and discourses that support and maintain it?

Theories claiming that social behaviours stem from inherent predispositions or social cognitions related to self-identity, as implied by much of the social psychology literature, are both inaccurate and misleading. Indeed there is an implicit assumption in much of this literature that modern Western society is the result of widely agreed upon principles and policies, and that industrial capitalism, and its more recent version neoliberalism, appear to be the economic system that most closely corresponds to human nature (Fromm, 1956/1991; Nafstad, 2002; Parker, 2007; Sloan, 1997; Teo, 2009). Cognitive processing of self-identity is influenced by the economics and politics of its respective era (Cushman, 1990, 1995; Ferraro *et al.*, 2005). Personality when viewed in the context of the barter economy was intertwined in relations with proximally close others, material products and the natural world. The emergence of money and the money economy dissolved this interdependence. Money, Simmel (1991a: 17–18) observed, now mediates all relations, creating a separation and distance between the individual and their social, material and natural worlds. In consumer culture the money economy drives an independent, autonomous, aggressive and highly competitive subject. This is by no means a natural state of affairs as implied by the social psychology literature. For example, the assumption that people seek to see themselves in a positive light, as proposed by theories of self-esteem, is by no means a universal feature of personality. People seek to see themselves in a positive light because they are compelled to turn themselves into a commodity, in order to achieve academic, career and romantic success.

The money economy, and now the neoliberal economy, is predicated on free and open markets, based on the theory that economic growth is most rapid when products, services and capital can circulate without hindrance (MacEwan, 1999: 31; Mandel and Novack, 1970: 76). The unceasing movement of capital around the global market speeds all related activities and makes them continuous; the freer the market, the faster money can flow (Simmel, 1907/1990). This circulation speeds up all related activity, so that any contentment with the attained state of affairs is considered stagnation or zero growth and punished in the competition between individuals and groups (Garhammer, 1998: 330–1). In this particular economic system, a system designed to enhance the movement of capital, producers, sellers and consumers are pitted against one another in what Lasch (1979: p. xv) describes as a war of competitive individualism. Mandel and Novack add:

> These economic circumstances generate unbridled individualism, egotism, and self-seeking . . . The members of this society, whatever their status, have to live in an atmosphere of mutual hostility rather than solidarity.
>
> (1970: 77)

The influence of neoliberalism has come to shape self-identity in various ways. Social identity theorists have superficially observed the effect of these economic conditions on social behaviour, as the following quote on inter-group behaviour and social identity illustrates:

> Intergroup behaviour tends to be competitive and ethnocentric. In intergroup contexts, people generally behave so as to gain or maintain an advantage for their own group over other groups in terms of resources, status, prestige.
>
> (Hogg and Abrams, 2003: 336)

This describes the prevailing behaviour of many people, where out-groups are viewed as rivals to be prejudiced against. However, inter-group theories fail to provide an interpretation of *why* individuals and groups seek to behave in this way. Aggression and competition between individuals and groups in consumer cultures has its basis in neoliberal ideology. In the end 'it is not individuals who are set free by competition; it is, rather capital which is set free' (Marx, 1857/1973: 650). For all of its observations, social identity theory does little to resolve or even enter into a debate on the origins of these social behaviours and nowhere in the literature is there an attempt to theorise contemporary social forces and the manner in which these have altered the experience of self-identity. Gough and McFadden note:

> Individuals within this theory (social identity theory) are conceptualized as self-contained units sharing sets of internal processes (cognitions, motives) that function in some universal way (categorization, comparison, differentiation) regardless of individuals' social, cultural and historical contexts. Consequently, prejudiced thoughts, emotions and activities are seen as residing within the individual with no theoretical exploration of their social origins or the diverse socially constructed ways in which these are legitimized and manifested.
>
> (2001: 202)

Furthermore, the social psychological literature asserts that self-identity is a 'product of the child's cognitive development rather than "environmental" factors' (Gough and McFadden, 2001: 131).

Given the constraints of these assumptions, what is needed is an explicit linking of self-identity to the particular conditions that characterise modern Western culture, which has become a consumer culture. Such an analysis would recognise that governments in modern Western societies now regard their citizens as *consumers* as opposed to *producers*, representing a significant shift in the mode of contemporary citizenship and the axis upon which self-identity is now constructed (Bauman, 2005; Munck, 2005; Smart, 2010; Storper, 2001). As Cohen (2003) and Munck (2005) note, the political promotion of the *citizen as consumer* simultaneously fulfils personal desire and civic obligation.[5] This has created a self-identity that is shaped via interactions with the marketplace, leaving it open to commodifying processes (Castells, 2004; Giddens, 1991). A good example of this has been changes in the provision of public services, often referred to as 'new public management', such as health, education, policing, security and welfare in countries like the United Kingdom. These publicly funded services are now subject to quasi-market mechanisms so that 'students, patients and welfare clients have been reconstituted in political discourse and media reporting as consumers or customers' (Smart, 2010: 47; see also Loader, 1999).

An economic and political system that views its citizens as consumers will have a corresponding influence on their internal states, including motivations, values, perceptions and beliefs. For example, 'freedom' in consumer cultures has become synonymous with free enterprise and consumer choice, which is guaranteed, so neoliberal theory claims, by free and unregulated markets (Cushman, 1995: 317; Smart, 2010: 30–44). Freedoms applying to speech, personal expression, the media, spiritual practice and association without discrimination or persecution, have become less important (Bauman, 1983). Neoliberalism is focused on fulfilling the economic self-interest of the individual and this has come to be reflected in people's primary motivations, such as the desire to turn oneself into a commodity (Baudrillard, 1970/1998; Cohen, 2003; Comaroff and Comaroff, 2001; Featherstone, 2007; Kotz, 2002; McDonald *et al.,* 2008). These motivations drive the need for self-esteem, self-enhancement and self-affirmation.

This particular view of freedom coupled with the commodification of social interactions and relations is in no way a natural state of affairs. They are freedoms and social interactions and relations that stem from and are linked to economic transactions of one kind or another. The commodification of social interactions and relations has created a social system where people treat each other as 'things' or 'commodities'. Instead of respecting the value of social interactions and relations, people treat each other as competitors or customers, depending on the economic relation they have with them (Augoustinos, 1999: 305; Freeden, 2003: 6–9; Mandel and Novack, 1970: 28). The neoliberal economic system creates an inverted or 'false consciousness', because people mistake contemporary social behaviours (such as impression management) as universal features of the human condition, when instead they are driven by a particular set of social and economic conditions (Slater, 1997: 113–14). We can see this in the way that people have come to view luxury products and services and how this view has shifted over time. What were once viewed as luxuries are now seen as necessities, such as owning a car, microwave oven, mobile phone or personal computer (Hamilton, 2002; Schor, 1999; Schwartz, 2005). To live life without these products and services would be viewed by many as a form of poverty (Bauman, 2004; Hamilton, 2002, 2003b; Hamilton and Denniss, 2005).

Social psychology takes a neutral approach to ideologies and discourses like consumerism (Sloan, 2001). Yet a deeper understanding of consumer culture's influence on social behaviour provides a number of important insights into the construction of self-identity. For example, it articulates the diverse constraints that shape reality construction, leading to false consciousness (Augoustinos, 1999: 309). This blinds many people to the flows of power, both destructive and productive, that impact on their everyday life (Sloan, 2001: 165). In his analysis of sites of consumption Ritzer suggests that the magical fantastic qualities designed into shopping malls, cruise ships and casino-hotels for example:

> lull people into a reverie that blinds them to the material realities that surround them . . . Thus, the dreams created by the new means of consumption can be seen as creating a 'false consciousness' among consumers in much the same way that such a consciousness was created among the proletariat in the heyday of producer capitalism. Adrift in a dream world of consumption, people are unable to see what is happening to them as well as the realities of the economic system in which they are immersed.
>
> (2009: 65)

False consciousness has been acknowledged in some sections of the social psychological literature. However, Augoustinos (1999) and Parker (2007) are critical of the way in which the concept has been applied. For example, Jost and Banaji (1994) and Jost (1995) treat false consciousness as a 'psychological cognitive phenomenon located in individuals' heads, rather than as a socially emergent product of capitalist society' (Augoustinos, 1999: 295). This singular focus on individual cognition blinds many social psychologists to a range of external factors that influence and shape the construction of self-identity, such as consumer culture.

The narcissistic self

Certain behaviours and emotional states have become peculiar to the social conditions that have come to characterise consumer culture. Social behaviour in the early phases of consumer culture – that which occurred in the late nineteenth and early twentieth centuries – was characterised by social emulation and conspicuous consumption (Sassatelli, 2007: 64–72). In contemporary consumer cultures self-identity has become more intimately linked with consumer products and services. This is a phenomenon that Slater (1997: 91) refers to as 'the cult of the self' in which 'other people and social relations are perceived only in terms of their implications for maintaining a self-identity'.

That personal preoccupation has become the overriding response to the anonymity, isolation and superficiality of consumer culture was investigated by Chris Lasch in his book *The Culture of Narcissism* (1979). Lasch's work is essentially a cultural critique of modern Western society, in which he invokes Freud's concept of narcissism to interpret the shift in Western culture from a productivist- to consumption-based society. Freud (1957) first conceptualised narcissism by referring to two types, 'primary' and 'secondary'. Primary narcissism is a normative developmental stage beginning in early infancy, while secondary or pathological narcissism is a label applied to adults who regressively take themselves as their primary love-object.

> Secondary narcissism . . . covers a range of different conditions . . . in which people are pathologically self-preoccupied; unable to relate; approach others not as ends in themselves but as means to selfish ends; resort to 'self-soothing' behaviours such as drug addiction, deliberate self-harm (including self-sabotage and the contamination of relationships) and promiscuous sex; (and) become self-defeatingly self-reliant.
>
> (Holmes, 2001: 36)

The 'diagnostic' features of narcissism as outlined in the *Diagnostic and Statistical Manual for Mental Disorders* (DSM) (American Psychiatric Association, 2000) include a number of formal criteria. The narcissist has an overblown sense of self-importance and entitlement. They are preoccupied with fantasies of success, brilliance, beauty and ideal love, and prefer to associate only with those of a high or higher status, and/or those who display special or unique qualities. A narcissist requires and desires excessive admiration, and they hold unrealistic expectations of themselves and others. Their self-centred, self-absorbed, self-conscious behaviour often creates problems in their relationships, as they consciously or otherwise exploit others for their own ends. A narcissist will similarly show a lack of empathy, sensitivity or acknowledgement of others' subjective experiences and may be envious, or believe that others are envious of them (American Psychiatric Association, 2000; Bourgeois *et al.*, 1993; McCann and Biaggio, 1989).

The extension of narcissism from its diagnostic and clinical roots to an instrument of personality and social psychological analysis is posited upon three main observations of the contemporary social world (Lasch, 1977, 1979, 1991; Pavia, 1998; Sennett, 1998; Silveria, 1990). First, self-identity has become a reflexive project – a problem requiring resolution. This contrasts with self–society relations in more traditional contexts where one's station was determined for life by the family one was born into, religion and cultural traditions (Cushman, 1995: 63; Giddens, 1991: 32–4).

Secondly, the modern citizen often feels powerless in the face of overwhelming global forces, the exponential growth in information, and the complex web of social, political and cultural networks that now constitute modern societies (Castells, 2000; Elliott and Lemert, 2009). Globalisation coupled with neoliberal economic prescriptions, particularly the deregulation of trade and financial markets, as well as the privatization of publicly owned assets and services, has led to the destabilisation of traditional institutions such as employment, which once provided community and security, and a stable foundation in which to anchor self-identity (Bauman, 2000, 2001b; Bourdieu, 1998; Neumark, 2000; Putnam, 2001; Riesman, 1961b; Sennett, 1977, 1998; Smart, 2010). In an attempt to wrest some level of control the individual retreats into psychic and bodily improvement and other personal preoccupations (Elliott, 2008: 8; Giddens, 1991: 171; Lasch, 1979: 30). Evidence for this can be seen in the shifts that have taken place in mass media consumption. The West, Halimi (1998) argues, is being turned off by an overdose of coverage of a world that offers them only powerlessness and frustration. In the US it is more profitable to provide local or domestic stories that focus on crime, sport and celebrity gossip in a way that entertains rather than informs and which chooses to ignore the international dimension of news. This widespread feeling of political cynicism and apathy celebrates an ideology based on self-reliance, a disregard for the poor and disadvantaged and a lack of concern with social harmony and cohesion (Chong *et al.*, 2001; Lane, 2001; Putnam, 2001; White, 2004).

Thirdly, consumption and its driving force, advertising, provides the supposed solution to the experience of disempowerment and isolation by offering attractiveness, health, intimacy and friendship through the 'purchase of the right kinds of goods and services' (Giddens, 1991: 172).

Lasch (1979) traces the culture of narcissism and the emergence of an increasingly narcissistic personality through changes in the way people work and use their leisure time. Traditional values associated with the Protestant work ethic, such as individual sacrifice for the good of the community, hard work, industry, thrift, saving and sobriety, were once seen as not only ensuring success, but a reward in and of themselves. Achievement in the nineteenth century was not merely measured against the achievement of others, 'but against the ideal of discipline and self-denial' (Lasch, 1979: 57). The ideal self was instituted in the notion of 'character' which compromised moral toughness and integrity and could be strengthened 'through hard work, self-sacrifice, religious observance, adherence to strict moral laws, the postponement of gratification, frugality, the rejection of overweening pride and self-congratulation' (Cushman, 1995: 64). In the modern era character has been replaced with personality, and values which celebrate individualism, the gratification of personal desires, self-absorption and bodily and psychic improvement (Baudrillard, 1970/1998: 45–6; Cushman, 1995: 64; Giddens, 1991: 171).

One example of this growing trend in narcissism was illustrated in a survey conducted by an Australian market research firm in 2004. The study randomly selected one thousand 18–30 year olds, asking them what they considered were the signs of success and accomplishment in life. Their responses, according to level of importance were: (1) designer clothes, (2) fame, (3) an understanding of the internet, (4) shopping in prestigious stores, (5) a university degree, (6) a million dollars and (7) recognition as an expert (Chalke, 2004).

Success in consumer cultures is also measured by corporate or career self-advancement, primarily achieved by competing with one's fellow workers in order to gain the attention and approval of one's superiors (Lasch, 1979: 57). The key to success in the workplace, and life in general, is predicated on mastering the art of impression management.

The transformation of the definition of success, and of the qualities believed to promote it is a long-term development, has arisen from general changes in the structure of society. These include the shifting emphasis from capitalist production to consumption, the growth of large organisations and bureaucracies, and the increasingly warlike conditions of social life (Lasch, 1979: 63). Unbridled aggression and competition between organisations, groups and individuals has become a defining feature of neoliberalism (Elliott and Lemert, 2009; MacEwan, 1999; Shaikh, 2005; Smart, 2003; Steger and Roy, 2010). The individual's mentality is no longer governed by rights, laws and obligations as it was in previous eras. Instead, neoliberalism seeks to govern the individual's mentality by fostering interests, desires, aspirations and most of all competition (Read, 2009: 5–6).

Neoliberal economic policies have led to greater volatility in the labour market, increased employment insecurity and a degrading of workplace conditions. As a consequence the worker has become increasingly atomised. Workplace behaviour is now characterised by a desire for upward mobility, achieved by employing techniques of impression management in order to compete with one's fellow employees, which has become the surest method of safeguarding occupational survival (Bourdieu, 1998; Harvey, 2005; McDonald *et al.*, 2008). This strategy requires that people 'become skilled at managing impressions, at assuming different roles, and at developing a magnetic personality' (Douglas, 2000: 269).

> Within large organizations, professional success requires a will to succeed according to the purely technical efficiency criteria of the functions one occupies, irrespective of content. It demands a spirit of competition and opportunism, combined with subservience towards superiors. This will be recompensed – and compensated – in the private sphere by a comfortable, opulent, hedonistic lifestyle. In other words, professional success becomes the *means* of achieving private comfort and pleasures that have no relation with the qualities demanded by professional life. These qualities are not connected with personal virtue, and private life is sheltered from the imperatives of professional life.
>
> (Gorz, 1989: 36)

In the workplace the narcissist will sacrifice group security and loyalties by categorising everyone as rivals. They will extol teamwork and cooperation, yet simultaneously hide deep antisocial impulses (Lasch, 1979: 64). They will praise respect for regulation and rules but secretly believe the rules do not apply to them, illustrating the fear of otherness that is characteristic of narcissistic behaviour. Evidence for this can be seen in workplace studies indicating declining levels of collectiveness (Deery and Walsh, 1999), social support and reciprocity among fellow workers (Sennett, 1998; van Horn *et al.*, 2001), and the rise of the narcissistic manager (Lubit, 2002). Added to this are self-commodifying and narcissistic trends such as 'personal branding' where people market themselves and their workplace skills as brands 'complete with promises of performance, specialized designs, and tag lines for success' (Lair *et al.,* 2005: 308). Personal branding and other forms of narcissistic behaviour ensure workplace success and subsequent access to status-defining consumption and lifestyles, in an employment climate that has become highly insecure. Read adds:

> The contemporary trend away from long term labor contracts, toward temporary and part-time labor, is not only an effective economic strategy, freeing corporations from contracts and the expensive commitments of health care and other benefits, it is an effective strategy of subjectification as well. It encourages workers to see themselves not as 'workers' in a political sense, who have something to gain through solidarity and collective organization, but as 'companies of one'.
>
> (2009: 7)

Rarely are such social forces and their historical antecedents explored in any meaningful way in the social psychology literature. Instead the majority of studies on narcissism in social psychology focus on personality traits deemed abnormal which are seen to stem from maladjusted internal states such as low self-esteem, poor self-regulation, aggression and impulsivity[6] (e.g. Bushman and Baumeister, 1998; Morf and Rhodewalt, 2001; Vazire and Funder, 2006). In contrast Lasch's (1979) analysis offers a potent social criticism of contemporary Western society that is both historically and culturally informed. Its lasting contribution is its insights into the destructive effects of aggressive and competitive individualism.[7] It also raises a number of pertinent questions, for example, why have aggression, competition, and in some cases conflict and violence continued to remain the default mode of social behaviour between individuals and groups in modern Western society? What is particularly perplexing is that social behaviour of this type is still the default mode in affluent societies where almost everyone has enough to eat, adequate shelter and clothing (Baudrillard, 1970/1998: 174–5). Drawing on the work of influential anthropologist Marshall Sahlins and his study of hunter-gathers, the primitive nomadic tribes of Australia and the African Kalahari, Baudrillard (1970/1998: 66–8) contends that we must abandon the idea that modern Western society is in any way 'affluent'. In primitive tribes affluence was measured by the quality and quantity of human exchange. In contrast, individuals and groups in consumer cultures are more likely to shun reciprocity so that social relationships add to the 'individual lack, since everything possessed is relativized in relation to others (in primitive exchange, it is *valorised* by the very relationship with others)' (Baudrillard, 1970/1998: 67). This has led to a 'psychological pauperisation' where affluence is equated with economic growth, and where actual poverty stems from the atrophy in relations between human beings (Baudrillard, 1970/1998: 65–8). Instead of an affluent society, Baudrillard argues that we live in a 'growth' society, which is wholly different. Citizens of a growth society achieve fulfilment and satisfaction by distinguishing themselves from others, by garnering status and by out-competing others for the coveted signs and symbols of success. These behaviours and others like it such as social comparison and impression management are designed to ward off the ever-present threat of anonymity.

Social psychology describes the ways in which individuals and groups compare themselves with each other. However, it fails to ask why it is that individuals seek to achieve distinction and social status, and why this has become the overriding motivation for many people. Social psychology assumes that these behaviours stem from inherent predispositions (personality). Instead, we argue that the psychological need for self-esteem, self-enhancement, self-affirmation and impression management behaviours stem from a political and economic system that celebrates and rewards these forms of thinking and behaviour as the surest methods for achieving success (whether it be success at school, money, career or romance). They also provide a buffer or solution to the threat of isolation, anonymity, powerlessness and the existential problem of solving one's self-identity. So that when the whole world becomes urbanised, when mass media and advertising become pervasive, then psychological needs grow exponentially, 'not from the growth of *appetite*, but from *competition*' (Baudrillard, 1970/1998: 65).

The distinctive self

Social identity theory posits that group membership is central to the definition of self-identity and that such memberships influence attitudes, conformity, attributions, stereotypes and organisational behaviour. While such an assumption, and the empirical evidence that supports it, is useful in providing a partial analysis of self-identity, its drawback is that it paints a one-dimensional picture of self-identity and its social interactions and relations. It fails for example to take into account the practice of consumption and how this is used to establish difference at both the individual and group level. Consumer culture influences and shapes the composition of social groups and those allowed access to them by providing the artefacts, experiences and knowledge which are used to signal status, good taste and cultural capital. As Lury (1996: 256) notes, consumer culture provides the context for the development of relationships, individual self-assembly and group membership.

Sporting, professional, family, educational or subcultural groupings are often formed around consumer brands and the lifestyles they promote (Bocock, 1992; Bourdieu, 1982; Giddens, 1991; Veblen, 1899/1994). This is particularly so in youth cultures, which are cultures of leisure and consumption organised around peer groups, where socialisation, solidarity, differentiation and status are expressed through consumer products (Lury, 1996: 196; Miles, 2000: 106–26; Wearing *et al.*, in press). Studies conducted on children and adolescents indicate that consumer products provide important symbolic value for impression management and acceptance in peer groups (Konig, 2008; Waerdahl, 2005). In one example of this phenomenon, Pugh (2009) conducted a three-year ethnographic study of public schools in California as well as fifty-four interviews with parents, finding that consumer products and experiences serve as tokens that children use to gain acceptance and belonging to a peer group. These tokens however must be the right tokens, such as shoes endorsed by well-known sporting stars, the latest in computer gaming or having watched the latest films at the cinema.

Difference, differentiation and social comparison in urban collectives rely to a large degree on the ability and skill to manipulate the signs and symbols of consumer culture in order to construct a viable self-identity.

> The principle of analysis remains as follows: you never consume the object in itself (in its use value): you are always manipulating objects (in the broadest sense) as signs which distinguish you either by affiliating you to your own group taken as ideal reference or by marking you off from your group by reference to a group of higher status.
>
> (Baudrillard, 1970/1998: 61)

The food that one eats, how meals are prepared, choice of restaurant, clothing and travel/holiday destination, where one lives, the type of dwelling one chooses to live in (or does not choose and must take by necessity due to lack of financial means), and its furnishings, are all representative of cultural markers of taste, status, lifestyle, attitudes and group membership. Bourdieu (1982) refers to these abilities and skills as 'taste', and taste he argues is a marker of social status. The development of 'good taste', or the acquisition of 'bad taste', places individuals and groups within a social hierarchy. These abilities and skills are practised in various fields including the arts (e.g. visual arts, performance arts, music, literature, dance or film), sport, food, architecture and interior design, to name a just a few (Bocock, 1993: 61). Lury adds:

> differential cultural consumption, or taste, both results from the class system and is a mechanism by which classes seek to establish their dominance within a society. Taste is thus . . . a process of differentiation, but it leads not only to the creation of distinctions between different categories of goods, but also to the creation of distinctions between social groups.
>
> (1996: 93)

The attainment of 'good taste' or the refinement of one's taste, and the knowledge associated with it, is referred to by Bourdieu as 'cultural capital'. Holt (1998) related the theory of cultural capital to the United States by investigating habits of mass consumption, rather than high culture as was Bourdieu's focus. He concluded that 'consumption continues to serve as a potent site for the reproduction of class' (Holt, 1998: 1). Cultural stratification, which has become a characteristic feature of contemporary Western society, stems in part from a system of scholastic production of consumers for products and services. Lizardo notes:

This system can best be described as an embodied cultural capital regime, in which the ability to indirectly decode the formal properties of cultural goods using habitualized schemes of perception and appreciation has replaced the capacity to directly acquire cultural works through purchase as the primary marker of status.

(2008: 32)

It is here that habitus provides a number of useful insights into social identity because of the implications that personal taste and cultural capital have for group membership and self-identity (Bourdieu, 1982). Habitus also challenges the traditional theories of social class based on family of birth, the ownership of capital and occupation. Habitus emphasises 'status consumption', reflecting modern Western society's transition from a society based on production to a society based on consumption. Giddens states:

In general it would be difficult to dispute that stratification within classes, as well as between classes, has come to depend not only on occupational differences but also on the differences in consumption and lifestyle . . . Modern societies have become consumer societies, geared to the acquisition of material goods. In some respects a consumer society is a 'mass society', where class differences are to a degree overridden.

(2006: 324)

Pakulski and Waters (1996) and Warde (1997) support Giddens's assertion that social class is becoming less of an important factor in understanding contemporary social groupings and classifications. Pakulski and Waters link the demise of social class to a range of social trends including political disengagement and declines in union membership. Sulkunen (1997: 1) adds: 'Consumerism as an ideology has been seen as displacing class awareness by promulgating an illusion of united interests of consumers instead of recognising conflicting interests in the sphere of production and distribution.'

Traditional class boundaries have also broken down as a consequence of the almost universal access to culture that citizens in Western society now enjoy through available technologies such as radio, television, film, information communication technologies and mobile phones. Particularly significant has been the increase in consumer buying power in the West over the last twenty years, so that overseas holidays, houses, professional household appliances and cars have become more affordable for many more people when compared with previous generations. Given that it is now possible for most employed people in Western society to afford a car, what then marks the underprivileged from the privileged is the type of car they can afford to purchase. Like Bauman's (2005) flawed consumers, the underprivileged in Western society are marked by their inability to engage in status consumption and the skills and competencies to be able to practise this (Pakulski and Waters, 1996).

The gendered self

Consumer culture reproduces two main female self-identities. The first is the domestic servant who brings joy and wellbeing to their family by purchasing happy, healthy products. In this characterisation, women's identities as wives and mothers[8] are bound up in their role as care giver, which is tied to their knowledge and use of household commodities such as food, cleaning products, furniture and kitchen/household appliances (Lury, 1996: 132). In the second more contemporary characterisation women's identities are constructed as liberated and narcissistic (Douglas, 2000). Taking advantage of the feminist movement that emerged in the 1970s, consumer culture began celebrating women's emancipation from their traditional roles inside the home. These traditional roles and identities were challenged and reconstructed as independent, interested in self-discovery and self-realisation. Women's self-identities became increasingly tied to body image and maintenance, as they were encouraged to assert their sexuality in more prominent ways. Advertisements began portraying women who knowingly and deliberately played with their sexual power and who were always 'up for sex' (Gill, 2008: 437). This sexual assertiveness was coupled with the celebration and promotion of other personality traits such as being confident, fun-loving and discerning – particularly in relation to women's products, services and the consumer spaces where they are sold (Douglas, 2000; Jantzen *et al.*, 2006; Scanlon, 2000a). This characterisation was personified in the 1980s advertising campaign conducted by the cigarette brand 'Virginia Slims' with its now famous tagline 'You've Come a Long Way, Baby'. This advertisement, Douglas (2000: 267) observed, 'equated liberation with the freedom to give yourself lung cancer' (see also Cushman, 1995: 69). This liberated narcissistic theme continues to be popular with advertisers today, as can be seen in L'Oreal advertisements, which use famous Hollywood actors such as Penelope Cruz and pop stars such as Beyonce to tell women to indulge themselves with face creams and lipsticks, 'Because I'm worth it'.

Advertisements such as these play an ideological role by making available certain self-identities for women, while constraining others (Sassatelli, 2007: 133). While women in consumer cultures have much greater economic independence and freedom to express and assert themselves, they are still constrained by a male hegemony which has become more nuanced and subtle in its discipline and power relations (Scanlon, 2000a). Feminine consumer culture is dominated by a heterosexual worldview in which feminine agency is subjugated to masculine desire. It uses heterosexuality as a cover to legitimise the narcissistic and hedonistic pleasures associated with consumption (Radner, 1997: 108). This can be seen in the mass media and advertising which celebrates a woman's greatest achievement as the gaining of approval for her physical attributes and fashions from men. Such approval is closely linked to feelings of self-worth and self-esteem[8] (Douglas, 2000: 270). Gill (2008: 436–8) argues that in more recent times this discourse has been challenged by advertisements that present assertive women who no longer need approval from men. Women are instead portrayed as seeking to please themselves only, 'and, in so doing, they just happen to win men's admiration'. The message here is that the purchase of a product or service will naturally capture men's attention. However, women are now more interested in fulfilling and satisfying their own desires and gratifications.

Women learn to construct a viable feminine self-identity, viable in terms of how others perceive them and their ability to create a positive impression, through their understanding and knowledge of consumer products and services.[9] They are encouraged to become experts in makeup, cosmetics, clothing, accessories, jewellery and hair styling, which function as the essence of femininity. Jantzen *et al.* (2006) for example found that appropriate selection and wearing of lingerie enabled women to demonstrate their competency in being able to manage an elaborate set of rules, conventions and classifications, demonstrating their mastery of modern femininity through the consumption of undergarments. This was seen as both a symbol and a tool for enhancing femininity, and indeed necessary to become a bona fide woman. So intimate is the relationship between women and commodities that women 'become women' because of their knowledge and ability to expertly apply makeup to their faces and bodies (Scanlon, 2000a: 7).

Men's self-identities are now also increasingly tied to their use of commodities as well.[10] Traditional consumer discourses associated production with men, and consumption with women. This representation is now beginning to break down as men are increasingly treated as consumers in much the same way as women (Bocock, 1993: 99). This shift began in the post-Second World War era as men's self-identities as husbands and fathers were tied to home-based construction, repair and maintenance through the purchase of power tools (Gelber, 2000). More recently, men have been encouraged by actors such as Matthew Fox, who typically plays characters that can best be described as 'rugged individuals', to purchase 'men's only' cosmetics, challenging long-held masculine stereotypes around the use of these products.

The use of commodities by both women and men is also centred very much on the home. Not only is the home a significant site for consumption and the construction and demarcation of gender, it is also an important site for the maintenance of romantic partnerships and family life (Sassatelli, 2007: 28–30 and 170–4). Houses are treated as major financial investments, typically the largest financial investment that most low to average income earners will ever make. Part of the significance of the home in consumer culture is its link with success, measured by one's house/apartment, its size, location and interior design and decoration. The surge of interest in real estate and home improvements reflects the neoliberal emphasis upon the 'home' as the site for individual aspirations and social status (Hamilton, 2002, 2003a; Hamilton and Denniss, 2005; Schor, 1999). One only has to look at popular magazines or turn on the television to see the massive interest in buying and selling homes, home decoration, home improvement and home design to see how fixated people in the West have become on all things real estate.[11] Gram-Hanssena and Bech-Danielsenb (2004) found that the choice and purchase of a house and the residential neighbourhood where it is located satisfies different symbolic values associated with social class and distinction. Choice of home decorations and furnishings were found to communicate more individualistic and self-expressive values, which illustrated the 'relationship between the interior of the house and the identity of the house owner' (Gram-Hanssena and Bech-Danielsenb, 2004: 18).

The role of the mass media in mobilising gendered self-identities, women's knowledge and expertise in the purchase and use of feminine products and services, and the way in which people's homes demarcate gender, points to the significance of consumer objects in the construction of gender in contemporary Western society. However, what we find in the social psychological literature is an almost total absence of any inquiry into the material conditions of life and their role in the social construction of gender. Social psychologists typically assume that gender is a biological or psychological essence (Gough and McFadden, 2001: 28–9; Magnusson and Marecek, 2010: 91), or what is commonly referred to as 'essentialism'. 'Essentialism is a way of understanding the world that sees things (including human beings) as having their own particular essence or nature which can be said to belong to them and explains how they behave' (Burr, 1995: 19). Examples of this in the social psychological literature can be seen in studies that view gender as a function of cognitive processing and categorisation (e.g. Bem, 1981), or cognitive development in childhood (e.g. Martin and Ruble, 2004). Studies such as these narrow the understanding of gender and its relationship to self-identity by failing to account for social forces, such as consumer culture, which reproduce gender for the purpose of commodification and profit. People come to experience themselves as psychologically gendered in everyday life through the purchase of consumer products and services and in the thousands of mass media and advertising messages they are exposed to each year. These normalise certain kinds of knowledge about gender while constraining others (Magnusson and Marecek, 2010: 92–3).

The discursive self

Like all societies, a society organised around consumption (and democracy) provides both benefits and drawbacks for its citizens. Its benefits include greater occupational and geographic mobility, choice of lifestyle, travel opportunities and spiritual practices – which have exploded in number and type. These freedoms and opportunities also extend to how we choose to see ourselves, and the images and impressions we wish to project to the world around us. We do this in the way we dress, our hairstyling and colour, choice of makeup and through our expression of taste. We may even undergo cosmetic surgery, have tattoos or travel to faraway countries and immerse ourselves in cultures and landscapes markedly different from our own. However, the construction of a viable self-identity through consumption is destined to be fleeting and temporary because of the relentless reinvention and repackaging of consumer products and services, along with the reinvention of their associated messages, narratives, images, values and lifestyles (Jameson, 1991: 4; Smart, 2010: 43–4). The fluid nature of self-identity in consumer culture replaces a previously more stable self-identity based on secure work and/or secure career (Smart, 2003: 74–7).

Jameson (1991) refers to the current period of capitalism as 'late', 'multinational' or 'consumer' capitalism. This period is unique in capitalism's history owing to the commodification of almost every cultural and political institution, as well as the commodification of social interactions and relations. It is a period of capitalism where surface appearance has become more important than actual substance, whether it be in fashion, visual art, buildings, political candidates or self-identity (see also Baudrillard, 1970/1998). Commodification and the superficiality of day-to-day life is driven by the exponential growth in information and images that pour forth in the mass media, advertising and through information communication technologies (Castells, 2000; Gergen, 1991). In a world where the mass media is now a major arbiter of reality 'the primacy of style over substance has become the normative consciousness' (Ewen, 1988: 2).

What has been lost is a centre which people can gravitate towards; an overarching moral authority that might guide the way people think and behave, and act as a basis for building character.[12] The very nature of consumer culture is its constant flux and transformation; as a consequence self-identity is set adrift (Bauman, 2001a; Sennett, 1998). Simmel notes:

> The fixed boundaries of social groups are dissolving more and more. The rigidity of caste and class ties and tradition is being increasingly broken – whether this be a benefit or a disadvantage – and the personality can circulate through a changing variety of situations, reflecting, as it were, the fluidity of things.
>
> (1991a: 30)

This constant shifting and movement in the dominant culture creates a sense of disorientation as people become unsure of their place in society, leading to a 'fragmentation' of the self (Jameson, 1991; Sennett, 1998). Part of the argument for the fragmentation thesis can be found in the notion of consumer discourses. Much instability in contemporary consumer culture stems from the symbolic mediation of social interactions and relations. Baudrillard argues:

> As a language, consumption is a way in which we converse and communicate with one another. Once we think of consumption as a language, we are free to deploy the whole panoply of tools derived from structural linguistics including sign, signifier, signified and code. As a result, instead of Marxian use-value and exchange-values, consumables become sign values.
>
> (1970/1998: 6)

If much of how we come to know ourselves is derived from the various consumer discourses communicated in the mass media and advertising then Baudrillard points to a very real dilemma in the constantly shifting nature of a sign's value, which is used to determine success, status, distinction, uniqueness, individuality and self-identity. On one hand the individual is trying to carve out a viable self-identity in a constantly shifting culture, while on the other they are caught up in a web of power relations influenced by consumer discourses they are scarcely aware of. These discourses give the impression of freedom through choice, however, as we shall see, the notion of consumer sovereignty and choice is not what it purports to be.

As previously discussed in Chapter 2, discourse can be language, text and practices that reflect socially accepted ways of thinking and talking about self-identity. They are bodies of knowledge (e.g. psychology), sets of rules and conditions established between institutions, economic and social practices, and patterns of behaviour (Foucault, 1981: 94). Politicians in contemporary Western society regularly point to consumer sovereignty and choice as the greatest benefits that flow from neoliberal economic policies. However, Marcuse (1964/2002), Ewen (1988) and Smart (2003, 2010) argue that increases in consumer choice merely give the impression of sovereignty. The selection of consumer products and services freely made by one individual or group are also made by millions of others whose values, beliefs, attitudes and behaviours are influenced and subject to the same production, distribution, retailing, marketing, mass media, branding and advertising processes (Dowd, 1991: 197; Jameson, 1991: 275; Smart, 2003: 75). Despite the attempted individualisation of consumer products and services, and the belief that status, distinction, uniqueness and individuality might be satisfied by participation in it, commodities are mass produced, mass marketed, mass sold and mass consumed (Ewen, 1988). This paradox has been described as the 'constraint of choice within the rhetoric of choice' (Tuffin *et al.*, 2000: 34).

Consumer discourses go beyond simply enticing individuals and groups to purchase a particular product or service; they provide a moral structure and guidelines for living from which self-narratives are constructed (Giddens, 1991; Hearn, 2008). For example, television and cinema communicate images and provide prepackaged scripts for thinking and talking about self-identity (Kellner, 1992; Sipiora, 2000; Stole, 2003). These discourses emphasise the construction of self-identity and lifestyle, as well as celebrating consumer experiences and sensations, which give rise to forms of self-expression, presentation and appearance (Bonner and Du Gay, 1992: 86; Featherstone, 2007: 89), eclipsing earlier ideals of character won through individual sacrifice, hard work, sobriety and thrift.

In their book *Channels of Desire: Mass Images in the Shaping of American Consciousness* Ewen and Ewen (1992) analysed the role of early twentieth-century mass media images and advertising in shaping thinking and behaviour and the forging of a hegemonic consumer society. Mass advertising images construct a mythological world of individualised consumers seeking out solutions to the problems of life through the purchasing of products and services. Throughout the twentieth century consumers in the West have been taught to equate consumption with citizenship and the demonstrable and necessary transformation of the self by celebrating particular personality traits, values, beliefs, attitudes and lifestyles (Kellner, 1992; Smart, 2010).

Despite the often intense debates in the social sciences on the enhanced freedoms, instability, isolation and anxiety that have come to characterise consumer culture, and their direct relevance to topics such as social identity, social influence, attitudes, persuasion, prejudice and affiliation, social psychology has remained mute on the majority of these debates. This is evident in the way that social psychology continues to subscribe to a concept of self-identity that has complete sovereignty over thinking, feeling and behaviour. This misguided perspective on self-identity is a consequence of social psychology's inability to take a reflexive stance on its own philosophies and assumptions, which has meant that in the absence of understanding these vital issues, it has come to reflect the dominant ideologies of capitalist/neoliberal economics in its conceptualisation of self-identity (Cushman, 1995; Moscovici, 1972; Parker, 2007; Rose, 1996; Sloan, 1997).

Theories of consumer culture challenge the very basis upon which social psychologists understand self-identity. Concepts such as self-knowledge, self-categorisation and self-concept become highly unstable and even redundant when viewed through the prism of consumer culture. As Ewen and Ewen (1992: 186–7) note: 'Today there is no fashion: there are only fashions . . . No rules, only choices . . . Everyone can be anyone.' These social and cultural trends, particularly the exponential increase in information via images, narratives and scripts related to self-identity, challenge the very notion that self-identity in contemporary Western society is experienced as a clearly defined set of 'self-schemas' that remain constant over time, or that group categories are static entities that provide us with a clear and unambiguous sense of who we are, or who we would like to be. Instead of confronting these difficult questions social psychology has been content to focus on the internal universe of the individual, from which it assumes social behaviour unproblematically stems. It does this by inquiring into predispositions, perceptions, attitudes, values, emotions and motivation (Rose, 1996: 4). These inquiries into various internal states make judgements about those that are healthy, and those that are pathological. Healthy states are deemed to be those aligned with the goals of rational and enlightened (economic) self-interest, reflecting the dominant conceptualisation of self-identity in neoliberalism (Aldridge, 2003: 55–7; Tuffin *et al.*, 2000: 33). Take for example this quotation from a textbook on applied social psychology:

> [H]ealth problems are related to unhealthy eating habits and a sense of not being able to control one's appetite, and environmental problems result in part from growing consumption levels and a tendency to pay attention only to one's immediate interests. Consequently, solutions and prevention of such problems require changes in attitudes, values, behaviour and lifestyles.
>
> (Steg and Rothengatter, 2008: 1)

We see here the assumption that the individual is responsible for their unhealthy eating habits and their inability to control their urges and desires. Such problems would not occur if the individual was a more rational consumer and more highly skilled in self-regulation. In dealing with the problem of unhealthy eating it recommends a more disciplined lifestyle by changing various internal states. The inability to make correct consumer choices in the marketplace stems from a faulty set of internal states requiring modification. If the offending internal states persist then they are deemed pathological. In effect the individual is blamed for these problems, while the social, cultural, economic and political conditions from where these problems emerge are largely ignored. If problems of unhealthy eating and obesity are to be effectively tackled by social psychologists then they need to go beyond just theorising internal states, to developing concepts and theories that describe and interpret the different forms of manipulation and seduction that lie at the heart of consumer culture.

The specific problem of unhealthy eating and others like it is also linked to the overarching ethics of self-identity set out by neoliberal economic policies. These policies seek to institute programmes of self-governance, which in the absence of their critique social psychology unwittingly supports (Rose, 1996: 116–49). By invoking Foucault's concepts of power/knowledge and discipline, Rose (1996: 152) explored the ways in which self-identity becomes an object, target and resource for certain tactics and procedures of neoliberal governmentality. Neoliberalism promotes enhanced individual freedoms, predominantly through market mechanisms and consumer choice. However, enhanced freedoms come with enhanced responsibilities. This ensures that social risks such as illness, addiction, unemployment and poverty remain the responsibility of the individual, instead of governments and the social and cultural conditions they create (Lemke, 2001: 201). As Tuffin *et al.* (2000: 35) put it, neoliberal policies seek to 'individualise risk factors'. The problem for democratic governments is how to produce self-governing individuals who are responsible, rational and enterprising, as opposed to passive, dependent and irrational (Lemke, 2001; Rose, 1996, 1999). Despite government promotion of 'consumer sovereignty', a society based on consumption is governed in much the same way as a society based on production. The emphasis on self-regulation is much greater under neoliberalism, due paradoxically to the deregulation and steady erosion of welfare policies by many Western governments. Deregulation in one sphere brings about the need for new regulations in others if the moral direction of the individual is to be influenced in any way (Sulkunen, 1997, 2009; Wickham, 1997). Fromm comments:

> In this century, at least in the developed capitalistic countries of the West, there is enough material satisfaction for all, and hence less need for authoritarian control. At the same time control has shifted into the hands of bureaucratic elites which govern less by enforcing obedience than by eliciting consent, a consent, however, which is to a large degree manipulated by the modern devices of psychology.
>
> (1962/2009: 63)

People's consumption patterns and habits are closely monitored and controlled through the promotion of morally correct values, beliefs and attitudes which people internalise. The governance of consumption takes many forms, however, the primary emphasis is on self-regulation and self-responsibility (Sulkunen, 2009). The governance of consumption is pervasive and its influence over a given population is potentially profound. Examples include public health campaigns promoting the dangers associated with smoking, alcohol and drug abuse, skin cancer, driving under the influence (which is not only unhealthy, but now deemed immoral), food labelling, film classification, hygiene standards both inside and outside the home, and the spatial design of gaming rooms in clubs and casinos (Sulkunen *et al.*, 1997). Other examples include the discipline of health and fitness in which governments and private companies work on people's thinking about the body, promoting certain behaviours in order to prevent ill health (e.g. obesity, heart attacks, high blood pressure and cancer), while selling health and fitness products, and the benefits associated with a desirable body, which can be made fit for impression management and its visual consumption by others.

> In this light, the consumer is the epitome of the liberal individual, and consumerism can be seen as a pre-eminent social training ground in its ethical production. It is where we apply ourselves, at the most intimate and detailed levels, the operations by which we understand ourselves in terms of choice.
>
> (Slater, 1997: 61)

Summary and conclusion

Self-identity in the social psychological literature is theorised as an individualistic, acultural, apolitical, ahistorical, free thinking, free acting entity. It is viewed as specifiable, measurable, ordered and rational (Howard, 2000: 387). Much of what is observed, measured and theorised by social psychologists, such as social identity, self-esteem, self-presentation, social comparison, self-enhancement and impression management, is shown here to be influenced and shaped by consumer culture and the capitalist/neoliberal ideologies that underpin it. A good example of this is the commodification of self-identity, or turning one's self into a commodity, which has become synonymous with achieving success in Western society. An understanding of commodifying processes related to self-identity provides a more far-reaching interpretation of why people seek to increase self-esteem (or at least attempt to avoid low self-esteem), why they engage in competition with other individuals and groups, why they seek to evaluate themselves by making comparisons with others and why they engage in impression management.

The advent of a more individualistic personality can be traced back to the shift from a productivist culture based on the Protestant work ethic and its values (individual sacrifice, hard work, industry, thrift, saving and sobriety) to a consumer culture characterised by the dissolution of traditional institutions, increased feelings of powerlessness, anonymity, isolation and a highly influential mass media and advertising industry that attempts to convince its audiences that they can wrest some level of control over life by retreating into bodily and psychic improvement (Giddens, 1991). We also explored the gendering process that is characteristic of consumer culture, which makes available certain gendered self-identities while constraining others. This challenges social psychological concepts of gender, which assume a biological or psychological essence (Gough and McFadden, 2001: 28–9; Magnusson and Marecek, 2010: 91).

We concluded the chapter by analysing the particular conditions that characterise 'late', 'multinational' or 'consumer' capitalism (Jameson, 1991), where there has been a loss of an overarching moral authority which people can gravitate towards, and a foundation from which to anchor self-identity. This has led to more fluid social groupings, challenging the basis of social identity theory. Consumer discourses have come to replace traditional institutions in Western society, providing an alternative authority to gravitate towards, which challenges the notion that self-identity can be experienced as a clearly defined set of schemas that remain constant over time, or that group categories are static entities that provide a clear and unambiguous sense of who we are. As Hayes (2003: 59) notes, psychology 'has been prone to the construction of an abstract and idealised subject divorced from the materiality and sociality of everyday life'.

4 Emotional and behavioural problems in consumer culture

Introduction

The purpose of this chapter is to build on the inquiry into self-identity conducted in Chapter 3 by tracing the links between emotional and behavioural problems and consumer culture. The subdisciplines of 'abnormal' and 'clinical' psychology are typically associated with research and practice on emotional and behavioural problems such as chronic stress, alcohol and drug abuse, prejudice, aggression, anxiety disorders and major depression. However, social psychological theory influences the study of emotional and behavioural problems in a number of ways. The first section of this chapter outlines some of the social psychological theory that has come to influence abnormal and clinical psychology. This is then followed by a critical analysis of the social-clinical literature through the lens of consumer culture and the significant role it has come to play in driving emotional and behavioural problems in contemporary society through the effects of the mass media and advertising, alienation and exclusion, and its obsessive focus on body image.

Emotional and behavioural problems in social psychology

History

Social psychology is not ordinarily associated with abnormal and clinical psychology. Nevertheless, formal links did once exist between the two subdisciplines. In 1921 the *Journal of Abnormal Psychology* became the *Journal of Abnormal and Social Psychology*. This arrangement ended in 1965 when the journal was split into two separate entities, the *Journal of Abnormal Psychology* and the *Journal of Personality and Social Psychology*. This split was reconciled in 1983 with the founding of a new journal, the *Journal of Social and Clinical Psychology* (*JSCP*) (Kowalski and Leary, 2000). Social psychological topics most commonly dealt with in *JSCP* include attribution, relationships, ego defences, emotion, health and the self (Snyder, 1988 cited in Kowalski and Leary, 2000: 14). The most popular areas of social psychology for clinical psychologists have been social cognition, the study of emotions and interpersonal processes. These topics have become important to abnormal and clinical psychologists because of the insights they provide in understanding individual differences in vulnerability to anxiety and attributional style (Leary, 2006; Maddux, 2010; Strauman *et al.*, 2007). Kowalski and Leary had this to say about the current application of social psychology to emotional and behavioural problems:

> Without question, areas within social psychology that focus explicitly on cognitive processes – for example, attribution, social perception and cognition, and attitudes – have most easily crossed the narrow bridge between social and clinical psychology. In fact, the cognitive revolution in psychology was an important impetus to the interface, as social and clinical psychologists alike recognized the usefulness of cognitive approaches to understand behavior.
>
> (2000: 16)

For the purpose of this inquiry we intend to focus on a select set of topics in the social-clinical literature beginning with self-identity and its sub-themes – self-schemas, self-esteem, self-comparison and self-regulation. This is then followed by a brief review of the theories of stereotyping, prejudice, aggression and violence.

Problems of the self: schemas, esteem, comparison and regulation

Problems or disturbances of the self or problems and disturbances with personality are implicated in various forms of psychopathology such as major depression, post-traumatic stress disorder, substance abuse and eating disorders. Self-schema theory is used by cognitive therapists to interpret personality, whereby personality is composed of 'basic schemas or interpersonal strategies developed in response to the environment'. Schemas are the basis from which people interpret the world around them. As such these can be 'highly selective, egocentric, and rigid'. An individual's schemas have the potential for 'cognitive vulnerability' if the person responds to their environment in a maladaptive or dysfunctional manner (Beck and Weishaar, 2005: 245; see also Riso and McBride, 2007). For example, an individual who desires to achieve and maintain a certain body image would be schematic on this attribute. This schema would influence the individual's beliefs about the importance of appearance and body image for their feelings of happiness and success (Buunk and Dijkstra, 2008: 254). The individual who is schematic for body image is therefore likely to scrutinise others' bodies, and media representations of the body for the purpose of comparison. If the individual's comparison of their body does not match the ideal they have constructed for themselves then they are likely to negatively evaluate their own body. Evaluations such as these will affect the person's self-concept and self-esteem.

Self-esteem is defined as 'one's attitude towards oneself or one's opinion or evaluation of oneself, which maybe positive (favourable or high), neutral, or negative (unfavourable or low)' (Colman, 2009: 681). Individuals with high self-esteem enjoy a number of psychological benefits. These include feelings of competence, self-confidence, an ability to handle criticism in a constructive manner and to successfully negotiate the vicissitudes of life. In contrast, people with low self-esteem feel incompetent, flawed in some way, inferior when compared to others, a failure, and lack confidence. As a consequence low self-esteem is implicated in various types of psychopathology such as major depression (Andrews and Brown, 1993; Tennen and Affleck, 1993; Wood and Lockwood, 2000), anxiety disorders (Leary *et al.*, 1995) and eating disorders (O'Dea and Abrahams, 2000). Low self-esteem is also linked with social problems such as aggression, antisocial behaviour and delinquency (Donnellan *et al.*, 2005). However, others argue that narcissism and unstable self-esteem are more accurate predicators of aggression than low self-esteem specifically (Baumeister *et al.*, 2000).

Drawing on the work of William James, Harter (1993) contends that self-esteem is linked to particular domains deemed important by the individual. Like self-schemas, if one perceives oneself as competent in the domains that one wishes to excel in then self-esteem will be high. Whereas if one proves unsuccessful in the domains one wishes to excel in then self-esteem will be low. Self-esteem is seen as particularly important for children, as it is claimed that this forms the basis of long-term mental health and wellbeing. The most prevalent domains deemed important by children and adolescents include physical appearance, academic performance, athletics, social acceptance and behavioural conduct (Harter, 1993: 88–9). Children and adolescents compare and scrutinise themselves and their peers on each of these domains, competing with one another to achieve high levels of status. 'Thus, how one measures up to one's peers, to societal standards, becomes the filter through which judgments are passed' (Harter, 1993: 94). The most important domain that people compare and compete with each other on is physical appearance (e.g. Wolsko, 2012). Appearance is difficult to avoid because it is always on display for others to observe, whereas academic competence for example is not (Harter, 1993: 96). Physical appearance is also deemed important because of the thousands of messages and images that people are exposed to everyday through the mass media and advertising, which extols the benefits and pleasures associated with beauty, attractiveness and glamour.

Research on people with low self-esteem has found they are more likely to engage in social comparison with others, indicating that a high degree of social comparison may in some way be maladaptive (Wheeler, 2000; Wood and Lockwood, 2000). People make social comparisons in order to 'evaluate their opinions and abilities by comparison respectively with the opinions and abilities of others' (Festinger, 1954: 118). People compare themselves for various reasons including increasing self-knowledge, testing the validity of one's perceptions, attitudes and beliefs, and to enhance some aspect of the self. Festinger (1954) initially hypothesised that people compare themselves with similar others – 'the similarity hypothesis' – who are marginally better than themselves. More recent research has found that people also compare themselves to dissimilar others in an attempt to enhance or protect subjective wellbeing (Suls *et al.*, 2002). Comparisons with dissimilar others involve both upward and downward comparisons with different types of comparison targets (Dijkstra *et al.*, 2010:

196). Downward social comparisons – comparisons with people worse off than ourselves – may reflect a desire to enhance self-esteem (Wills 1981, 1991, cited in Suls *et al.*, 2002: 161–2; Wood and Lockwood, 2000: 100), whereas upward social comparisons may reflect a desire to see similarities between ourselves and others of a higher social or cultural standing. In this type of comparison we may wish to see ourselves as a member of the elite, or at least sharing some attributes with them (e.g. Jones and Buckingham, 2005). Upward social comparisons also have the potential to result in feelings of inferiority, dissatisfaction and decreases in self-esteem (Richins, 1995). Other emotions elicited in the social comparison process are jealousy and envy.

> In envy producing situations, a person observes the possessions, attributes, or relationships of another and wishes he or she possessed the object (and that the other person did not). The possession could be, in fact, a material object such as a house, car, or money, but it could also be a human attribute such as an extraverted personality or even friendship or romance with another person.
>   (Tangney and Salovey, 2010: 249–50)

The social comparison process is also linked to social identity. Social comparisons with similar others are typically made within in-groups, which play an important role in anchoring a person's perceptions, attitudes and beliefs (Hogg and Vaughan, 2005: 124). As previously discussed in Chapter 3, group membership influences self-esteem so that membership of a higher status group will typically correspond with higher levels of self-esteem (e.g. Brown and Lohr, 1987). However, stigmatised groups have been found to protect their self-esteem by employing a number of strategies. These include attributing negative feedback to prejudice, comparing oneself only to others in one's in-group as opposed to out-groups, and selectively devaluing those aspects in which one's in-group fares poorly (Croker and Major, 1989).

Social comparisons may also lead to feelings of 'relative deprivation' – a sense of having less than we feel entitled to. Two types of relative deprivation have been identified in the literature: (1) 'egoistic' (individual or personal), and (2) 'fraternalistic' (group). Egoistic deprivation derives from an individual's sense of deprivation relative to similar others, whereas fraternalistic or collective deprivation derives from comparisons with dissimilar others, or members of out-groups (Tyler and Smith, 1998). Relative deprivation theory assumes that disadvantaged individuals and groups will naturally recognise the injustice of their situation. This however is not always the case (Smith and Ortiz, 2002). Tyler and Lind (2002) argue that group-based deprivation leads to discontent only when it is perceived that unfairness has occurred in the allocation of resources (procedural justice), as opposed to unfairness in the amount of resources actually allocated (distributive justice) (see also Folger and Konovsky, 1989). Tyler and Lind (2002) note that disadvantaged groups believe that market approaches to the allocation of resources are fair, despite the glaring inequities that exist between the rich and poor in Western countries.

The argument is that people regard the procedures of the marketplace as fair . . . they believe that the market allocates resources to people in a neutral unbiased way, based on how hard they work and how intelligent and well educated they are. Because the procedures of the market are fair, people do not focus on whether individuals or groups in fact receive fair outcomes.

(Tyler and Lind, 2002: 66)

Another major area of social-clinical research related to the self is 'self-regulation' or 'self-control'. Self-regulation refers to a person's ability to alter their responses to emotions, thoughts, temptations and behaviours. Research on self-regulation stemmed initially from a series of experiments testing children's abilities to delay gratification (Mischel, 1974). Dale and Baumeister note:

Many forms of self-regulation (including delay of gratification) involve a conflict between an immediate, short-term goal and a long-term one, and self-regulation succeeds when the person can resist the immediate impulse and pursue what is best in the long run.

(2000: 144)

Self-regulation functions by aiming to meet an ideal standard that people compare themselves against (Doerr and Baumeister, 2010). These standards might include an ideal weight, academic grades or how much alcohol one should consume at a friend's party. One of the obvious problems with the self-regulation literature is that it does not debate the basis on which people make judgements about which standards are acceptable or appropriate in any given time or situation. Moreover, it fails to ask what goals are deemed appropriate for a person to aim towards. Given that human beings do not live in a social or cultural vacuum, standards are not only influenced by one's thinking but also by the ideologies and discourses that are dominant in a particular culture at a particular time.

Given the wide array of choices available in consumer cultures, self-regulation plays an important role in successfully negotiating the potentially negative consumer choices that people are confronted with everyday, particularly those activities/substances which have shown to have addictive qualities such as gambling, drug taking, alcohol, spending money and food. The failure to self-regulate is therefore viewed as a maladaptive response to one's environment and is often listed among the diagnostic criteria for mental disorders in the *DSM* (Dale and Baumeister, 2000: 145). One area of self-regulation that Dale and Baumeister (2000) focus on is emotions. In the context of psychotherapy a strategy for dealing with a failure or inability to self-regulate might involve teaching clients to acknowledge and express emotions in a more healthy and constructive manner. However, relying on, promoting or encouraging internal self-regulation, while certainly useful, does little to address the social, cultural, political and economic problems that also play an important role in understanding and treating emotional and behavioural problems. Howard notes:

We are living in a very 'me-centred' period of history and many counselling and care theorists attend to individual dilemmas and dynamics with scant attention to the society and culture of which we are apart.

(2004: ix)

A now widely publicised example of this is the link between eating disorders in young people and the 'thin ideal' they are exposed to in the mass media and advertising. Evidence for this can be seen in rates of eating disorders which are more often diagnosed in girls and women because of the greater pressure placed upon them by the mass media and advertising to conform to celebrated standards of weight, height, body shape and appearance (Dijkstra *et al.*, 2010: 199).

Stereotyping, prejudice and aggression

In his 1922 book *Public Opinion* Walter Lippman examined the difficulties that people are confronted with in trying to make sense of life in an increasingly complex society. To negotiate this complexity Lippman believed that people turn to solace in simplistic explanations.

For the real environment is altogether too big, too complex, and too fleeting for direct acquaintance. We are not equipped to deal with so much subtlety, so much variety, so many permutations and combinations. And although we have to act in that environment, we have to reconstruct it on a simpler model before we can manage with it. To traverse the world men must have maps of the world.

(Lippman, 1922/1965: 20)

These maps have become known as stereotypes, which Gordon Allport (1958) described as erroneous generalisations that reflect the law of least effort. Tajfel (1969: 81–2) defined stereotypes as 'the attribution of general psychological characteristics to large human groups'. They are devices for making quick unthinking assessments or generalisations, forming a basic means by which individuals organise their social cognition (Pettigrew, 1981). Social psychologists have long argued that human minds think with the aid of categories, grouping things together in order to make sense of them, whether they are objects or people. These categories form the basis of prejudgment. While social categorisation is an effective strategy for understanding a complex world it also has the potential to cause fear and great harm for people, particularly those that experience prejudice, discrimination, aggression and violence as a consequence.

The basic problem with stereotyping is that it does not take into account the wide variation that actually occurs within individuals and groups. Not only are stereotypes typically inaccurate, they have the potential to increase self-consciousness in the target group which may have detrimental effects on the target's self-concept and self-esteem. For example, in one experiment, university students were required to carry out two tasks in succession; trying on swimsuits followed by a difficult maths test. The results revealed that women scored lower on the maths test than their male counterparts. It was concluded that women were much more likely than men in the study to adopt the perspective of an outside observer scrutinising their appearance. For women the pressures to conform to a particular stereotypical body image were found to be much greater than for men. This meant that the women in the study were much less focused on the task of taking a maths test (Fredrickson *et al.*, 1998): evidence of the greater pressure which girls and women are subjected to by societal expectations.

Prejudice is defined as a preconceived judgement without consideration of the relevant evidence. Like stereotyping, it is thought to be based on faulty or inadequate information, or the faulty or inadequate processing of information. It is an especially 'unfavourable judgement based on group membership' such as race, colour, religion, sex, sexual orientation, disability, mental illness or age (Colman, 2009: 596). Aronson *et al.* (1999: 501) define prejudice as 'a hostile negative attitude toward a distinguishable group of people, based solely on their membership to that group'. People who hold prejudicial attitudes are more likely to behave in a discriminatory manner towards those individuals and groups they have an unfavourable judgement of. The effect of prejudice on the target group is potentially damaging. These effects may include social stigma (the devaluing of one's group by society), feelings of low self-worth and low self-esteem as a consequence of internalising society's negative evaluations, increased levels of anxiety due to stereotype threat (the inadvertent confirmation of a negative stereotype), being denied fair treatment and access to basic societal rights and resources, attributional ambiguity (a heightened scrutiny and sensitivity of one's treatment by others) and a self-fulfilling prophecy (Hogg and Vaughan, 2005: 369–74). A number of interpretations have been put forward to explain prejudice, although the most popular theories in the social psychological literature appear to be those based on some form of social categorisation. Examples of this stem from two of social psychology's most iconic studies, the Robbers Cave State Park experiments (Sherif and Sherif, 1953), and Tajfel's (1970) 'minimal group paradigm'.

The most damaging behaviour to stem from stereotyping, prejudice and discrimination is aggression and violence (Hogg and Vaughan, 2005: 376–7). One of the earliest interpretations of aggression and violence was the frustration–aggression hypothesis developed by Dollard and colleagues (Dollard *et al.*, 1939). According to their theory aggression stems from some form of frustration, which occurs when one is unable to satisfactorily achieve a desired goal. This theory was superseded in the 1970s as learning (behavioural) theories grew in popularity. Learning theories assume that aggression is a learned behaviour, whether through reinforcement or modelling the behaviour of others (e.g. Bandura, 1977). More recent interpretations of aggression and violence have turned to social-cognitive and information processing models, which paint a more multi-dimensional picture. These models work on the assumption that aggression results from person (genetic predisposition, self-schemas, beliefs, attitudes, self-regulation failure, gender, alcohol, etc.) and situational (learning, provocation, frustration, social stress, relative deprivation, etc.) variables combining to produce aggressive behaviour (Anderson and Huesmann, 2007; Mummendey and Otten, 2001).

Emotional and behavioural problems in consumer culture

Media and advertising 1: work and spend treadmill

The mass media (e.g. television, film, internet, magazines, newspapers, radio and music) and advertising are both products for consumption and a major driver of the ideology of consumer culture[1] (Elliott and Ritson, 1997; Hackley, 2002). The mass media and advertising celebrate and encourage a consumer ideology, which states that the meaning of life is to be found in buying things and experiences (Bocock, 1993). There is some useful albeit superficial research in the social psychology literature that attempts to make some meaningful links between emotional and behavioural problems and the pernicious influence of the mass media and advertising (e.g. Mutz and Goldman, 2010). However, in the majority of social-clinical analyses the mass media and advertising are reduced to a singular environmental variable. With regards to links between stereotyping and the mass media, for example, social psychology's approach 'is generally investigated in scientistic terms, with an excessive reliance on experimental data at the expense of, say, any exploration of the intellectual and cultural history, or relevant work done in media studies' (Pickering, 2001: 34).

Consumer culture theorists view the mass media and advertising as a vehicle to promote an ideology, which encourages people to find happiness and solutions to the problems of life in the acquisition of products and services. From this perspective, the mass media and advertising 'constitute the most significant forms and channels of cultural representation and exchange' (Pickering, 2001: 32). They have a profound influence on people's motivations and the way they construct their needs, desires, attitudes and stereotypes. They establish and reproduce social and cultural norms and are a powerful means by which the elite such as politicians, senior governmental officials, business leaders and media-owners control information, which is used to influence people's thinking in support of their political and economic interests (Herman and Chomsky, 1994).

The primary purpose of advertising is to persuade an audience to purchase a particular product and/or service. It does this by making people feel more self-conscious (Ewen, 1976/2001: 37–9), convincing them they live in a state of relative deprivation and that they need to compete with others in order to maintain their lifestyle and personal prestige (Smart, 2010: 77). Rather than validating personal and social experiences, mass media and advertising exploit them by making people feel more fearful, anxious, envious, jealous, unfulfilled and discontented (Richins and Dawson, 1992; Smail, 2005; Wykes and Gunter, 2005). Advertising attempts to convince its audience that the purchase of the right kinds of products and services will ameliorate these negative feelings by providing solutions to life's problems and/or by offering attractiveness, health, intimacy, friendship, etc. Lastly, advertising seeks to convince its audience that the experience of spending their leisure time in spaces for consumption and purchasing a product or service is enjoyable, pleasurable and entertaining – a leisure activity that contributes to wellbeing (Coleman, 2004).

In his book *Captains of Consciousness: Advertising and the Social Roots of Consumer Culture* Stuart Ewen (1976/2001) traces the history of advertising from the 1900s to the 1930s. During this period business leaders and politicians came to the realisation that mass production would not survive without a corresponding mass consumption that was necessary to stave off the ever-present threat of economic stagnation. 'In response to the exigencies of the productive system of the twentieth century, excessiveness replaced thrift as a social value. It became imperative to invest the laborer with a financial power and psychic desire to consume' (Ewen, 1976/2001: 25). In order to achieve these twin aims, corporate public relations advocated for shorter working hours and higher rates of pay so that workers would have enough time and money to consume. This was coupled with a massive increase in advertising of all types to implant in workers the necessary desire to purchase non-necessary products and services. Rather than allowing workers the freedom to control the means of production, business leaders and politicians advocated for the self-actualisation[2] of workers 'among the uncontestable fruits of the new industrial cornucopia' (Ewen, 1976/2001: 27). As production mechanisms became more efficient, work became increasingly routine and monotonous; 'consumer culture presented itself as the realm within which gratification and excitement might be had – an alternative to more radical and anti-authoritarian prescriptions' (Ewen, 1976/2001: 189). To mobilise workers' psychic desire to consume and to elicit the instinctual anxieties redolent of social intercourse, prominent psychologists (e.g. Walter Dill Scott, John Watson and Edward Bernays) and other social scientists of the period were recruited to provide expertise on how advertising could achieve these aims. 'In mass advertising, the consciousness of a selling point was precisely the theorized "self-consciousness" of the modern consumer . . . This self-consciousness was clearly identifiable with the continuous need for product proliferation that informed modern industry' (Baritz, 1960: 39).

While a shorter working week, higher wages and advertising solved the problem of mass production, the shift towards mass consumption led to the development of a set of new problems (not least environmental degradation stemming from overconsumption of the Earth's resources and the pollution this generates, which will be discussed in more detail in Chapter 6). The growth in mass media and advertising led to a huge increase in the social comparison messages and images that the average person was now regularly exposed to. As previously discussed, people make comparisons with similar others and dissimilar others via upward and downward comparisons (Suls *et al.*, 2002). In a consumer culture the exposure to upward social comparisons has come to dominate, so that the sky is now the limit, which has very real effects on people's self-esteem and the lifestyles they choose to pursue (Bauman, 2000: 76).

The majority of advertising messages and images present idealised visions of life, of beautiful, happy, healthy people surrounded by wealth and luxury, enhanced by flattering camera angles and lighting, who engage in witty, sparkling conversations which are carefully scripted and edited (Richins, 1995). Increasingly popular with audiences is living life vicariously through the rich and famous, which has become a common theme of many television programmes. The people these programmes are based on typically live self-obsessed hedonistic lifestyles that are then mimicked to lesser degrees as consumer products and services have become more affordable, and as cosmetic surgery becomes more widely accepted (Hamilton, 2002). The effect of this constant exposure to upward social comparisons has led to an increase in material and personal expectations, raising the benchmark by which people judge themselves and others. Many more people now desire success, particularly celebrity status, and to live an idealised consumer lifestyle not unlike the rich and famous.

> We ask ourselves what these 'people' have done to merit their circumstances and wonder how we can get them too. The information about their possessions and status is thus relevant and integrated into our expectation of what ought to be, raising it somewhat.
>
> (Richins, 1995: 603)

Given the inequities that exist in capitalist/neoliberal economies, most people will never experience the sorts of luxury lifestyles the rich and famous enjoy (even if they can increase their indebtedness to finance larger homes, luxury/sports cars, overseas holidays and designer clothing). Also, most people will never experience the sort of personal success that is likely to turn them into a celebrity so that many people who miss out end up feeling cheated, unsuccessful or inferior in some way (Smail, 2005: 61–2).

The exposure to upward social comparisons has had a profound effect on social behaviour in the realms of work and leisure. One effect of this has been the 'work and spend treadmill' (Cross, 1993; Schor, 1991, 1999), which represents the triumph of the marketing, mass media and advertising industries in influencing millions of people's thinking and behaviour in Western consumer cultures. The work and spend treadmill begins with the 'scaling up' of individual needs and desires via social comparisons communicated through the mass media and advertising, resulting in unsustainable debt for many consumers (Hamilton, 2002, 2003b; Schor, 1999). As Hamilton (2002: 5) notes: 'The desire to emulate the lifestyles of the very rich . . . The scaling up of "needs" often outpaces the growth of incomes so that many people who are wealthy by any historical or international standard actually feel poor.' The unsustainable nature of this debt was made painfully apparent during the 2008 global financial crisis as banks around the world foreclosed on millions of home loans. Many people confused needs with desires and borrowed more money than they could afford to repay. This perverse behaviour was encouraged by the banks and other creditors whose shameful predatory lending tactics was driven by the greed of their leaders and shareholders.

This scaling up of desires is vividly illustrated in the changing moral attitudes towards money as evidenced by the growth in personal credit and debt prior to the global financial crisis. During this period the typical UK household falling into debt difficulty owed more than £25,000, compared to £10,000 three years previously

(Wilson, 2003). What is striking about these figures is that they do not include mortgage repayments. In Australia more than half of 18–24 years olds accrued credit or personal loan debts worth more than $14,000 (Griffiths and Renwick, 2003). In the US Schor (1999) found that between 1990 and 1996 personal credit card debt doubled. The fallout from this surge in personal debt has been a steady increase in bankruptcies in all three countries from 1990 to 2006. From 2007 to the present, bankruptcies have increased dramatically, placing extreme financial pressure on individuals and families. For example, social research published by the UK Office for National Statistics shows that divorce rates in 2011 went up for the first time in seven years. Relate, one of the largest UK counselling charities, observed: 'It's no surprise that the divorce rate is rising given the pressures that couples and families are under. We are seeing more people than ever coming to Relate because of money worries' (Rogers, 2011). The UK Office for Budget Responsibility is predicting that by 2015 average household debt is forecast to rise to £77,209. All of these studies place the blame for spiralling debt on spending sprees and a desire to live a luxury consumer lifestyle stimulated by the upward social comparisons that people are now exposed to in the mass media and advertising. Schor notes:

> A mere car now carries a slightly downscale image, as people shift to sport utility vehicles. The trend includes urban spas, personal trainers, limousine rides ... professional quality everything – from cookware to sports equipment.
>
> (1999: 15–16)

Partly as a result of this desire for luxury consumer lifestyles, British, Australian and North American workers now work some of the longest hours in the world. A study conducted by Reeves (2003) in the United Kingdom found that 42 per cent of survey participants regularly worked more than forty-eight hours a week, and that 51 per cent worked longer hours than they did five years ago. In the United States, Schor (1991: 29) found evidence that the average employed person was working an additional 163 hours a year or the equivalent of an extra month a year. This increase occurred over a twenty-year period (1970–90), and was found to cut across class, income bracket and gender. More recent data from the US indicate that, despite the massive growth in unemployment and under-employment since the 2008 global financial crisis, US workers continue to work more hours than the average worked by those living in other Organisation for Economic Co-operation and Development countries (OECD, 2011a). In Australia, many workers have now joined their US and Japanese counterparts by working some of the longest hours in the world (Campbell, 2001; Fear and Denniss, 2009; Pocock *et al.*, 2001). Working longer hours Beder (2001) argues is motivated by a desire to consume more – bigger and better – and where the purchase of products and services has become the last remaining method of ensuring commitment in an increasingly secularized Western society where the Protestant work ethic has now faded into history.

In order to bring costs down for the consumer, production mechanisms in most businesses are placed under severe pressure to increase output and sales at a reduced cost. This has had a radical impact on the hours, speed and intensification of working life (Aldridge, 2001; Anderson-Connolly *et al.*, 2002; Bertman, 1998; Bunting, 2005; Davis, 1998; Gleick, 1999; Pocock *et al.*, 2001; Schor, 1991). Not only do many employees now work longer hours, they are also working 'harder' and 'faster'.

Many of the these problems have only intensified since the 2008 recession, as millions of people have lost jobs, while those that remain in the workforce are required to take up the slack as the numbers of people in their organisations have shrunk (Kadet, 2011). For those people still in employment, the increasing number of hours worked and the greater speed and intensification of work has been found to be a major contributor to emotional and behavioural problems. Chronic exposure to workplace stress, longer working hours, downsizing and employment insecurity have been linked to psychosomatic illness, anxiety disorders and major depression (Chartered Society of Physiotherapists, 2004; D'Souza *et al.*, 2003; James, 2007; Kivimaki *et al.*, 2000; Strazdins *et al.*, 2004; Wang, 2005). Deteriorating employment conditions, a concomitant feature of neoliberal economic policies, have been linked to increases in the consumption of, and in some cases addiction to, alcohol, tobacco, legal and illegal drugs (Kivimaki *et al.*, 2007; Kouvonen *et al.*, 2005).

People who feel what they earn from their employment is not enough to keep pace with their constantly stimulated consumer desires turn to spending on credit. Prior to the global financial crisis credit and charge card debt in Australia rose from $571million in 1985 to $18billion in August 2007 (Reserve Bank of Australia, 2007). In the United States credit card debt rose from $1000.6billion in June 1996 to $2442.3billion in June 2007 (Federal Reserve, 2007), while in the United Kingdom consumer credit lending rose from £45billion in December 1993 to £213billion in February 2007 (Credit Action Group, 2007). This debt is on top of already record levels of mortgage debt to finance larger and more luxurious homes. As de Graff *et al.* (2005: 24) note, 'the average size of new homes is now more than double what it was in the 1950s, while families are smaller'. As we have mentioned, the massive increase in debt has led to record numbers of people experiencing financial stress and bankruptcies, which are linked to stress-related disease, marital conflict and in some cases family breakdown (de Graaf *et al.*, 2005; Griffiths and Renwick, 2003; Hamilton and Denniss, 2005; Schor, 1999). Despite the economic, social and psychological fall out from this spending binge and the cataclysmic recession that followed it in 2008, the upward social comparisons that people are exposed to through the mass media and advertising continue unabated.

The simultaneous goals of attaining financial success and status through work, surrounding oneself with luxury possessions in an attempt to emulate celebrity lifestyles, cultivating the right personality and attaining bodily perfection have become pervasive concerns for many people in consumer cultures (Kasser, 2003; Kasser and Ahuvia, 2002; Kasser and Kasser, 2001; Kasser and Ryan, 1993, 1996; Kasser *et al.*, 2004). However, as rates of material wealth have increased there has been a corresponding decrease in subjective wellbeing. Meyers (2000) and de Graaf *et al.* (2005) report the paradoxical finding that, as levels of affluence in the United States have climbed upwards, there has been a corresponding increase in human suffering. In the period 1960–2000 rates of divorce in the United States increased by 100 per cent, teenage suicide increased by 300 per cent, violent crime increased by 400 per cent and the prison population increased by 600 per cent. In a similar finding Diener *et al.* (1999) investigated levels of subjective wellbeing in the United States from 1946 to 1989, comparing it with rates of income over the same period. While personal income steadily increased over this period levels of subjective wellbeing have steadily fallen. Other evidence of this paradox has been reported by James (2007) who quoted a World Health Organisation (WHO) study which found that over one-quarter of Americans suffered some form of emotional distress in the previous twelve months, compared to one-sixth of Nigerians. Although the United States is forty times richer then Nigeria, it is by some margin more emotionally distressed.

Children and adolescents growing up in consumer cultures are particularly vulnerable to the pernicious messages and images communicated in the mass media and advertising. Mayo (2005) and Griffiths (2005) found that many cases of substance abuse, eating disorders, anxiety disorders and major depression in young people stem from an inability to gratify consumer desires and to conform to the thousands of idealised messages and images produced by the mass media and advertising industries. In a similar vein, McCreanor *et al.* (2005) found that young people are heavily influenced by the advertised identities sold by alcohol companies, which is linked to increased rates of alcohol consumption, addiction and their associated psychological distress, such as anxiety disorders and major depression. Mass media and advertising have also been found to place chronic strains on parent–adolescent relationships, as adolescents pit their wants and desires against their parent's ability to fulfil them (de Graaf *et al.*, 2005). The problem for parents is that children are socialised into a life of consumption and internalise consumer ideologies from an early age (Bocock, 1993: 82–3). Children are taught to relate to themselves and others as commodities (Schor, 2004; Seiter, 1993). In the United States the typical child watches twenty-eight hours of television a week, which adds up to 20,000 advertisements each year (American Academy of Paediatrics, 2001). These advertisements teach children to associate happiness and wellbeing with the purchase and ownership of consumer products and to compete with other children by comparing their acquisitions with others (Goldberg *et al.*, 2003; Gunter and Furnham, 1998; Schor, 2004; Sipiora, 2000). By the time children reach adolescence such associations and social comparisons have become firmly engrained (Schlosser, 2002).

Media and advertising 2: needs and desires

As more and more groups in the world become aware of the goods on offer by having their desires stimulated, formed and articulated by the mass media and modern advertising, so the number of people who form their sense of purpose and identity through consumption expands.

(Bocock, 1993: 111)

Consumer cultures are cultures organised around the stimulation of desires as opposed to the satisfaction of needs (Baudrillard, 1970/1998; Bauman, 2001a, 2004; Gorz, 1989). The deregulation of markets has led to the deregulation of desires, which are critical to stimulating continual economic growth. Desires are expertly manipulated by the mass media and advertising industries, creating fear and anxiety, by playing on people's feelings of personal inadequacy and desire to manage favourable impressions in the minds of others (Bauman, 1989: 189; Ewen, 1976/2001). Advertising attempts to convince its audience that the purchase of the right kinds of products and services will provide solutions to their anxieties and inadequacies. Nevertheless, while these solutions emancipate constructed problems in one area of life they have the potential to become genuine burdens in others, underscoring the highly ambivalent nature of consumer culture (Sassatelli, 2007: 106).

As Bauman (2001b: 17) notes, the 'rationality of consumer society is built on the irrationality of its individualized actors'. Governments and public policy-makers are ensnared in this ambivalence as they seek to stimulate economic growth via consumption, while trying to manage its inherent risks, and ameliorate the worst of its effects (e.g. addiction, obesity, indebtedness, bankruptcy, etc.) in an effort to protect public health (Sulkunen, 2009). These 'diseases of the will' represent 'failures of responsible self-control and self-management' (Sedgwick and Valverde, 1999, cited in Rose, 1999: 266). NGOs and governmental agencies deploy health and education programmes in the hope of modifying people's consumer behaviours by discouraging a total unleashing of their desires. Yet they must fight against a multi-billion-pound tide of mass media and advertising messages that entice, encourage and cajole consumers to do the very opposite. In the end it is economic growth that wins out (Hamilton, 2003a), and economic growth can only be maintained by consumers who believe they deserve to have more and better of everything (Gorz, 1989: 115; Smart, 2010: 148).

The irrationality of the individualised actor in consumer culture is attributed in the social-clinical literature as a failure in self-regulation. By ignoring the influence of the mass media and advertising and the economic and political ideologies that promote economic growth at all costs, social psychologists end up blaming the individual for their inability to control their desires, impulses, urges and temptations (e.g. Strauman *et al.*, 2010: 85). This problem Cushman (1990, 1995, 2002) argues stems from capitalism's theory of the person, which social psychology implicitly maintains and supports. The self in this respect is understood to be the container of a 'mind' and more recently a 'self'. This self is constructed as an 'empty' vessel for the purpose of staving off economic stagnation. People become containers to be filled up with products and services, ensuring economic growth and prosperity. The problem for society and the individual is the risks associated with the construction of a self that is 'empty', so that the filling up with consumer products and services becomes compulsive or addictive. Prior to the late nineteenth-century temperance movement, the compulsive consumption of alcohol for example was not considered pathological. Behaviours once considered normal are now, when taken to excess – gambling, eating, drug and alcohol consumption, shopping – considered pathological. People today suffer problems that were unheard of a hundred years ago, such as anorexia nervosa, body dysmorphic disorder and obesity. Addiction is made problematic not because compulsive activities represent an inability to modify one's responses to emotions, thoughts, temptations and behaviours (e.g. Dale and Baumeister, 2000). Instead addiction is made problematic in conditions where freedom and self-identity are coupled with consumer choice, and the exponential increase in consumer buying power that citizens in the world's wealthiest countries now enjoy. Giddens writes:

> Once institutional reflexivity reaches into virtually all parts of everyday social life, almost any pattern or habit can become an addiction. The idea of addiction makes little sense in a traditional culture, where it is normal to do today what one did yesterday . . . Addictions, then, are a negative index of the degree to which the reflexive project of the self moves to centre-stage in late modernity.
>
> (1992: 75)

In order to combat weakness in self-regulation the social-clinical literature highlights the efficacy of cognitive therapy or emotional coaching as a means for strengthening its capacity (Doerr and Baumeister, 2010: 78; Strauman *et al.*, 2010: 104–5). However, both of these treatments/clinical interventions focus on changing cognitions and behaviours, while ignoring the inducements consumers are offered to bypass rational self-regulation. For example, the numbers of people struggling with or going bankrupt due to credit card debt has increased dramatically over the last forty years. Ritzer (1995) argues that, due to America's culture of individualism, the individual is blamed for social problems that stem from credit card indebtedness. And yet the real culprits are government and financial institutions which promote and advertise easy credit, financial imprudence and reckless consumer spending in order to stimulate economic growth.

If rational self-regulation is to be truly effective in stemming some types of psychological distress, then social psychologists need to acknowledge and account for in their theories the unquestioned ideology of economic growth and the manner in which it is maintained through the unleashing of consumer desires. Chronic stress due to overwork, obesity due to overeating and alcoholism due to overdrinking for example, can only be understood by investigating the ways in which consumer desires are constructed around work, eating and drinking, and the manner in which the mass media and advertising promote irrational behaviours around these. By diagnosing people with 'self-regulation failure' social-clinical practitioners are asking their clients to become complicit in their own subjugation for giving in to temptation and impulse, instead of blaming the economic and political system that maintains itself through irrational behaviour (Fromm, 1956/1991; Kaye, 2008: 174). Moloney and Kelly note:

> when seeking to account for the likely origins of their own experiences of ill-health, contemporary Westerners may have a propensity to discount the

harmful effects of those social and material adversities with which they may be struggling, and instead attribute their problems to their own apparent lack of will power, or internal moral resolve.

(2008: 280)

Media and advertising 3: stereotyping

The mass media and advertising play a major role in reproducing stereotypes. In their comprehensive historical analysis of stereotyping in Western consumer cultures, Ewen and Ewen (2006: 3) propose that stereotyping is the product of a political process facilitated by the mass media and advertising: 'Within recent history, the media's capacity to spawn mass impressions instantaneously has been a pivotal factor in the dissemination of stereotypes.' The basic assumption in the social psychology literature is that stereotyping, prejudice and discrimination are cognitive errors, and these are related to perceptions of group membership, which are universal and inevitable (Henriques, 1984: 75–81; Pickering, 2001: 31), and they have the individual serving as its primary cause (Dixon and Levine, 2012: 6–7). The social psychology literature shows a lack of interest in the provenance of stereotyping, how it has changed over time and the role that consumer culture plays in its content and maintenance. Gough and McFadden note:

> There is little concern here with the social origins and content of stereotypes (regarded as the province of sociology or politics); their existence is simply accepted and the emphasis is on how – and to what extent – people use these in social perception and identity formation.
>
> (2001: 131)

The fundamental problem for social psychology is its interpretation of stereotyping using theories that have their basis in social cognition and personality, since they provide a de-limited account of the phenomenon. Social cognition is based on an 'individual/social dualism in which what happens inside people's heads frames what is happening in the social world' (Parker *et al.* 1995: 35; see also Henriques, 1984). In this line of thinking stereotyping and prejudice illustrate a basic human flaw – the limited ability to process information leading to thinking that is irrational, biased or distorted in some way. Social cognition rests on a rationalist model of human behaviour (Parker *et al.*, 1995: 61), so that irrational thinking in the form of stereotyping and prejudice can be overcome with its opposite: rational thinking.

Social psychology has set itself the task of understanding how limited, faulty and biased thinking occurs in the form of stereotyping and prejudice, and how it might be replaced with more correct rational forms of thinking. This is the basic approach that underpins cognitive therapy. In this theoretical model individual mental processing becomes the target of analysis. However, the focus on mental processing means that social psychology leaves out an analysis of the social and cultural aspects of stereotyping and prejudice. Pickering notes:

The problem raised by revisionist social psychology in its approach to stereotyping stem from the splitting apart of the two opposed dimensions in the stereotype concept, so that the psychological process of stereotyping becomes conceived as decontaminated from the politics of stereotypical representation.

(2001: 37)

In contrast, studies conducted in the critical psychology, health studies and behavioural science fields acknowledge that the mass media and advertising play a significant role in the reproduction of stereotyping (e.g. Haynes *et al.*, 2005; Sieff, 2003). To ignore this influence in the formation of stereotypes is to ignore one of the most vital aspects of contemporary social and cultural life (Pickering, 2001). For example, Taylor *et al.* (1995) found that minority groups in the United States are commonly underrepresented and stereotyped in magazine advertising. In a content analysis of popular US magazines Hispanic Americans were found to be underrepresented based on the size of their population in the US. Previous research indicated that Hispanics are often portrayed in magazine advertising as uneducated blue-collar workers who are family orientated (Faber *et al.*, 1987, cited in Taylor *et al.*, 1995: 612). Asian Americans are portrayed as hardworking, well educated and talented in maths and science, whereas African Americans are rarely portrayed using complex technical products, confirming the stereotype they are poorly educated (Taylor *et al.*, 1995: 619).

The film industry also relies heavily on the use of stereotypes, providing people with stories that encourage them, 'without reflection, to see certain things, certain people, in predetermined ways, regardless of countervailing evidence' (Ewen and Ewen, 2006: 8). One of the most commonly relied upon stereotypes used in film is the characterisation of people suffering psychological distress as dangerous, deranged and potentially violent (e.g. Angermeyer and Schulze, 2001). 'Movie stereotypes that contribute to the stigmatization of mentally ill persons include the mental patient as rebellious free spirit, homicidal maniac, seductress, enlightened member of society, narcissistic parasite, and zoo specimen' (Hyler *et al.*, 1991: 1044). A good example of this was Heath Ledger's depiction of The Joker in the Batman film *The Dark Knight* (Camp *et al.*, 2010), for which Ledger posthumously won the Academy Award for Best Supporting Actor. Much of the public's understanding of mental illness, and mentally ill people, is informed by the mass media which often depict the illness and the people that suffer it in an inaccurate and unfavourable light (Wahl, 1992, 1995).

Alienation and exclusion

Consumer culture alienates people from one another. This problem arises from its ideological emphasis on individualism (Baudrillard, 1970/1998; Fromm, 1956/1991; Marcuse, 1964/2002). The producer society achieved its goals through collective action, whereas consumption is achieved in isolation. Even when consumers act together it is ultimately a solitary activity that 'leads to distinction and differentiation, not to social solidarity' (Ritzer, 1998a: 5). Individualism is enshrined in neoliberal economic policies ostensibly in the notion of consumer sovereignty where freedom and democracy are practised in personal consumer choice, providing the means for individual self-liberation and the continual fashioning of self-identity (Cushman, 1995: 6; Smart, 2010: 141). Bonner and du Gay (1992: 86) note that under consumption's regime of the self 'consumers are constituted as individuals seeking to maximize the worth of their existence by assembling a lifestyle, or lifestyles, through personal acts of choice in the marketplace'.

The individualistic ideology mobilised by neoliberalism and practised in the act of consumption has had wide-ranging effects on social behaviour. Research conducted by Putnam (1995, 2001) in the US for example revealed declines in the numbers of people participating in civic organisations and other forms of collective action such as parent–teacher associations, local political party membership, Boy Scouts, the signing of petitions, church services, sports coaching and labour unions. Declines in participation were also found to extend to informal socialising such as spending time with family and friends. These changes, Putnam argues, are due to the increase in dual-income families and the extra time they spend at work in order to earn higher incomes to increase consumer purchasing power (in effect the work and spend treadmill).[3] This is coupled with the solitary nature of popular leisure activities such as television, DVDs, the internet and computer gaming.[4]

The other major factor that alienates people from one another in consumer cultures is the process of commodification (e.g. Schmitt, 2003: 93–111). Commodification perverts the way we see ourselves and others, as social interactions and relations in the productive and consumptive sphere are predominantly valued for their economic exchange. One of the most vivid examples of this is illustrated in the behaviour of tourists who travel to other geographic locations in order to consume exotic environments and people commodified by the tourism industry (e.g. MacCannell, 1992; Ponting, 2009). Consumer culture is alienating because it 'develops needs according to the logic of commodity production rather than the logic of human development' (Slater, 1997: 125). Braverman adds:

> It thereby comes to pass that while population is packed ever more closely together in the urban environment, the atomization of social life proceeds apace. In its most fundamental aspect, this often noticed phenomenon can be explained only by the development of market relations as the substitute for individual and community relations. The social structure, built upon the market, is such that relations between individuals and social groups do not take place directly, as cooperative human encounters, but through the market as relations of purchase and sale. Thus the more social life becomes a dense and close network of interlocked activities in which people are totally interdependent, the more atomized they become and the more their contacts with one another separate them instead of bringing them closer.
>
> (1974: 192)

Elliott and Lemert (2009) link globalised consumer culture and the individualism it promotes to a range of emotional and behavioural problems such as narcissism (see Chapter 3), anxiety, aggression and violence.[5] Global consumer culture has created many more opportunities for independence and freedom of expression than any previous era, however, it has resulted in increased feelings of isolation and insecurity in the labour market and in social interactions and relations, which are beset by chronic levels of social comparison. Wolsko writes:

> A high degree of personal insecurity is fundamentally guaranteed in a milieu where human beings define their 'selves' as independent, autonomous agents, who strive for self-esteem by competitively asserting their own uniqueness, power, and positivity over other distinct social and natural entities.
>
> (2012: 342)

Through interviews and biographical material, Elliott and Lemert (2009) conclude that the cause of isolation stems from the extension of market relations into every aspect of modern-day life. This extension has colonised and commodified public spaces and public goods such as water, electricity, railways, education, healthcare, and policing, as well as human interactions and people's personal and intimate lives such as romance, sex, friendships, music, ideas, literature and art. Commodification emphasises 'individual self-interest at the expense of reciprocal or collective values' (Wheelock, 1999b: 30). People respond by retreating into a privatized world of individual desires while denying their dependency on others (Elliott and Lemert, 2009: 41). The rationality of neoliberalism and its compensatory consumption, Gorz notes,

> constitutes an incentive to withdraw into the private sphere and give priority to the pursuit of 'personal' advantages, and thus contributes to the disintegration of networks of solidarity and mutual assistance, social and family cohesion and our sense of belonging. Individuals socialized by consumerism are no longer socially integrated individuals but individuals who are encouraged to 'be themselves' by distinguishing themselves from others and who only resemble these others in their refusal (socially channelled into consumption) to assume responsibility for the common condition by taking common action.
>
> (1989: 47)

This emphasis on individualism has resulted in a society (Western society) where passive aggression has become a means of survival, as competition between individuals, organisations and institutions has become increasingly ruthless, and where those who have missed out come to resent those who are better off (Braverman, 1974: 180; Elliott and Lemert, 2009: 185–95; Wheelock, 1999b: 30). A vivid example of this can be seen in the growing gap between rich and poor, both within and between countries.[6] In the world's wealthiest countries people compete with one another to accumulate the signs and symbols of consumer success (Baudrillard, 1970/1998). However, the means by which success is achieved – jobs, careers and incomes – is now haunted by the spectre of fragility and precariousness (Perelman, 2005; Sennett, 1998; Wheelock, 1999a). Employees face the ever-present threat of becoming a flawed consumer (Bauman, 2005: 36–42 and 68). Much of the distress experienced by the unemployed, the underemployed, those living on welfare and the working poor stems from their inability to fully participate in consumer culture. As this quotation from Bauman illustrates, self-esteem is mediated as much by the material conditions of everyday life as it is by internal dispositions, attributions and group memberships as is claimed in the social psychological literature.

> [A]s the propriety of human existence is measured by the standards of decent life practised by any given society, inability to abide by such standards is itself a cause of distress, agony and self-mortification. Poverty means being excluded from whatever passes for a 'normal life'. It means being 'not up to the mark'. This results in a fall in self-esteem, feelings of shame or feelings of guilt . . . resentment and aggravation, which spill out in the form of violent acts, self-deprecation, or both . . . It is this inadequacy, this inability to acquit oneself of the consumer's duties, that turns into bitterness at being left behind, disinherited or degraded, shut off or excluded from the social feast to which others gained entry.
>
> (Bauman, 2005: 37–8; see also Cruikshank, 1996)

Given that consumer choice is one of the central pillars of neoliberalism, without an adequate financial income such choices become redundant. Freedom and membership to Western society is therefore predicated in monetary terms. The inability to practise choice through consumption, and thereby freedom in the eyes of society, has the potential to act as a potent source of ostracism, leading to feelings of frustration, anger, aggression and violence (Bauman, 2005). In a particularly revealing study on the links between race and consumption, Lamont and Molnar (2001) conducted a series of interviews with marketing professionals who specialise in the African-American market. What they found is that participation in consumer culture is a key means for marginalised groups to gain membership of mainstream society.

> [C]onsumption is uniquely important for blacks in gaining social membership. Their experience with racism makes the issue of membership particularly salient, and consuming is a democratically available way of affirming insertion in mainstream society. This is facilitated by the prevalence of a market driven notion of equality, and an equation of social membership with purchasing power.
>
> (Lamont and Molnar, 2001: 42)

Aggression and violence are therefore present whenever there are groups denied the symbolic status, social meaning and lifestyles of others who have sufficient access to economic and cultural capital.[7] Lower status individuals and groups, those without access to economic and cultural capital, are more likely to experience identity-threatening stressors, and therefore more likely to behave in aggressive and violent ways, or to become involved in criminal activities and enterprises (Thoits, 1991). Given the massive inequities in wealth that neoliberal economic policies have created, its redistribution via criminal violence has become 'one of the few serious options for the poor'. The authorities, particularly in the United States, have responded by 'criminalizing whole communities of impoverished and marginalized populations' (Harvey, 2005: 48). Poverty, instead of being seen as a problem of social inequality, comes to be seen as a problem of law and order, and the individual's personality (Bauman, 2011). The consequence of this in the US has been a massive increase in the prison population, so that the number of people under supervision of adult correctional authorities reached a staggering 7.1 million at the end of 2010 (US Department of Justice, 2011).

Hall *et al.* (2008) conducted an ethnographic study of adolescent and young adult males who regularly engaged in deviant and criminal behaviour in low income areas of northern England. They found that deviant and criminal behaviours, and their associated identities, were closely intertwined with a desire to acquire consumer products that signified power and status. Conspicuous consumption was found to be used as a device for positioning oneself in competition with other adolescents and young adult males, as well as providing hedonistic enjoyment of the products themselves. Deviance and criminal behaviour were found to be motivated by the social meaning and distinctions that consumer products accord. A study carried out for the Youth Justice Board of England and Wales came up with a similar finding. The authors found that consumer culture not only made robbery more lucrative, it was found to be a key motivation for participating in criminal activity in the first place. For many teenagers mobile phones are a must-have status symbol and some young people are prepared to turn to crime in order to get them (Fitzgerald *et al.*, 2003).

Both of these studies highlight the desire of young people to attain symbolic status associated with consumer products, and that living without such symbols is likely to produce feelings of envy, jealousy and uselessness stemming from social comparisons. This issue has received little systematic attention from social psychologists (Tangney and Salovey, 2010: 261), due mainly to their unwillingness to investigate the social and cultural origins of the social behaviours they document, such as social comparison, relative deprivation and aggression, which are viewed primarily as cognitive phenomena (e.g. Berkowitz, 1972). While cognitions are clearly implicated in social comparisons, relative deprivation and aggression, their actual origins lie outside the individual's mind in the growing gap between rich and poor and in the denial of consumer status symbols and the lifestyles that signal these. Bauman notes:

> If the welfare state is now underfunded, falling apart or even being actively dismantled, it is because the sources of capitalist profit have drifted or have been shifted from the exploitation of factory *labour* to the exploitation of *consumers*. And because poor people, stripped of the resources needed to respond to the seductions of consumer markets, need currency and credit accounts (not the kinds of services provided by the 'welfare state') to be of any use in consumer capital's understanding of 'usefulness'.
>
> (2011: 16)

In social psychological studies where environmental/external conditions are accounted for, they are reduced to singular variables such as heat, cold, noise and crowds, implying that these factors in conjunction with a person's personality and perceptions are the causes of aggression and violence. In analysing the recent history of neoliberalism and the various types of capitalism that preceded it, it becomes clear that relative deprivation, aggression and psychological distress arise out of the inequities that it creates and its peculiar form of social organisation, which pits people against one another in a winner-takes-all competition (Bauman, 2011; Howell and Mamadou, 2007; Mirowsky and Ross, 2003; Smail, 2005; Wilkinson, 2005).

The effect of this competition on children and adolescents is particularly dramatic. Youth in-groups and out-groups are determined largely on the basis of ownership and display of high-status consumer products, or conforming to the ideals set by consumer culture through fashions and trends (Lury, 1996; Miles, 2000; Milner, 2005; Pugh, 2009). Even when adolescents attempt to rebel against these and other societal pressures, the marketing industry instantaneously repackages these for sale back to the adolescents who believe they represent some form of authentic societal resistance[8] (Wearing *et al.*, in press). A poll conducted on primary and high school teachers found that children who cannot afford the latest brands face bullying and/or exclusion by their peers. The poll found that 85 per cent of teachers believe that possession of fashionable products is important to their pupils, with 93 per cent saying brands are the top influence on what children buy. Seventy per cent of teachers believe the cause of 'brand bullying' is the intensive targeting of children and adolescents by the marketing and advertising industries[9] (Association of Teachers and Lecturers, 2008). This phenomenon is particularly problematic for children of flawed consumers as the ability to consume ties in with peer group acceptance and the development of a viable self-identity (Griffiths, 2005; Mayo, 2005). In responding to the pressures placed on children and adolescents of flawed consumers, parents attempt to 'shield' their children by reducing spending on themselves in order to protect their child's self-esteem and sense of belonging (Pugh, 2004, 2009; see also Durrer and Miles, 2009; Varman and Vikas, 2007).

While the majority of basic consumer products and services are now within reach of most people, including the underclasses in Western society, inequality still exists, however it has become an inequality that is largely symbolic in nature. Symbolic inequality reveals itself in 'taste', which has become a form of indirect social discrimination. Bourdieu and Wacquant (1992: 172) refer to this as 'symbolic violence', defining it as a form of social harm 'exercised upon a social agent with his or her complicity'. Choice of lifestyle denotes an association with either refined or coarse tastes, creating a cultural/symbolic hierarchy, which is additive to the more visible structural/material forms of inequality (Carlisle *et al.*, 2008). Researchers in the area of mental health have pointed to inequalities in financial resources as a source of psychological distress (Mirowsky and Ross, 2003; Smail, 2005; Wilkinson, 2005). However, disadvantaged groups face the 'double jeopardy' of been placed in a lowly social position because of their inability to make investments in self-identity in the same way that groups high in economic and/or cultural capital can. Symbolic inequality or symbolic violence have 'consequences for the psychological wellbeing of disadvantaged groups' (Carlisle *et al.*, 2008: 631).

Our inquiry into symbolic inequality and violence illustrates the inherent limits of social psychological theory to fully take account of the drivers of emotional and behavioural problems. To begin with it ignores distal power relations such as political economy, viewing these as irrelevant (Smail, 2005). As we have tried to illustrate so far, the inability to access economic and cultural capital is a major source of psychological distress, highlighting that many emotional and behavioural problems are caused by material circumstances, not individual psychological conditions (Smail, 2005: 32–9). Secondly, this has a knock-on effect in terms of the solutions and interventions that the social-clinical literature then prescribes, so that material and symbolic inequality are individualised as cognitive vulnerabilities or maladaptive responses to environmental stressors. 'The temptation for psychologists whose stock in trade is the practice of "cognitive-behavioural therapy" is to convert powerlessness into a "sense of disempowerment" that can be "treated" by persuading people to see things in a different light' (Smail, 2005: 39). The underclasses in consumer cultures are effectively blamed for the circumstances they find themselves in as they come to be judged as the aggregate product of poor individual choices: 'proof of the "choice incompetence" of its members' (Bauman, 2005: 76).

> In our 'society of individuals' all the messes into which one can get are assumed to be self-made and all the hot water into which one can fall is proclaimed to have been boiled by the hapless failures who have fallen into it. For the good and the bad that fill one's life a person has only himself or herself to thank or to blame.
>
> (Bauman, 2001b: 9)

The body

Consumer culture treats the body as the most precious of objects and resources (Baudrillard, 1970/1998: 129; Featherstone, 2010: 197). It has become a point of focus for the mass media, advertising, fashion and fitness industries which link it to health, sex appeal and sophistication (Bocock, 1993). Evidence of the body's significance in modern life can be seen in the therapeutic cult and sacrificial practices that now surround it (e.g. Dworkin and Wachs, 2009; Sassatelli, 2010). The secular spiritual awakening associated with modern society led to the body's rediscovery and liberation from previous eras of puritanical repression (Baudrillard, 1970/1998: 129). 'Once thought to be the locus of the soul, then the centre of dark perverse needs, the body has become fully available to be "worked upon" by the influence of high modernity' (Giddens, 1991: 218).

In consumer cultures the body is viewed as a potent device for marketing self-identity and for the purpose of impression management (Featherstone, 1991: 171). As Sassatelli (2010) observes, the fit body has become a status symbol. Other evidence of the body's importance to the marketing of self-identity can be seen in the growing popularity and acceptance of cosmetic surgery. Large numbers of women are now having breast implants purely to enlarge or reshape their breasts and 'who consider any health risk worth the resulting boon to their self-esteem and market value' (Bordo, 1993: 20). In consumer cultures the closer one's body approximates the idealised images of youth, health, fitness and beauty, the higher its exchange-value becomes (Dworkin and Wachs, 2009; Featherstone, 1991). This 'means that the body itself becomes something of a "fetishised" commodity, one that has to be attractively "packaged", "marketed", and "sold"' (Williams and Bendelow, 1998: 73).

The massive growth in body images now transmitted through the mass media and advertising has significantly increased body consciousness (Bordo, 1993; Ewen, 1988; Wykes and Gunter, 2005). This has led to the construction of the 'body-as-image' so that it is no longer constituted, experienced or managed as a '*natural* body, but as a floating sign system or sign-commodity, an always imperfect but perfectible *spectacle* to be worked upon in the pursuit of a better *look*' (Malson, 2009: 139). As a consequence, self-identity is now intimately linked and bound up with one's body image, influencing self-esteem and self-confidence (Featherstone, 1991; Giddens, 1991; Shilling, 2003). 'In contemporary consumer culture, consumers' perceived responsibilities include careful monitoring and controlling not only of the physical appearance of their bodies, but also of the various foods, substances, and environmental conditions to which their bodies are exposed' (Thompson and Hirschman, 1995: 144).

Now that the body has become fully available to be worked upon, facilitated in large part by its commodification by the fitness industry (Dworkin and Wachs, 2009), it has become a reflection of its owner. Bodily neglect is viewed as a lowering of one's status and one's acceptability as a person (Slater, 1997: 92), it is an indication of neglect, laziness, low self-esteem and moral failure (Featherstone, 1991: 186). An inability to live up to celebrated bodily ideals makes the vast majority of people, in particular women, unhappy with their bodies (Bordo, 1993; Dijkstra *et al.*, 2010; Wykes and Gunter, 2005). Exposure to mass media and advertising images in the form of upward social comparisons has raised comparison standards for attractiveness and led to lower satisfaction with one's own attractiveness (Richins, 1991). Individuals are made to feel anxious and vulnerable, constantly monitoring themselves for bodily imperfections (Featherstone, 1991: 175). For example, exposure to 'thin ideal' images has been linked to body dissatisfaction, lowered self-esteem and negative emotions, particularly in young women (Mazzeo *et al.*, 2007; Wykes and Gunter, 2005). Wykes and Gunter note:

> mass media representations of femininity and especially the female body not only set limits and controls on women's self-worth and the value assigned to them but nurture falsities by allying sexual and social success to size. However, those false standards serve powerful ideological and commercial interest groups which profit from encouraging the beauty aesthetic.
>
> (2005: 220)

The pressures exerted by consumer culture encourage and promote an instrumental attitude to be taken towards the body (Dworkin and Wachs, 2009; Featherstone, 1991). 'The positive benefits of bodily transformative work are endlessly extolled' (Featherstone, 2010: 200). Each minute part of the body is exposed to a range of targeted solutions[10] (Lury, 1996: 134–5), offered by myriad products, services and techniques now available for purchase to renew the body (and self-identity). The reward for ascetic body work is a more beautiful body, a more beautiful self-identity and greater psychological wellbeing (Featherstone, 2010).

The moral imperative that encourages body work places demands and pressures on the consumer that are contradictory. On one hand consumers are invited to gratify their impulses and indulge in the hedonistic joys of food, drink and passive/sedentary leisure pursuits, while on the other they are disciplined to delay and suppress their desires in order to attain the perfect body.

> Consumer culture continually excites and encourages us to 'let go' indulge in our desires – for sugar, fat, sex, mindless entertainment. But at the same time burgeoning industries centered on diet, exercise, and body enhancement glamorize self-discipline and code fat as a symbol of laziness and lack of will power. It's hard to find a place of moderation and stability in all this, easy to fall into disorder.
>
> (Bordo, 1993: p. xxi)

Eating disorders such as anorexia are evidence of the extreme measures that some will go to in order to delay and suppress their desires, whereas obesity is an extreme example of giving in to one's desires. 'Both are rooted in the same consumer culture construction of desire as overwhelming and overtaking the self. Given that construction, we can only respond either with total submission or rigid defense' (Bordo, 1993: 201). The mandate for discipline clashes with the mandate for pleasure (Williams and Bendelow, 1998: 75). 'In short, neoliberal governmentality produces contradictory impulses such that the neoliberal subject is emotionally compelled to participate in society as both out-of-control consumer and self-controlled subject' (Guthman and Du Puis, 2006: 444).

The social-clinical literature has shown a partial willingness to debate the role played by the mass media and advertising in eating disorders (e.g. Levine and Murnen, 2009; Polivy and Herman, 2004). However, much of this literature focuses on individual pathological variables such as cognitive vulnerability, ridged body schemas, self-focused attention, poor self-regulation, low self-esteem and attachment avoidance as potential causes. This approach is coupled with a focus on the categorisation of symptoms into a taxonomy of disorders (e.g. Dijkstra *et al.*, 2010: 197–9; Strauman *et al.*, 2010: 95–6). It views consumer culture as a merely contributory, facilitating or modulating variable. In contrast, critical feminist scholars argue that consumer culture is not simply contributory, but *constitutive* of eating disorders in modern Western society (e.g. Bordo, 1993; Malson, 1998, 2009; Saukko, 2009). Consumer culture exerts an enormous amount of pressure via inducements and punishments that facilitate the internalisation of values and beliefs that emphasise strict bodily surveillance and the linking of self-identity with bodily appearance (Thompson and Hirschman, 1995: 151).

Social psychology's contribution to understanding eating disorders and disturbed body image has broadened individual psychology's focus on intra-individual factors. It has achieved this by exploring eating disorders in relation to social-identity, group dynamics, social comparisons, attributions and attitudes. While this widened focus has expanded the understanding of these forms of distress, it neglects to inquire into the social origins of these problems and the dominant societal ideologies in which these disorders arise. For example, analyses that apply social comparison theory to understand eating disorders and disturbed body image (e.g. Buunk and Dijkstra, 2008; Dijkstra *et al.*, 2010; Thompson *et al.*, 1999) fail to acknowledge and understand the historical antecedents of these behaviours and how they have changed over time as a consequence of shifts in social, cultural, political and economic conditions. Secondly, the social-clinical literature fails to inquire into *why* people express a fundamental desire to compare themselves to others in the particular ways they have observed and documented in their research.

We argue that it is not the social comparison processes *per se* that are the cause of distress but what it means for the individual in the context of living in a consumer culture; a culture that commodifies the body and self-identity, and where achieving the ideal body weight, height and shape have the potential to profoundly affect one's marketability and one's exchange-value within the family, peer groups and in society at large. Having the wrong body weight, height and shape can have very real material consequences. Bodily appearance has the potential to affect one's sexual desirability, career success, friendships, group memberships and the ability to create positive impressions in the minds of others. The desire to do whatever it takes to achieve the correct body, whether conforming to a strict diet or undertaking cosmetic surgery, has become a rational response to overwhelming societal pressures. Eating disorders and a disturbed body image are far from being aberrant and idiosyncratic features of pathological individuals – individuals with disordered personalities. Instead, eating disorders highlight the history, pressures, incitements and structures of power in consumer cultures that reward a minority, and punish the majority based on the appearance of their bodies (Heyes, 2009: 73). Excessive fat for example is punished because it illustrates the individual's inability to effectively govern their body by exercising freedom through consumer sovereignty and choice. Such people are unable to take responsibility for the risks to their health that their choices pose and are therefore identified as having little value in a consumer society (Guthman and Du Puis, 2006: 443).

Summary and conclusion

This chapter began with an exploration of social psychological theory applied to abnormal and clinical psychology, starting with a brief history of relations between the subdisciplines. Abnormal and clinical psychologists draw on social cognitive theories in their understanding of individual differences in vulnerability to anxiety and attributional style. These theories include self-schemas, self-esteem, self-comparison and self-regulation. Abnormal and clinical psychologists have also been drawn to the social psychological theories of stereotyping, prejudice and aggression. Theories of stereotyping and prejudice emphasise 'faulty' thinking (or errors in thinking) and the holding of narrowly conceived points of view. Aggression and violence are theorised as an interplay between individual differences (personality) and situational factors (environment).

In critiquing the social-clinical literature it was argued that consumer culture, in particular the mass media and advertising, has led to massive increases in upward social comparisons, and that symbolic meaning and symbolic hierarchies play an important role in the aetiology of some emotional and behavioural problems. Feelings of success, wealth and affluence are in effect the accumulation of coveted consumer symbols (Baudrillard, 1970/1998: 31). An inability to access these has the potential to become a source of psychological distress.

One of the strengths identified in the social-clinical literature has been its acknowledgement of the role played by interpersonal relationships and social norms in relation to psychological distress, and the social nature of treatment strategies such as psychotherapy and therapeutic groups. Yet despite these attempts to conceptualise a broader 'social' understanding of distress, social psychology continues to displace the responsibility for distress onto the individual sufferer, as opposed to social forces such as consumer culture, which influence the day-to-day conditions in which distress arises. As Smart argues in relation to problems associated with overconsumption:

> There is a tendency to displace problems from the realm of social structure onto individuals, to translate problems into individualized pathological, psychological and biological conditions, to the detriment of an understanding of the cultural and economic factors that actually promote excessive consumer activity.
>
> (2010: 150)

This narrowly conceived perspective stems from social psychology's individual–social dualism, so that the 'notion of problems being located in an individual removes any responsibility from society' (Parker *et al.*, 1995: 61). This can be seen in the highly ambivalent nature of consumer culture, which places people in an impossible position, where they are encouraged to simultaneously express their deepest desires while punishing themselves for losing control, and then ultimately being blamed by society for the disordered behaviours that stem from their inability to regulate these. Social psychology assumes that psychological distress and psychopathology stem from an individual's inability to correctly rationalise and regulate their faulty thinking and behaviour. The impact of social forces is rarely questioned so that distress is viewed as an internal problem.

While there is some utility in social-clinical theories within treatment strategies, aiming solutions solely at the individual limits the potential scope and creativity by which these problems might be solved. Looking further afield to those factors outside the individual, and ensuring that people have some power to determine those aspects of life they deem important, provides a more effective avenue for assisting the psychologically distressed. For example, if the theory of social comparison is to be clinically useful then it needs to be reconstructed in light of the pressures exerted by consumer culture through the mass media and advertising, and the ideologies of individualism, narcissism and commodification which have become key drivers of insecurity and alienation in modern Western societies. As Fromm (1956/1991: 70) proposes, rather than helping the individual adjust to society, social psychologists should be adjusting society to suit the needs of the individual.

5 Consumer culture and space

Introduction

The purpose of this chapter is to illustrate how consumer spaces and the wider consumer transformation of urban/suburban environments in the West has come to influence social behaviour, and how these insights intersect with theories in social psychology. A characteristic feature of consumer cultures is the increasing variety of spaces designed to facilitate consumption and leisure experiences such as shopping malls, shopping arcades, supermarkets, franchised outlets, cinema complexes, casinos, bars, clubs, theatres, theme parks, cruise ships, restaurants, fast-food chains, cafés, hotels, holiday resorts and airports. Indeed, many of the world's major and not-so-major cities have become objects of consumption themselves as tourists flock in their millions to experience their various sights and spectacles.

The shift in the West away from economies based on production towards economies based on consumption has spatially transformed Western cities and the nature of everyday life. However, these spatial transformations and the social change they have wrought rarely figure as topics of research in the social psychological literature, despite the significant influence they have on social behaviour. As the following inquiry will illustrate, the spaces where people consume and the wider spatial transformation that has taken place in the Western world's urban/suburban environments is critical to understanding the changing nature of social interactions and relations, and of social behaviour more generally.

Social psychology and space

Social and environmental psychology

The question of geographic space in the science of psychology typically falls under the remit of 'environmental psychology', which is defined as the 'study of psychological aspects and effects of the physical surroundings, including especially the built environment, in which people work and live' (Colman, 2009: 253). Space, particularly consumer and urban/suburban space, is used to produce and consume things, to conduct interactions, build relationships and to maintain personal and social identities. The ways in which space is conceptualised, designed and used, and the meanings applied to it, come to define the people who live in them.

Social psychologists have, to some modest degree, recognised the value of understanding spatial influence on social behaviour (e.g. Altman, 1976; Proshansky, 1976; 1981; Steg and Gifford, 2008). One of the earliest commentaries on the relationship between social and environmental psychology by Altman (1976) identified a number of topics that he saw as being of interest to both subdisciplines. These topics include privacy, personal space, crowding and attitudes. Given that social psychology is the more mature subdiscipline, Altman argues that it potentially has much to offer its younger cousin, particularly in the area of methodology. Nevertheless, environmental psychology has much to offer in return:

> I believe that the philosophical trends implicit in environment and behavior research can have a healthy impact on Social Psychology. Whether Social Psychology is in or out of the 'crisis' about which so many have spoken is irrelevant. The point is that we have neglected to examine systematically the philosophical underpinnings of our field – what it is we study, our causal models of inquiry, etc. The study of environment and behavior poses some provocative questions and can highlight and force us to examine such philosophical assumptions.
>
> (Altman, 1976: 111)

Darley and Gilbert (1985: 949) however are less sanguine. In their chapter titled 'Social Psychological Aspects of Environmental Psychology' the authors claim that environmental psychology lacks integration and that it is more useful to think of it as a federation of various active research areas that has yet to develop an adequate set of analytic techniques or theoretical postulates. Environmental psychology, they add, must seem like an 'odd enterprise' to an academically committed experimental social psychologist, and that some of the research carried out and published in the subdiscipline is not of an acceptable methodological standard. The authors also dismiss environmental psychology's concern to produce social change and the seeking of solutions to social problems, as it reminds them of those social psychologists who once belonged to the activist wing of the group that once surrounded Kurt Lewin (Darley and Gilbert, 1985: 982–3).

Person–environment interaction

In our reading of the social-environmental psychological literature we identified three main theories that are commonly invoked. They include cognitive behaviour, social norms and person–environment fit. The following review of the social-environmental research is in no way exhaustive. Instead we seek to outline some of the salient points that we have identified in some of this research for critique later in the chapter.

In the first of the 'cognitive-behavioural' studies Moos *et al.* (1981) investigated the differences between psychiatric patients and staff in their perceptions of different rooms in a psychiatric hospital. The research design employed a number of scaled questionnaires to test participants' reactions to the dayroom, dining room, lecture room, bedroom, bathroom and meeting room. Reactions to the rooms differed for both patients and staff depending on personal perceptions; these perceptions were categorised into four main dimensions: aesthetic appeal, physical organisation, size and temperature ventilation. In a more recent study of perceptions/reactions to different physical environments O'Brien and Wilson (2011) tested participants' capacity to judge the safety of unfamiliar neighbourhoods. The authors had their participants observe photographs of unfamiliar neighbourhoods, asking them to rate their social quality. The findings indicated that social quality depended mainly on the general upkeep of physical structures.

Jorgensen and Stedman (2001) measured 'sense of place'[1] by administering a sense of place scale to a sample of lakeshore property owners in northern Wisconsin. The scale was designed to measure the participants' thoughts, feelings and behavioural commitment to their lakeshore properties. The authors found the participants' attitudes provided greater interpretation than the other measured dimensions (feelings and behavioural commitment) when it came to understanding their sense of place. In a later study Stedman (2002) presented a model of sense of place based on social psychological theory. He found that place satisfaction is strongly based on cognitive attributions made about the place (see also Proshansky *et al.*, 1983).

In a chapter analysing the relationship between social and environmental psychology Aiello *et al.* (1981) suggest that perception, cognition, attitudes and group processes are topics that are common to both subdisciplines and that all of these factors play an important role in understanding crowding, personal space and intimacy regulation. Like the majority of authors in this area, Aiello *et al.* argue that personality is a key construct in understanding how people will react to different physical and social environments (see also Baum *et al.*, 1981). Evans and Lepore (1993) and Evans *et al.* (1996) conducted two studies on crowding (see also Evans *et al.*, 1989). In the first study the authors investigated social withdrawal in situations of crowded housing and how this might affect social interaction with others outside the house. Under laboratory conditions Evans and Lepore found that participants' living in crowded housing are less likely to offer support to a confederate in need. This lack of social support was linked to the participants' social withdrawal, caused by living in crowded conditions. In the second study the authors investigated the relationship between residential crowding and psychological health and how the manipulation of interior design might mitigate this negative relationship. They found that residents of crowded homes with greater architectural depth – the number of spaces one must pass through to get from one room in the house to another – are less likely to socially withdraw because of its buffering effects.

Social-environmental research has also investigated the role that 'social norms' play under different environmental conditions. Social norms are defined as 'socially or culturally accepted standards of behaviour, which have become accepted as representing how people "ought" to act and what is "normal" (i.e. appropriate) for a given situation' (Hayes, 1993: 159). Argyle *et al.* (1981) examined the influence of situational variables on social behaviour, with a particular focus on personality–situation interaction. They began with the premise that people have set expectations – social norms – which guide their behaviour in particular spaces. These norms give rise to situated behaviours such as 'territoriality' (where people make claims over certain spaces), 'crowding' (the stresses that this places on people), 'privacy' (the level of control over personal information and interactions), 'personal space' (the perception of what constitutes one's personal space) and 'barriers' (the placing of physical barriers that impede interaction) (Argyle *et al.*, 1981: 274–8). Minam and Tanaka (1995) investigated how different physical environments support and constrain group behaviour finding that implicit rules (i.e. context specific social norms) govern the use of different spaces in school buildings, a university cafeteria and an urban residential area. In a similar study Aarts and Dijksterhuis (2003) assessed the influence of a library in eliciting silence as a normative behaviour associated with this particular space. Aarts and Dijksterhuis study is emblematic of the types of studies conducted in the social-environmental field where the focus is on the influence of other people in the regulation of behaviour, as opposed to the physical environment itself. As Darley and Gilbert (1985: 973) note: 'Of all the many aspects of our environment, we are most severely and most often affected by the other persons who surround us'. Aarts and Dijksterhuis's study also conforms to mainstream precepts in its use of an experimental research design and its testing of the relationships between different sets of interacting person–situation variables.

Another popular theoretical approach in social-environmental psychology is 'person–environment fit theories'. The basic premise here is that behaviour is influenced by the degree of compatibility between a person's personality and their environment (Edwards *et al.*, 1998: 28). The individual – that is their personality – is either congruent or incongruent with a particular space and individual traits such as the Big Five will play an important role in mediating behavioural outcomes (Harms *et al.*, 2006; Suls *et al.*, 1998). A good example of a person–environment fit study was conducted by Diener *et al.* (1984) who investigated the relationship between personality and the situations that people consciously choose to place themselves in. They predicted that congruence between the situation and personality is likely to give rise to positive affect. Yet despite the intuitive appeal of the affect-congruence hypothesis, and some data supporting its propositions, the authors found that overall the relationship was weak and that it offered little predictive quality.

Consumer culture and space

The commodification of social interactions and relations in consumer space

The rise of consumer culture has not only fundamentally transformed the way we think about and construct a viable self-identity, it has also fundamentally transformed the way in which we plan, design, construct, organise and manage the spaces we live in (Lefebvre, 1974/1991a, 1947/1991b). As Harvey (1985: 222) notes: 'Capitalism has to urbanise in order to reproduce itself', and it is through this process of urban/suburbanisation over the last 300 to 400 years that capitalism and consumer culture has been able to flourish. Zieleniec notes:

> The concentration of labour, of the means and mode of production, circulation and consumption made the urban the new and predominant spatial form. The urban became the hub in which, through which, and from which modern capitalism originated and was perpetuated.
>
> (2007: 15)

What is immediately apparent in most medium to large Western cities is their increasing commodification and the number and size of spaces devoted to consumption. This has had the effect of commodifying an increasing number of social interactions and relations. In his investigation of public life in eighteenth-century Paris and London, Sennett (1977) found that people once mingled freely in public spaces such as theatres, ale and coffee houses, streets, coaching inns, parks, and markets, which was part of a distinctive culture of sociability. As the population of cities quickly grew during this period so did networks of sociability and civility in which information was exchanged and conversation and debates between strangers became a regular occurrence in public spaces. It was during this era that large urban parks were built for promenading and social exchange, and streets were made fit for pedestrians. In order to facilitate interchange in public spaces, distinctions of rank were set aside so that people could experience interactions with one another without 'revealing much about their own feelings, personal history, or station' (Sennett, 1977: 82). It was in these public interactions that a relatively healthy community life was able to flourish.

The growth in capitalism and industrialisation in the nineteenth century led to a spatial transformation of cities and a distinct shift in the nature of public interactions. Spaces for work (production) were divorced from spaces for leisure (consumption). New districts were created for the purpose of separating people into different social classes. 'This was the beginning of a "single function" urban development. Each space in the city does a particular job, and the city itself is atomized' (Sennett, 1977: 297). Technological innovations such as the motor car further dispersed the population and public spaces were transformed into thoroughfares which people moved through rather than visited and interacted with their fellow city dwellers. Sennett found that capital had come to reconfigure urban spaces so that they became more rational and efficient with respect to its circulation, production, exchange and consumption (Marx cited in Harvey, 2001: 81). Changes in the spatial structure of cities in the nineteenth century, was coupled with the rise of 'personality' and an increasing cultural emphasis on the narcissistic investment in the self. The distinction between the public and private spheres of life began to dissolve during this period and social interactions and relations were geared towards revealing a person's inner self as opposed to spontaneous playful interchange in public spaces. This resulted in a retreat from civic life into more private realms of intimacy, which has now become characteristic of contemporary city life in the West (Sennett, 1977: 313–27).

The process of spatial transformation and subsequent social change that began in the nineteenth century accelerated in the West as political economies shifted from production (industrial) to consumption (post-industrial[2]) (Zukin, 1991). Drawing on the work of Georg Simmel, Miles (2010) argues that as a consequence of spatial changes designed to stimulate consumption, a superficial sense of social interaction and relations compared with previous historical eras came to dominate. The reason for this is that social interactions and relations became increasingly commodified; their purpose was to 'serve the calculative needs of money which thereby prioritises modes of interaction through exchange' (Miles, 2010: 17).

The impoverishment of social interactions and relations has been driven by a number of key factors. First, the privatisation of public space in the form of shopping malls 'constructs relationships between individualized consumers and a market detached from local physical space'. The owners of shopping malls seek to control diversity, which has the potential to threaten monetary exchange (Voyce, 2006: 274). Secondly, the increasing growth in suburban sprawl acts as a spatial barrier to social interactions and relations. For example, grocery stores and main streets in the US were once filled with people who were familiar to one another. As more and more people chose to live in the suburbs, or were priced out of urban areas owing to their gentrification, main streets declined and the majority of suburbanites began to shop in large impersonal malls.

> Although malls constitute America's most distinctive contemporary public space, they are carefully designed for one primary, private purpose – to direct consumers to buy. Despite the aspirations of some developers, mall culture is not about overcoming isolation and connecting with others, but about privately surfing from store to store – in the presence of others, but not in their company. The suburban shopping experience does not consist of interaction with people embedded in a common social network.
>
> (Putnam, 2001: 211)

In his book *Enchanting a Disenchanted World* Ritzer (2009: 2) analyses the settings where consumption takes place, which he defines as the 'new means of consumption'. The new means of consumption are settings that either came into existence or rapidly grew in prominence at the end of the Second World War. These include shopping malls, theme parks, ski resorts, chain stores, franchises, fast-food restaurants, electronic shopping centres, superstores, night clubs, cruise ships, casino-hotels and airports. In contrast to the main or high street that was primarily designed to function as a space for buying and selling, the new means of consumption are designed and decorated to lure and enchant the consumer by offering a delight-filled leisure experience. These cathedrals of consumption offer settings that are magical and/or fantastic, in order to elicit a sense awe and reverence in those who visit them. Underneath the enchanting surface of these sites however is a process of capitalist rationalisation that has altered social interactions and relations.

In the new means of consumption, face to face relationships have been reduced (e.g. at the drive-in window of a fast-food restaurant) or eliminated completely (e.g. in online shopping, home shopping networks, and at self-service storage centres). With the advent of the current recession, personnel have been reduced at many cathedrals of consumption, making personal interaction even less likely. The interaction that remains tends to be superficial. Few people today go to the new means of consumption for the social relationships offered by those who work there. Rather, they go to get what they want as quickly and impersonally as possible.

(Ritzer, 2009: 37)

Interactions in consumer spaces are designed to facilitate relations with products and services, as opposed to people. In the process of exchange between the consumer and the employee the emphasis is on speed, efficiency and increasingly self-service (Ritzer, 2009: 37). The shopping mall and other consumer spaces like it are impersonal settings where the consumer usually deals not with the owners but with employees, who are strangers and rarely encountered again (Shields, 1992: 102). Furthermore, 'consumers often share physical spaces of consumption such as a concert or exhibition halls, tourist resorts, sport activity sites, shopping malls and cafeterias, without having any actual social interaction' (Uusitalo, 1998: 221). When interactions do occur between consumers and employees they are generally of a simulated nature, so that in the process of interaction the employee is likely to be following a predetermined script. As a consequence, the interaction is typically devoid of genuine spontaneity and engagement. The result, Ritzer notes, is that

authentic interactions rarely, if ever, take place. In fact, so many of our interactions in these settings (and out) are simulated, and we become so accustomed to them, that we lose a sense of 'real' interaction. In the end, it may be that all we have are the simulated interactions. In fact, the entire distinction between the simulated and the real may be lost; simulated interaction may be the reality.

(2009: 105)

In situations where monetary exchange dominates, individuals become estranged from one another as products and services are bought and sold in a sphere of anonymity (Simmel, 1991a). Transactions in the marketplace typically occur between stranger and stranger. The advent of the telephone, television and the internet (as well as credit cards) have accelerated this process as many people choose to consume in the privacy of their own home (Ritzer, 2009: 130–4).

This general disconnection from meaningful social interactions and relations in consumer and urban/suburban spaces of the West is part of a wider phenomenon that Giddens refers to as 'disembeddedness'. Disembeddedness is defined as 'the lifting out of social relationships from local contexts and their recombination across indefinite time/space distances' (Giddens, 1991: 242). Modernity, Giddens

(1990: 18–19) argues, 'tears space away from place by fostering relations between absent others, locationally distant from any given situation of face-to-face interaction. Under these conditions place becomes increasingly phantasmagoric'; that is, locales become penetrated and shaped by social and cultural influences quite distant from them, and different influences appear one day and are gone the next. The disembedding process is a consequence of globalisation, which Giddens (1990: 64) defines as 'the intensification of worldwide social relations which link distant localities in such a way that local happenings are shaped by events occurring many miles away and vice versa'.

The effect of disembeddness is that self-identity in late modernity is less anchored to proximally close spaces as the influence of global events, ideas, ideologies and fashions come to dominate. The altering of social interactions and relations that this precipitates is not entirely the result of increased mobility (although this certainly plays a role) but rather place has become 'thoroughly penetrated by disembedding mechanisms, which recombine the local activities into time/space relations of ever widening scope' (Giddens, 1991: 146). Under these conditions meaningful attachments to place are weakened, so that social interactions and relations, as well as the influence of social institutions and active civic engagement atrophy (Giddens, 1991: 144–9; Putnam, 2001: 204–15; Sennett, 1977: 296–312; Voyce, 2006: 274). Rodaway notes:

> The subject's world of meaning, language, agency, rationality and desire disappear and are replaced by . . . the seduction of ready-made packages of meanings (or signs). The subject is made passive, hedonistic and loses its biographical and geographical grounding.
>
> (1995: 252)

The disembedding from place can be seen in the massive growth of 'non-places' that have emerged as a consequence of the changing patterns of consumption in the West. Non-places are defined by Ritzer (2007: 36) as 'a social form that is generally centrally conceived, controlled, and comparatively devoid of distinctive substantive content'. Non-places are scattered throughout large Western urban/suburban environments and include such ubiquitous consumer spaces as shopping malls, airports, fast-food restaurants, and other franchised outlets. Non-places are generic, as opposed to unique, have weak local geographic ties (they are not embedded in the local geography), are highly rationalised in their operations and for the people who work and consume in them they are dehumanising.[3] This is because dehumanising relationships are more likely to occur in 'generic, interchangeable non-places like fast food restaurants, (which are) characterized by their lack of ties to specific geographic locales and time periods and the sense that one is simply flowing through them' (Ritzer, 2007: 72). The effect of non-places on social interactions and relations is to nullify them.

> [S]ettings become places or *non*places (or somewhere in between) because of the thoughts and actions of the people who create, control, work in, and are

served by them . . . even human beings (and their services) become people or
*non*people (and *non*services) as a result of the demands and expectations of
those with whom they come into contact.

(Ritzer, 2007: 79)

Non-places disembed people from their locales, casting them into an ever-changing
symbolic universe that leads to the formation of ego-centred individualism (Ritzer
et al., 2005: 303). Consumer spaces are designed to increase mobility, flexibility
and interchangeability, undermining a sense of living in a specific or unique
locale. People feel less rooted to these spaces because of the lack of connection
they have with the owners and employees who work in them and their generic
features, which are devoid of uniqueness and replicated throughout the world
(Augé, 1995; Ritzer, 2007: 72; Zukin, 1991: 27).

These various disembedding mechanisms and their spatial transformations
undermine the ability to create a stable self-identity as locales which people
identify with become fragmented and/or constantly superseded (Urry, 1995:
219). Under these conditions social identity becomes much more fluid owing to
locationally distant influences. The nature of these time/space shifts hardly figures
in the social psychology literature, yet this issue is of key importance to social
identity theorists because of the implications that these shifts have for the nature
of group memberships. Group memberships based on traditionally conceived
social bonds, and networks tied to distinctive places that people have developed
an identification with over long periods of time, have given way to much weaker
short-term affiliations characterised by constant and rapid change, which has
contributed to group expansion, differentiation and dissolution (Bauman, 1992,
2004; Gergen, 1991; Kvale, 1992a; Lechner, 1991; Sennett, 1998). Social-
environmental psychologists have overlooked this social trend because their
research is largely focused at the level of the individual, who is treated as a self-
contained unit that is antecedent to the environment/context they find themselves
in (Sampson, 1989). Space is treated by social-environmental psychologists as an
empty vessel in which humans and human-made structures are placed and which
people perceive and react to based on their personality. They cognitively process
space by categorising and assigning meaning. In contrast, consumer culture
theorists assume that capitalist/neoliberal ideologies constitute forms of spatial
organisation, design and governance for the purpose of producing corresponding
social interactions and relations designed to increase efficiencies in production
and spending on consumption (Davis and Monk, 2007; Harvey, 2001; Lefebvre,
1974/1991a; Simmel, 1950b, 1991a).

There is also the problem that much of the empirical evidence that social-
environmental psychologists base their theories on stems from laboratory and/or
experimental based methods where social behaviour is lifted out of its social and
cultural context. Research of this nature is limited to an analysis of effects that are
'proximal, local, short-term, and decomposable' (Danziger, 2000: 329). A good
case in point is the way in which social-environmental theory fails to account
for the influence of commodification on social behaviours, which are driven by

the capitalist/neoliberal spatial ordering of urban/suburban environments. This is particularly evident in consumer spaces where the overriding emphasis is on the selling of products and services, and the consumption of their spectacles, reinforcing the commodification of social interactions, which creates a separation and distance between people (e.g. Voyce, 2006). We can see this in the commodification of labour as well where employees working in non-places are turned into 'non-people'. 'Of course, a nonperson is a person but one who does not act as if he or she is a person, does not interact with others as a person, and perhaps more important is not treated by others as a person'[4] (Ritzer, 2007: 79; see also Talwar, 2002). These non-interactions and non-relations reinforce the ego-centred individualism that social psychology treats as an unproblematic universal feature of social behaviour (see Chapter 3).

Social psychology's impoverished theory on this topic extends also to its accounts of globalisation, which is only sparsely dealt with in the literature. One of the few social psychologists to foresee the impact of globalisation on social psychology's theory of the person was Edward Sampson. Sampson's (1989) contention is that social psychology has not gone far enough in connecting theories of the person with social change in the form of globalisation. Social psychology he argues is still committed to an understanding of the person rooted in theoretically outmoded thinking. Drawing on the work of Michael Sandel, Sampson argues that social psychology needs to move away from a theory of the person based on a liberal individualistic conception, one in which the person is theorised as antecedent to society, towards an alternative view of the person as constituted by society.

> Policies and behaviors of states and persons far removed from our own habitats have profound implications for our longevity, economic status, and the very quality of our lives . . . Our lives are elements in several dramas that can no longer be understood simply by focusing narrowly on our inner experiences or personal preferences . . . The functional unit whose understanding we must seek is no longer the individual as currently understood, but something more globalized in its form.
>
> (Sampson, 1989: 917)

In line with Sampson's (1989) thinking what is needed is a view of the person that takes account of these fundamental social forces and shifts in the experience of time and space that globalisation has wrought. While the majority of social psychologists have remained indifferent to globalisation and the worldwide spread of consumer values,[5] the topic has not been completely ignored in the social psychology literature. However, the small number of social psychologists who have engaged with the topic of globalisation since Sampson's initial work would certainly not be considered members of the 'mainstream'. Kenneth Gergen (1991) is one example here who argues that the growth in information communication technologies has led to a profound change in the way we understand the self.

Emerging technologies saturate us with the voices of humankind – both harmonious and alien. As we absorb their varied rhymes and reasons, they become part of us and we of them. Social saturation furnishes us with a multiplicity of incoherent and unrelated languages of the self. For everything we 'know to be true' about ourselves, other voices within respond with doubt and even derision. This fragmentation of self-conceptions corresponds to a multiplicity of incoherent and disconnected relationships.

(Gergen, 1991: 6–7)

Like Gergen, McKenna and Bargh (2000) argue that the internet has altered our understanding of the self in the way it has changed social interactions. They point to the opportunities that internet users now have to engage in greater identity and role construction.[6] This is due to the internet's anonymity and the mitigation of physical proximity and the opportunities this affords when it comes to avoiding face to face encounters, as well as being able to control the time and pace of social interactions. In a similar vein Chiu and Cheng (2007) investigated how symbols of diverse cultures, now found in cities all over the world, have the potential to activate two or more cultural representations simultaneously. The authors chose to focus on consumer brands as examples of cultural representations, because they have become the most ubiquitous cultural symbols in the era of globalisation. Using the example of a Starbucks café, once sited in Beijing's 'Forbidden City' palace museum, the authors contend that visitors to the museum upon seeing this symbol of American culture in a quintessentially Chinese setting may activate two cultural representations simultaneously. This juxtaposition has the potential then to enlarge the distinctions between different identity options and choices that are available for self-identity construction. Globalisation, the authors note, 'has compressed the felt distance between cultures and created contradictory spaces; increasingly, symbols of multiple cultures are seen in the same space' (Chiu and Cheng, 2007: 97). In concluding, all three studies (Chiu and Cheng, 2007; Gergen, 1991; McKenna and Bargh, 2000) are important contributions to the social psychology of consumer culture because they seek to understand the implications of globalisation, the spread of consumer values, and the spatial and temporal reordering they have wrought, by focusing on its effects on everyday social interactions and on the experience of self-identity. This is unusual because social psychologists have typically shown little interest in any of these topics – 'globalisation', 'consumer values' and 'everyday social interactions' – however, they are fundamental if we are to understand social behaviour in all of its complexity (e.g. Tuffin, 2004: 165–6).

The governance of consumer and urban/suburban spaces

Despite the proclaimed freedoms associated with consumer sovereignty and choice, there exists in the West a range of institutions (e.g. governments, government agencies, private corporations, social, medical, economic and legal authorities) that govern social interactions and relations in consumer and urban/suburban spaces in line with neoliberal principles of rationality (Rose and Miller, 1992; Shankar *et al.*, 2006). As previously noted, citizenship was once tied to a set of obligations reflecting membership of a collective. This has now been replaced with the 'citizen as consumer' whose duty is to exercise choice in order to further individual gratification and wellbeing. This mode of citizenship has become the basis for shaping self-identity and fulfilling psychic and cultural needs (Cohen, 2003; Dean, 2010: 72; Rose, 1999: 230–1). Neoliberal programmes of government, unlike their fascist, communist or theocratic counterparts, do not seek to control the population by directly suppressing freedoms, instead they 'govern at a distance' by creating locales and persons capable of economic self-regulation (Dean, 2010; Lemke, 2001; Read, 2009; Rose, 1999; Rose and Miller, 1992).

Two main objectives are pursued by the various institutions and authorities that seek to govern consumer spaces in neoliberal economies. The first is the stimulation of desire and subsequent consumer spending. The second is to maintain spending and related consumer activities by providing a safe and secure environment, achieved by excluding elements of the public that do not conform to the 'consumer as citizen' ethic.

In order to stimulate spending, consumers are offered attractive entertaining spaces that attempt to recreate a 'dream world', which acts as a powerful influence over consumer behaviours. Consumer spaces facilitate this by seeking to flatter consumers, offering access to magical/fantastic/luxury surroundings, where they are made to feel they belong to an elite or special class of people (Miles, 2010: 103). Other techniques applied in consumer spaces that seek to manage people's emotions include the creation of 'bright, cheery, and upbeat environments' (Ritzer, 2009: 83). In order to cultivate heightened emotional responses the marketing, mass media and advertising industries, in conjunction with the owners and managers of consumer spaces, create images, narratives and environments that engage the senses with powerful mythologies (Baudrillard, 1970/1998).

Ritzer (2009) divides consumer spaces into two main categories – 'heterogeneous' or 'purified'. Heterogeneous spaces are diverse and geographically unique, such as a bustling street bazaar or marketplace. These spaces are vibrant and/or chaotic as people haggle over products and bustle their way through tightly packed streets or marketplaces. They are lively spaces with social interactions to match. Purified consumer spaces are carefully constructed cathedrals of consumption such as franchises, fast-food restaurants, shopping malls, discounters, superstores, cruise ships, casino-hotels and theme parks. These spaces are designed to create a spectacle, an extraordinary space that in some instances gives the consumer a sense of colossal boundless space. The emphasis in purified spaces is on the control and management of the consumer experience. Christopherson notes:

> The quintessential features of these environments are separation from the larger urban environment, limited pedestrian access, multilevel functionality integrated spaces through which users are channelled via walkways and high levels of security. Although these spaces may provide spectacle – puppet shows, musical performances, fashion shows – all activities are programmed and intended to enhance the central uses of space.
>
> (1994: 418)

In recent years, more and more consumption now takes place in virtual spaces. The development of information communication technologies has enabled consumer outlets to transcend the boundaries and barriers between physical spaces of consumption and the home. Ritzer (2009: 118) terms this phenomenon an 'implosion', which he defines as the 'disintegration and disappearance of boundaries as formerly differentiated entities collapse in on each other'. The collapse of consumption into the home can be seen in the growth of infomercials, home shopping networks, online malls and internet shopping, which are designed to entice consumers with an endless array of products and services available for sale at any time of the day and night, and which can be purchased from anywhere in the world, with a minimum of inconvenience. Both physical and virtual spaces of consumption rely on the perception of a colossal phantasmagoria of products and services to arouse the interest of the consumer (Ritzer, 2009: 129–50).

The notion of what constitutes a consumer space has also been enlarged, as whole cities are now marketed to visitors/tourists as commodities to be consumed (Miles, 2010). The result is that urban areas have been redefined as consumption experiences (Christopherson, 1994: 413). Cities all over the Western world compete with one another in order to attract visitors/tourists by spending large sums of money developing urban precincts, with significant investments made in cultural capital as a way of countering the economic effects of deindustrialisation and the loss of manufacturing employment to developing countries. A key strategy here has been to build consumer attractions such as sporting stadiums, theatres, galleries, convention centres and entertainment venues, as well as organising 'urban spectacles on a temporary or permanent basis'[7] (Harvey, 2001: 355). A global cultural economy of space now emanates from the Western world in which supply and demand have been replaced by seduction and desire (Terkenli, 2002).

As governments and private corporations seek to increasingly commodify public and private space the citizen consumer is positioned as an 'increasingly passive agent observer, fascinated, entranced and entangled with the images of the contemporary objective world. The consumer is thus made to desire, the landscape is made to seduce' (Terkenli, 2002: 229). However, the image of the city conferring cultural capital on its visitors/tourists subsumes an uncomfortable experience that lies underneath. This image hides much of the city's social life where young, poor, unemployed, homeless, indigenous, disabled and the mentally ill[8] are actively excluded (Christopherson, 1994; Miles, 2010: 39–54). Consumer spaces also maintain a 'false consciousness' through the use of spectacle, which is designed to hide the origins of consumer products and services, lest their magical mystical qualities be contaminated by their human relations such as developing world sweatshops.

The exclusion of undesirables has become a key strategy in the governance of consumer spaces. Neoliberal governmentality divides the population into two main categories. The first is the 'citizen as consumer', the self-governing, responsible, independent and enterprising individual whose life revolves around an active engagement with the market and consumption. The second is 'targeted populations', these are people deemed to be irresponsible, helpless, dependent and who are unable to adequately manage their own risks, and so require government discipline in the form of 'technologies of agency' (Dean, 2010: 194–7). City planners, designers, administrators and private corporations seek to create spaces that exclude these targeted populations by inhibiting 'those activities, behaviours or processes deemed negative to an efficient capitalist accumulation process' (Zieleniec, 2007: 118; see also Voyce, 2006). The citizen as consumer is also a highly targeted and disciplined entity, however, they are governed in much more subtle and nuanced ways (they are governed at a distance) that avoid the direct coercive strategies used on targeted populations. In this respect the citizen as consumer is still ultimately bound by the structures determined for them by the various institutions that govern consumer culture (Miles, 2010: 58). Sassatelli comments:

> Going shopping may thus be represented as a *legitimate and disciplined form of leisure* in so far as it exemplifies the distant but polite encounter between free moneyed individuals, which corresponds with the ideal of the free market and the dominant tendencies of capitalist culture.
>
> (2007: 165)

The active governance of consumer and urban/suburban spaces has increased over the last fifty years in cities all over the Western world, as private corporations in conjunction with national, state/county and city planning authorities seek to serve the needs of capital by commodifying space. The commodification of space, particularly the massive increase in property speculation and the transformation of previous public spaces into consumer spaces, has functioned to exclude those groups without means (the targeted populations). A good example of this was Margaret Thatcher's privatisation of council housing in the United Kingdom during the 1980s. The initial stages of this scheme – the 'Right to Buy' scheme – were positively received by council housing residents, however, it was eventually taken over by property speculators who saw quick profits, which led to greatly inflated prices, making adequate and affordable housing for lower income groups out of reach. Once the transfer was accomplished 'housing speculation took over, particularly in prime central locations, eventually bribing or forcing low-income populations out to the periphery in cities like London and turning erstwhile working-class housing estates into centres of intense gentrification' (Harvey, 2005: 164).

Gentrification refers to the process by which relatively affluent groups of people looking to enhance their lifestyle, or for investment purposes, purchase older housing stock in the inner city once occupied by lower income groups (Lees *et al.*, 2007). Gentrification is a form of conspicuous consumption expressed via the symbolic investment in housing, designed to communicate a particular inner urban lifestyle in order to solidify one's cultural capital and class position (Jager, 1986). The renovating of inner-city areas all over the Western world by the upper and upper-middle classes acts a geographical distinction that accords cultural and symbolic capital to the new occupiers. However, it has become an instigator of social conflict and spatial segregation as people on lower incomes are expelled to live in outer suburban ghettos, or forced to leave the city altogether, and they end up living in areas with a lack of employment opportunities and services, further stigmatising the residents (Baudrillard, 1970/1998: 57; Smith, 1992; Smith and Williams, 1986).

The trend for private developers and corporations to purchase once freely accessible public spaces, turning these into consumer precincts such as shopping malls, has also become a means of excluding targeted populations. These quasi-public spaces are controlled by private interests making use of sophisticated surveillance and monitoring technologies to keep targeted populations out. One example of this is 'economic zoning', which is designed to exclude fringe groups from public spaces while enticing 'rightful occupants' (the citizen as consumer) via target marketing, advertising and surveillance (Voyce, 2006: 260). The increasing numbers of spaces now given over to consumption have led to the erosion of public spaces as private developers seek to capitalise on public–private partnerships.

The active exclusion of targeted groups from consumer spaces also occurs in many newly built residential suburbs as upper and upper-middle class residents seek to live in 'gated' suburbs or communities[9] policed by private security firms. The popularity of gated suburbs stems from the loss of faith in the ability of public institutions to provide a degree of security, as well as in being able to happily and safely live in a socially diverse harmonious community (Boddy, 1992). The fear and anxiety now associated with public space has led to the rise of gated suburbs, fortified houses,[10] privatised parklands and other privatised urban/ suburban islands, which are now vigilantly watched over by growing bands of private security firms (Davis and Monk, 2007).

From this brief inquiry into the governance of consumer space we have attempted to illustrate how consumer and urban/suburban spaces in the West reinforce the centrality of cultures based on consumption. This occurs via its implosion into the home, the commodification of city spaces designed to attract visitors/tourists, in the encouragement and promotion of consumer spending by offering fantastic/magical/luxurious spaces such as shopping malls, theme parks, cruise liners, theatres, etc., and in the exclusion of and prejudice against targeted groups from freely accessing consumer spaces, and what were once freely available public spaces.

As was previously noted the essential problem for social psychology in accounting for these various social forces is its conceptualisation of space, which it treats as a neutral container of things that are somehow unaffected by the ideologies and discourses that underpinned their planning, design, construction, organisation and management. In this respect social-environmental theories of social behaviour are narrowly conceived; its focus rarely moves beyond the confines of the individual/group and the effect of specified environmental variables on behaviour such as heat, noise, light, ventilation, crowds and buffering effects. The material aspects of space are ignored in favour of a mentalist approach where social behaviour in different spaces is seen to be influenced by individual perceptions, personality traits, sense of place and social norms. This research has been achieved by maintaining an ontology (individualism) and epistemology (positivism) which aspires to an illusion of certitude by employing simplified research questions, necessarily made so, to be methodologically manageable; or as Darley and Gilbert (1985: 983) are at pains to stress, an 'acceptable methodological standard'. Thus, under the banner of acceptable methodological standards we find operationally delimited definitions of geographic space and a blunted understanding of the ways in which it shapes and influences social behaviour.

Our inquiry into the ways in which consumer space is governed also provides alternative insights into exclusion and prejudice, which it has shown to be both ideologically and discursively driven and then practised in forms of spatial organisation, design and management, as can be seen in the increasing privatisation of public spaces for the purpose of consumption and the commodification of cities more generally. Issues of conflict, oppression and prejudice are of major concern to social psychologists, however, theories in this area fail to account for the role that political and economic ideologies, discourses and institutions play in these social problems, and the ways in which they are manifested in the design of consumer and urban/suburban spaces. It is clear from the consumer space literature reviewed here that prejudice is caused by much more than just an attitude or set of norms that reside inside the minds of individuals and groups. Or that prejudice might simply be understood as an irrational or faulty cognition, a problem with personality, or a bias towards one's own in-group in the case of social identity theory.

Summary and conclusion

Despite Altman's (1976) proposal that environmental psychology could potentially provoke in social psychology a closer inspection of its philosophical assumptions, the research identified here as falling into the category of social-environmental psychology propounds theories that have their basis in behaviourism. Three theories were reviewed including cognitive behaviour, social norms and person–environment fit. These theories treat the physical environment as a 'stimulus' and a person's behaviour (based on their personality, perceptions and/or group memberships) as a 'response'. As well as being underpinned by a behaviourist perspective with a nod to various aspects of cognitive processing, these theories treat space as an empty container devoid of ideological or discursive influence.

By drawing on spatial theories from the consumer culture literature we argued that everyday social interactions and relations have become increasingly commodified, their purpose being to serve the calculative needs of money, which prioritise modes of interaction through exchange based upon an instrumental mentality (Miles, 2010: 17). This has led to an impoverished sociability as people are estranged from one another. Coupled with disembedding mechanisms – 'the lifting out of social relationships from local contexts and their recombination across indefinite time/space distances' (Giddens, 1991: 242) – it was argued that self-identity has become less anchored to proximally close spaces and places, making it much more fluid and unstable owing to locationally distant influences. Social forces such as the commodification of space and globalisation, which have been shown to have significant effects on the formation of self-identity, hardly figure as topics of research and theory in the social psychology literature.

We concluded the chapter by analysing the ways in which social behaviour is governed in consumer and urban/suburban spaces. Despite social psychological theories that propose free thinking, free acting agents, the population in neoliberal economies are governed at a distance via the spatial design of consumer and urban/suburban spaces. These spaces are designed to stimulate consumer spending through the use of spectacle and the creation of magical luxurious environments. These spaces also function to prejudice and exclude those without financial means and those likely to cause fear, anxiety, alarm and/or embarrassment; all of whom are disqualified from participating in consumer culture. These historical, political and economic forces challenge social psychological theories of prejudice and exclusion, which are understood to function inside the individual's mind. Social psychological theories fail to account for the ways in which geographic space in the West is designed to facilitate the movement of capital, which has corresponding effects on social behaviour.

6   Conclusion

Introduction

The purpose of this concluding chapter is twofold. In the first section we discuss the environmental limits of consumer culture and the challenge this presents to social psychology in its attempt to meaningfully contribute to a more environmentally sustainable future. In the final section we undertake a broad summary of the main points, arguments and implications for social psychology stemming from our inquiry into consumer culture.

The environmental limits of consumer culture

Over the last five decades the world's leading environmental scientists have been warning the world about the impending environmental catastrophe resulting from unsustainable levels of consumption. The global think tank the Club of Rome, first formed in 1968, was instrumental in bringing this issue to worldwide prominence. In 1972 the club commissioned the publication of the highly influential book *The Limits to Growth* (Meadows *et al.*, 1972), which argued that year-on-year economic growth in the West would eventually exhaust the world's natural resources. Smart (2010: 184) adds: 'there has been an increasing accumulation of scientific evidence on and growing international concern over climate change and other forms of environmental degradation arising from a resource and energy intensive consumption-driven way of life'. The United States, for example, makes up approximately 4 per cent of the world's population, and yet it consumes 26 per cent of the world's energy and emits approximately 25 per cent of the world's carbon emissions. While the United States is the largest culprit in terms of population, per capita rates of consumption and pollution in other Western consumer-driven nations such as Australia, United Kingdom, France, Italy, Spain, Germany and Canada are no less problematic and disastrous for the planet's ecological systems.

Despite the clear scientific links between rates of consumption and environmental degradation, the majority of Western governments, regardless of political persuasion, have been reluctant to show any type of leadership on this issue. Over the past three decades Western governments and their citizens have remained locked in a vicious cycle of economic growth fuelled by unsustainable levels of consumption. This is because consumer cultures are essentially cultures based on 'economic growth', their politics and economics are geared toward this purpose, so that 'dysfunctional' consumption (overconsumption) has now far outstripped its 'functional' counterpart (consumption based on needs), making the current economic system parasitic upon itself (Baudrillard, 1970/1998: 41). The dilemma of consumption is that any attempt by government to limit economic growth and the concomitant consumer lifestyles would lead to large-scale resistance, particularly from powerful business/corporate lobby groups, and eventual political defeat (Durning, 1992; Jackson, 2008). This has become the basic problem of consumer cultures worldwide – its intimate link with 'economic growth', which is tied to the planet's capacity to provide the natural resources that consumer products and services are made from and to absorb the massive amounts of waste (e.g. air, land and water pollution) that consumption produces (Durning, 1992; Jackson, 2008).

Most prominent environmental scientists and organisations now agree that the only way to successfully deal with environmental degradation is for human societies to strike a balance between a level of consumption that provides survival, security and some comfort, while simultaneously sustaining the Earth's natural resources for present and future generations (e.g. Ehrlich and Ehrlich, 2004; Halweil *et al.*, 2004; Suzuki, 2003). In order to strike this balance Western nations will need to counter the problem of 'overconsumption', that is, consumption which outstrips the sustainable capacity of the Earth's natural resources (Renner, 2006). Overconsumption is defined as the consumption of products and services 'at a level over and above that which is necessary to maintain a reasonable standard of living and at a rate that is greater than can be environmentally sustained in terms of resource provision and the handling of waste' (Humphery, 2010: 184; see also Hamilton, 2002, 2003b).

Consumption and its relationship to environmental degradation have not been lost on social psychologists, who have conducted or identified research relating to the overconsumption of energy, water and other natural resources (e.g. Gifford, 2005; Gregory and Di Leo, 2003; Kurz *et al.*, 2005; van der Pilgt, 1996). This research has been complemented by studies that investigate consumer behaviours in relation to the purchasing of products that use recycled packaging, avoid excessive packaging or products that use more environmentally friendly ingredients (Linn *et al.*, 1994; van der Pilgt, 2006). This research and others like it provide insights into a range of intra-psychic variables (e.g. values, habits, attitudes, beliefs, decision-making, perceptions and motivations) related to responsible environmental behaviours, and the success or otherwise of environmental education/awareness programmes in promoting more sustainable forms of consumption.

While this research has a certain degree of utility, it is ultimately flawed because it attributes problems like overconsumption to cognitive processes, when they are in fact symptomatic of a much wider social problem. What is needed is a social psychology that tackles the 'causes' of overconsumption, which are to be found in the values propagated by consumer culture and the political and economic ideologies that maintain it. If social psychology seeks to become a serious player in helping to solve the world's environmental problems then it will need to engage with the broader historical, social, economic, political and cultural forces that drive consumer culture. Attempts to influence and support more sustainable forms of consumption will require research and practical programmes that go above and beyond the investigation of intra-psychic variables and the prescription of environmental education/awareness programmes, environmental labelling or devising incentives to stimulate pro-environmental consumer behaviours.

The most fundamental of these broader social and cultural factors that drive overconsumption in the West is neoliberal economics. As the economists Hamilton and Denniss (2005: 7) note, neoliberalism and its market-based reforms 'promote higher consumption as the road to a better society', based on the belief that the best way to advance a country's interests is to 'maximise the growth of income and consumption' (Hamilton and Denniss, 2005: 7; see also Hamilton, 2003a). Not only does neoliberalism promote lifestyles based on overconsumption, its constant drive to open up new markets for capital accumulation, and its view that everything can in principle be treated as a commodity, has meant the natural world in all its forms is constantly under threat from those who seek to exploit its potential monetary riches (Harvey, 2005: 160–1). This threat has become increasingly serious due mainly to the constant neoliberal rolling back of environmental regulation and legislation, particularly in the United States. As Harvey (2005: 175) notes, neoliberalisation 'happens to be the era of the fastest mass extinction of species in the Earth's recent history'.

Given the dangers that environmental degradation now poses to human survival, economists and financial analysts now concede there are clear and defined environmental limits to economic growth, and that the sooner policy-makers and multinational corporations realise this, the sooner the world's economy can begin the challenging process of transitioning to new post-growth, post-consumerist models (Das, 2011; Hanley *et al.*, 2001; Pearce *et al.*, 1992).

Social psychologists have the potential to make a meaningful contribution to resolving the challenge of environmental degradation by focusing on research and practice that supports the transition towards a post-growth, post-consumerist society. In the latter part of his book *Growth Fetish* Hamilton (2003a: 205–40) discusses how Western economies might manage this shift, providing one possible avenue – albeit general in nature – for mapping alternative theoretical perspectives, research and practice for social psychologists to pursue. Many of the topics raised by Hamilton speak not only to the issues of overconsumption, but to other issues raised in this book so far, such as the work and spend treadmill, the pernicious influence of the mass media and advertising, prejudice and exclusion.

Social psychologists need to move out of the shadows of their self-imposed irrelevance. As Hill (2006) argues, social psychology has been dominated by empirical experimentation on micro-theories. Research and theory applied to social problems such as human rights violations, AIDS, politically motivated violence and developing world poverty are few and far between. Instead, social psychologists prefer to focus their attention on irrelevant issues such as factors that influence restaurant tipping (Hill, 2006: 628).

One of the ways that social psychology can become relevant once again is to become a more informed critic of political economy, specifically neoliberalism, and the many social and environmental problems it has created (Harvey, 2005). Neoliberalism trumpets enhanced freedoms for the individual through greater consumer choice and sovereignty, however, its interests are clearly bound up with multinational corporations and financial capital (Couch, 2011). Furthermore, the trumpeting of enhanced freedoms via consumer sovereignty and choice has become inherently problematic in that it tends towards material comfort and conspicuous consumption over necessity (Gronow, 1997). Therefore, there needs to be a clear and unequivocal rejection of neoliberalism's 'economic growth at all costs' mantra constantly voiced by politicians and business leaders (Hamilton, 2003a: 211; Hertz, 2001: 113). This will require a 'displacement of economic rationality by other forms of rationality' (Hamilton, 2003a: 214–15); a rationality based on fulfilling a reasonable standard of living, as opposed to the overwork and spend culture which currently dominates the West, driven by a desire to increase personal consumption (Schor, 2008). Erich Fromm has suggested that the economic system in the West needs to shift from a system based on 'maximal' consumption to a system based on 'optimal consumption' (Thomson, 2009: 109). Hamilton adds:

> The move to shorter working time would be much more than a workplace policy; it would form the centrepiece of far-reaching social change. In the first place, people would be freed to spend more time with their families, in their communities, and pursuing the activities that they find personally fulfilling. Second, the declining emphasis on paid work would be accomplished by a waning preoccupation with consumption activities and together these would constitute an assault on the role of consumption in constructing identity.
>
> (2003a: 219)

As outlined in Chapter 4, overconsumption is driven in large part by the mass media and advertising. In order to counter its promotion and encouragement of overconsumption it is recommended that advertising and sponsorship be banned in all public spaces, and that further restrictions be placed on the quantity of advertising that people, in particular children, are exposed to through the mass media (Hamilton, 2003a: 219). We are already seeing changes in public policy and legislation in the West on this issue. For example, NGOs comprising concerned parents, teachers, academics, health and medical practitioners have sought to resist aspects of consumer culture by calling for restrictions on 'junk food' advertising to children, as one method for stemming the obesity epidemic in young people[1] (e.g. Mackay *et al.*, 2011).

In the domain of education Hamilton (2003a) recommends that philosophy, ethics and history play a much more prominent role in high school and university curriculums in order to cultivate an 'art of living' instead of lives based on the pursuit of wealth, material acquisition and the seeking of celebrity status. However, it is precisely these education courses that are marginalised by the commodification[2] of education where quality is measured by the 'earning potential of graduates and little importance is attached to the extent to which education can transform students into well-developed human beings who have a deeper understanding of themselves, their societies and the world' (Hamilton, 2003a: 221).

Social psychology can play a supportive role here by conducting research, trialling programmes and becoming a stakeholder in support of changes in public policy and legislation related to economic growth, working hours, mass media, advertising and education. This however will require that social psychology shifts from a subdiscipline that advises on behaviour change only, and its emphasis on individual action and responsibility, to a subdiscipline that engages in social policy debates and social and political criticism (e.g. Uzzell, 2010). In many cases this will require challenging powerful business lobbies, which spend billions of pounds every year on marketing, media, advertising and political lobbying programmes which support and encourage overconsumption (Harsch, 1999: 566; Stevenson, 2002: 309; Urry, 2010: 200–8). It will also require challenging entrenched government ideology and public policy, much of which is built on a foundation of economic growth and consumption.[3] This is not an insignificant challenge for social psychology which has long colluded with big business, government and consumerist values in the West (Baritz, 1960; Curtis, 2002; Cushman, 1995; Moscovici, 1972; Parker, 2007; Sloan, 1997).

It is important to note however that not all social psychologists shy away from engaging with issues of social policy and social criticism. As well as drawing on alternative theoretical frameworks, critical social psychologists frequently engage with and take positions on important and contemporary debates in society. This contrasts with mainstream social psychology which prides itself on its objective scientific stance (Gough and McFadden, 2001: 2). Just some of the social issues and debates that critical social psychologists have raised in their research and practice include racism (Henriques, 1984), apartheid (Hook, 2011), mental illness (Hare-Mustin and Marecek, 2009; Kidner, 2007), social class (Ostrove and Cole, 2003), homosexuality (Clarke, 2007; Feminist Lesbians Group, 2005; Gough, 2002), capitalism and neoliberalism (Sloan, 2001; Nafstad and Blakar, 2012; Nafstad *et al.*, 2007; Tuffin *et al.*, 2000), asylum seekers (Goodman, 2008) and social justice (Aron and Corne, 1994; Fox *et al.*, 2009; Sloan, 2000). Critical social psychology along with other alternative movements within the discipline of psychology (e.g. humanistic psychology, community psychology and discursive psychology) provides an important point of departure for psychology scholars wishing to place issues of an ethico-political nature at the heart of their research and practice.

Towards a social psychology of consumer culture

The purpose of our inquiry has been to critically analyse and expand the leading positions in social psychology from the perspective of classical and contemporary theories of consumer culture. We began with a discussion on the lack of theorising in social psychology around the macro issues of consumer culture. These issues include its links with political economy, globalisation, commodification, lifestyle choice, the mass media, advertising, urban/suburban planning and alienation. Social psychology's current focus on consumption is narrowly placed on the analysis of responses to specific products and services, and to their marketing. Drawing on the work of Kasser and Kanner (2004) three main reasons were given for this. They included psychology's focus on intra-psychic variables while eschewing variables that lie outside the person, which is reflected in the dominance of social cognition in social psychological theory generally. Secondly, psychology has tended to collude with consumerism, allowing it to be co-opted by the interests of business, advertising, public relations, mass media and marketing. This collusion was traced back to the early twentieth century in the work of prominent psychologists of the time such as Walter Dill Scott, John Watson and Edward Bernays. The third reason is that psychology has generally taken an ambivalent attitude towards social policy and social criticism. This is in line with social psychology's 'natural science' epistemology, which maintains an illusion of moral and political neutrality in pursuit of a dream that it will eventually discover a set of universal laws governing social behaviour.

In our initial inquiry into consumer culture we discussed its prominent place in everyday life. Evidence of its significance can be seen in the amount of time people spend shopping and watching television every week, the amount of money spent on consumer products and services, and the way in which public spaces in the West are geared towards consumption. This was followed by a conceptual exploration of consumer culture, through a reading of Ritzer *et al.* (2001) and Featherstone (2001). In scanning the terrain of consumption Ritzer *et al.* (2001) proposed that it covered four main topic areas, from which our inquiry focused on three. These included consumer objects (products and services), consumer subjects (consumers) and consumer sites (spaces and places where consumer products are bought and sold). Featherstone's (2001) conceptual analysis pointed to the changes in societal values wrought by consumer culture, outlining the ways in which citizens of the West in the early twentieth century were trained to let go of their Protestant ethic of individual sacrifice, hard work, thrift and delayed gratification, embracing a new ethic based on the expression and satisfaction of long-suppressed desires, pleasures and to spend money now and save later. Like Ritzer *et al.* (2001), Featherstone (2001) also pointed to the ways in which urban/suburban spaces have been redesigned over the course of the nineteenth and twentieth centuries to facilitate the movement of capital in order to increase consumption. Other features of consumer culture highlighted by Featherstone (2001) include the massive growth in the marketing, public relations, mass media and advertising industries whose aim is to encourage and maintain consumption in the West. This is coupled with a growth in population and pollution, and the increasing depletion of natural resources that is now blighting the globe as a consequence of consumer-driven lifestyles in the West.

In seeking to analyse consumer culture from a political economy perspective we explored its position within the broader ideology of capitalism and free market economics (neoliberalism). Consumer culture came to dominate the West in the years following the Second World War as consumption was used by governments as a means to reconstruct the economy, which had hitherto been geared towards military production. In order to stimulate consumer spending government and business through the mass media and advertising linked it to citizenship, national pride and patriotism. Although a form of global free market economics existed prior to the Great Depression of the 1930s, it was resurrected in the 1980s by Margaret Thatcher and Ronald Reagan. Both leaders enacted a raft of new economic policies that included the deregulation of financial institutions, the freeing up of capital restrictions around the globe, privatising government enterprises and undermining collective labour associations. The free market was promoted as a superior mechanism for resolving social and economic problems, as well as increasing personal freedoms and economic prosperity through consumer choice and sovereignty. As neoliberalism has expanded around the globe, the free market and its relentless commodification has come to mediate virtually every aspect of day-to-day to life, including the ways in which people think and behave. As Harvey (2005: 3) notes, neoliberalism 'has pervasive effects on ways of thought to the point where it has become incorporated into the common-sense way many of us interpret, live in, and understand the world'.

In order to provide a theoretical and philosophical basis for critiquing and expanding social psychological theory, we reviewed the consumer culture literature with a focus on the topics of self-identity, emotional and behavioural problems, and geographic space. This review was divided into four parts: historical precursors (Marx, Simmel, Veblen, Fromm), poststructuralist theories (Foucault, Baudrillard, Bourdieu), social theories (Giddens, Bauman, Lefebvre), and feminist theories (Scanlon, Bordo). Starting with the work of Karl Marx we traced his theories of commodity fetishism, false consciousness (originally developed by Marx's collaborator Engels) and alienation. Simmel along with Veblen highlighted the shift from religion to the money economy as the new mediator of social interactions and relations. Both pointed to the growth in urbanisation and the desire for recognition and distinction as a way of transcending urban anonymity, which they observed in social emulation and conspicuous consumption. Our review of the historical precursors was completed with an analysis of Erich Fromm's work. Fromm, one of the few social psychologists to have analysed consumer culture, pointed to the ways in which it has led to the commodification of self-identity and the experience of alienation this has created.

Breaking away from the main tenets of Marxist theory, poststructuralism proposes that consumer culture is 'a process governed by the *play of symbols*, not the satisfaction of material needs' (Bocock, 1993: 75). This quotation sums up the basis of Baudrillard and Bourdieu's interpretation of consumption, as both highlight the way in which consumer products and services are used as cultural markers of taste and to communicate one's place in a social hierarchy, as well as choice of lifestyle, values and self-identity. Baudrillard highlighted the increasing prominence of the body in consumer culture, which has become intimately linked with self-identity. The body is also used as a means through which self-identity is marketed and sold. In our review of Foucault we focused on his theory of governmentality and discourse applied to consumer culture and neoliberalism. We also explored the ways in which space is governed in Western urban/suburban environments, which is designed to stimulate consumer spending and to discipline, police and control 'targeted groups'.

In our review of social theories of consumer culture we focused on the work of Anthony Giddens, Zygmunt Bauman and Henri Lefebvre. Giddens and Bauman tracked the changes in social experience that have taken place in conjunction with the shift from a society based on production to a society based on consumption. This shift has seen the demise of a relatively stable self-identity that was anchored to traditional institutions such as work, family, religious observances and social class, which provided a degree of social solidarity. This has been replaced by a reflexive self-identity that floats among the multiple identities, images and diverse lifestyles that consumer culture offers, increasing feelings of instability, anxiety and risk. Bauman reiterated that consumption is no longer an instrumental activity aimed at satisfying basic living and material needs, instead it has become a means of gratifying desires which are open-ended and infinite. Our review of Lefebvre focused on his work linking social life with spatial organisation, in which he points to its increasing commodification in capitalist economies and its use as a means for exclusion, prejudice and injustice.

In our review of feminist theories of consumer culture we explored the work of feminist and consumer culture theorists Jennifer Scanlon, Susan Bordo and others. Analysing consumer culture through a feminist lens highlighted the ways in which it demarcates the genders. Consumer culture perpetuates a narrow view of feminine identity, one that is subjugated to the sexual desires of men, and which is used to sell products and services. This is most actively promulgated through the gendering of products and services and in the images and narratives communicated in the mass media and advertising. These representations open up and constrain certain female identities, which have become intimately tied to the body and idealised images of beauty and sex appeal.

We began our inquiry of the leading positions in social psychology by focusing on its theories of self-identity. Its initial forays here drew on an eclectic range of theoretical perspectives including structuralism, psychoanalysis, sociology and interactionism. However, these perspectives were eventually discarded in favour of a social cognitive perspective that gained popularity and eventual dominance in the 1970s and 1980s. Social cognition assumes that social behaviour is determined by individual cognition in actual, implied or imagined social situations. This assumption plays a central role in social identity theory, the leading theory of self-identity in social psychology. This theory assumes that self-identity is informed by the ways in which people cognitively categorise themselves and others into social groups. It purports that cognitive categorisation influences self-esteem, as well as providing an interpretation of other social behaviours such as competitiveness and aggression between individuals and groups, social comparison making, the seeking of self-enhancement and engaging in impression management.

In critiquing these leading positions it was argued that competitiveness, aggression, social comparison, self-enhancement and impression management are not universal social behaviours that have existed across time and space, or indeed representative of inherent predispositions or group categorisations, as is claimed in the social psychology literature. Instead, the formation of self-identity in the West is shaped and mediated to a large degree by consumer culture and its links with capitalist/neoliberal ideologies. This can be seen in its privileging of certain individualistic personality traits such as flexibility, competitiveness, aggression, enterprise, entrepreneurship, innovation, emotional intelligence and extraversion, which are linked to motivations to acquire money, power, status, fame and beauty. These traits and desires are shaped by consumer culture forces such as the commodification of self-identity, which can be seen in the encouragement to market and sell one's self and in learning to view it as a cultural resource. As a consequence, self-identity has become much more narcissistic when compared to previous historical eras, as can be seen in the popular retreat into psychic and bodily improvement (Giddens, 1991: 171). Narcissism has become the overriding response to feelings of powerlessness and isolation in a globalised world. This can also be seen in the desire for distinction and status, which has become the overriding response to the population growth in urban areas and the feelings of anonymity it creates, and in the desire to construct a viable self-identity as can be seen in the mastering of good taste and the garnering of cultural capital. The formation of gender identities was found to be influenced by the mass media and advertising, which is obsessed with beauty and body image. Lastly, we explored the ways in which consumer ideologies and discourses have led to a more reflexive, anxious and unstable self-identity, which challenges social psychological interpretations which claim that people are free thinking, free acting agents.

Conducting an inquiry through the prism of consumer culture expands social psychological theories of self-identity because it not only describes the contemporary societal conditions in which it is formed, but it also provides insights into its origins. For example, it provides an interpretation of why individuals and groups compete with one another to the degree that they do, engage in impression management, and why people are becoming more individualistic and less caring of others. It tells us why people seek to establish difference at both the group and individual level and the ways in which this influences the process of group memberships, the formation of attitudes, conformity and stereotypes, which social identity theory fails to interpret in any comprehensive manner. Furthermore, it tells us why women's identities are intimately tied to body image and maintenance – overturning the assumption that gender is a psychological essence (Gough and McFadden, 2001: 28–9). It challenges the relevance of social identity theory by exposing its failure to account for recent social trends such as the breakdown in traditional institutions and the fluidity of social groups and self-identities in consumer cultures, which are constantly being formed and dissolved owing to information communication technologies and globalisation. In this respect, social psychological theorists need to take into account that self-identity is 'not necessarily rigid or clearly separate from others, with hard or fixed boundaries' (Pickering, 2001: 29). There are important implications for this as argued by Cushman:

Significant sociopolitical change in the last decade of the twentieth century will continue to be ineffective unless a political movement can take into consideration the current configuration of the self and develop ways of reconfiguring the self so that it will be at once more socially cooperative and less vulnerable to consumerism, less rigidly masterful and bounded and not as empty as our present configuration.

(1995: 90)

In the second major topic of investigation we built on our previous inquiry into self-identity by tracing the links between emotional and behavioural problems and consumer culture. To begin with we reviewed the social psychological literature that informs abnormal and clinical psychology. The theories in social psychology focused on cognitive processes have been most commonly utilised in clinical and abnormal psychology. These include self-schemas, self-esteem, self-comparison and self-regulation. We also reviewed theories of stereotyping, prejudice, aggression and violence. All of these theories are based on the assumption that emotional and behavioural problems such as depression, anxiety, prejudice and aggression stem from irrational or faulty cognitions such as highly selective, egocentric and rigid self-schemas, or negative attributional styles.

In our critique of the social-clinical literature we sought to expand upon its limited interpretations of emotional and behavioural problems by highlighting the role played by consumer culture through the mass media and advertising. We argued that the dominance of the mass media and advertising in everyday life in the West has led to massive increases in upward social comparisons, which has had a profound effect on work and leisure behaviour as evidenced by widespread indebtedness, bankruptcies and overwork, all of which have been empirically linked to psychosomatic illness, anxiety disorders, major depression and addictions. We further explored the mass media and advertising by analysing the ways in which it stimulates false needs and desires (creating a false consciousness), and its reproduction of stereotypes; as well as the ways in which it promotes and encourages its audiences to develop irrational consumer habits, which for some people have led to addiction, obesity, indebtedness and bankruptcy. By highlighting the links between consumer culture and emotional and behavioural problems we sought to provide an alternative to social psychological interpretations of emotional and behavioural problems, which are viewed as failures in self-regulation. Its intra-psychic perspective unwittingly blames the individual for social forces that it has little control over. It proposes that emotional and behavioural problems stem from an individual's inability to regulate their behaviour. While we agree that self-regulation plays a part in this equation, it is an impoverished theory because it fails to account for the consumer ideologies and discourses that influence irrational or self-destructive behaviours. The same problem is encountered in social psychological concepts of stereotyping, which are theorised as a propensity to make quick unthinking assessments by grouping people into erroneous categories. Again, this is an impoverished theory because it fails to account for the content and sociocultural origins of stereotyping, which can only be fully understood by analysing the effect that images and narratives promulgated by the mass media and advertising have on people's thinking and behaviour towards others.

We continued our inquiry into emotional and behavioural problems by investigating the links between consumer culture and alienation and exclusion. We explored the alienating effects of consumer culture and neoliberalism, which emphasise self-interest at the expense of reciprocal or collective values (Wheelock, 1999b: 30). This was evidenced by declines in the numbers of people participating in civic organisations and informal socialising, the solitary nature of popular leisure activities and the commodification of human interactions and relations which do not take place in a show of solidarity, but are instead mediated through the competitively designed market as relations of purchase and sale (Braverman, 1974: 192). Alienation is experienced by those without the financial means to participate in consumer culture, by which they are excluded from attaining symbolic status. We argued that symbolic inequality has significant effects on self-esteem influencing one's social identity. Symbolic status is also a marker of one's economic and cultural capital, which in turn influences the groups that one is able to join or not join. Symbolic inequality was also found to be linked to aggression, violence and crime, so that those people without it will seek to gain it in whatever way they can. The inability to access economic and cultural capital is a major source of psychological distress, highlighting the ways in which emotional and behavioural problems are shaped as much by material circumstances (Smail, 2005: 32–9), as they are by an individual's cognitions and personality.

To complete our inquiry into emotional and behavioural problems we explored consumer culture's obsession with the body, which it treats as the most precious of objects and resources (Baudrillard, 1970/1998: 129; Featherstone, 2010: 197). The body has become a point of focus in the mass media, advertising, fashion and fitness industries, and is used to market and sell self-identities. This has significantly increased 'body consciousness' and levels of anxiety and vulnerability in relation to it. Consumer culture encourages and promotes body work in the form of fitness, dietary, fashion and beauty regimes, as well as cosmetic surgery, all of which have become moral imperatives. These pressures are implicated in eating disorders and disturbed body image. Social psychology has broadened individual psychology's understanding of these disorders by pointing to their links with social identity, group dynamics, social comparisons, attributions and attitudes. However, despite this broader perspective social-clinical theory neglects to account for the contradictory pressures exerted by consumer culture, in understanding eating disorders and disturbed body image and the political and economic ideologies that drive it.

In the third major topic of investigation we explored how consumer spaces and the wider consumer transformation of urban/suburban environments in the West influence social behaviour. To begin with we reviewed social psychological theory used in environmental psychology. These include cognitive-behavioural, social norms and person–environment fit theories. The basic assumption underpinning these theories is that social behaviour is influenced by personality and perceptions which interact with differing physical environments.

In our critique of the social-environmental literature we began by exploring the commodification of social interactions and relations in consumer space and the broader effects of the capitalist/neoliberal shaping of urban/suburban spaces. Capitalism has to urbanise in order to reproduce itself (Harvey, 1985: 222); therefore urban/suburban spaces are designed to serve the calculative needs of money, prioritising interactions through modes of exchange, as opposed to interactions based on solidarity and reciprocity (Miles, 2010: 17). In consumer spaces more specifically, consumers are directed to purchase products and services, as opposed to interacting with other consumers and employees. Consumer spaces are not about overcoming isolation and connecting with others, but about privately choosing and consuming products and services (Putnam, 2001: 211). The alienation inherent in these interactions is particularly acute in exchanges between consumers and employees, which are often impersonal, scripted and devoid of genuine spontaneity and engagement. This general disconnection from meaningful social interactions and relations in consumer and urban/suburban spaces is part of the wider phenomenon of disembeddedness, which is driven by information communication technologies and globalisation. Under conditions of disembeddedness local space becomes penetrated and shaped by social and cultural influences quite distant from it. These alienating and disembedding mechanisms challenge the basic assumption of social identity theory, by questioning the function of group memberships in informing self-identity, as these have become increasingly fleeting and unstable, due in part to the dissolution of local space as a stable anchoring point. What has come to replace self-identity based on stable group memberships anchored to a particular locale is a much more fluid self-identity influenced and shaped by events, cultures, ideologies and social movements that are distant from it. As a consequence self-identity has become less anchored to its locale and the other people and groups who inhabit it.

Our inquiry into consumer culture also calls into question the social-environmental notion of the individual as a self-contained unit that is antecedent to society (Sampson, 1989), who responds to their environment based on their personality and perceptions. In contrast, consumer culture theorists propose that self-identity and social behaviour are constituted in part by capitalist/neoliberal ideologies through their influence over the spatial organisation, planning and governance of cities in the West. This spatial reordering produces corresponding social interactions and relations designed to increase efficiencies in production and spending on consumption.

Following on from our discussion of the spatially alienating and disembedding effects of consumption, we analysed the ways in which consumer and urban/suburban spaces in the West are governed by neoliberal principles of spatial rationality. In an effort to create cities that confer cultural capital on their inhabitants and to seduce visitors/tourists to spend time and money in them, governments and private corporations seek to exclude groups which do not conform to the 'citizen as consumer' ethic. These 'targeted groups' imperil efforts to create magical, fantastic, luxurious or genial spaces for consumption, as they cause fear, alarm, anxiety and embarrassment. Various strategies are mobilised to exclude targeted groups, including the use of surveillance, the employment of private security, the building of 'gated' suburbs, the gentrification of urban areas once occupied by lower income groups and the redevelopment of public spaces, which are turned into quasi-private spaces such as shopping malls, shopping precincts, business parks, luxury apartments or theme parks. The governance of consumer and urban/suburban spaces challenges social-environmental theory, which treats space as an empty container devoid of political and economic ideologies. Social-environmental theories ignore the ways in which dominant ideologies and discourses underpin the creation and management of urban/suburban spaces. Concepts of geographic space linked to consumer culture theory also challenge social psychological theories of exclusion and prejudice, which illustrate the ways in which these phenomena are spatially influenced and therefore much more complex than simple social cognitive theories allow.

In conclusion, we have illustrated the ways in which theories of consumer culture intersect with the leading theories in social psychology such as self-identity, social identity theory, self-esteem, impression management, narcissism, self-comparisons, stereotyping, prejudice, aggression, eating disorders, disturbed body image and social norms. Our inquiry has illustrated the potential for theories of consumer culture to both critically deconstruct and expand social psychological theory, adding to the existing literature on critical social psychology. Moreover, we have illustrated how social psychology may become relevant once again by getting to grips with one of the most powerful contemporary social forces in the form of consumer culture.

Above and beyond a need to engage with theories of consumer culture, there is a need for social psychologists to better understand the role of political economy in shaping and influencing social behaviour. At present, social psychological theories fail to account for the influence of distal powers such as consumer culture and the politics and economics that maintain it. These are forms of power (or influence) exerted at a distance from the individual and the group, however, their effects are proximate and profound (Smail, 2005). So obscure and taken for granted are these powers exerted by political and economic ideologies, and the public policies and programmes that evolve from them, that most people are unaware of their effects on their day-to-day life. Social psychology perpetuates this ignorance by failing to help people understand 'how their conduct is constrained by the action of powers well beyond their ken', because it 'focuses them instead on an "inner world" of ideality that doesn't even escape the confines of their own skulls' (Smail, 2005: 32). Moreover, social psychology's theorisation of a self-identity composed of unalterable predispositions that lie outside of history, culture, politics and economics is

> often used to suggest that social changes cannot take place because they would be contrary to human nature. We could trace one aspect of this idea of unalterable human nature in the growth of the cult of individualism coincident with the demands of a free market.
>
> (Leonard, 1984: 30)

Social psychology's narrow perspective on social behaviour not only constrains its theory, it also constrains its practice. At present its practice deals only with the symptoms of social problems as manifested in disordered forms of social behaviour, as opposed to understanding their underlying causes, as was illustrated in relation to social psychological prescriptions aimed at stemming environmental degradation; or the ways in which social psychologists blame addiction on a person's inability to self-regulate. As Smail (2001: 160) argues, distal causes of emotional and psychological distress require distal cures. In this respect social psychology needs to become much more politically active if it is to have any meaningful impact on solving some of the world's most pressing problems. It can do this by lobbying for public policy that protects people from the worst aspects of consumer culture and neoliberal economics. This will obviously require a greater commitment to social criticism and a much more meaningful engagement with public policy processes, an understanding of how they are influenced and the practical programmes that evolve from them.

Notes

1 Introduction

1 The field of 'leisure studies' failed to make much of an impact in sociology, even less so in psychology. However, there has been an increasing interest in the mass media, sport, cultural studies and consumerism because of the influential role these phenomena now play in understanding modern Western society (Marshall, 1998: 364).

2 We take our definition of political economy from Hahnel (2002: 1) who defines it as the study of 'economics within the broader project of understanding how society functions'.

3 Social psychology has been no exception (see Pepitone, 1981).

4 In a conversation with Jerome Bruner on the topic of psychology's movement away from applied research, Martin Seligman in his foreword to the edited collection *Positive Psychology in Practice* (Linley and Joseph, 2004: p. xii) noted that Bruner once told him: 'About 60 years ago the chairmen of Harvard, Princeton, and Penn got together at a meeting of the Society of Experimental Psychologists and agreed that they would hire no applied psychologists. This set the hiring pattern of many of the great departments to this very day.'

5 A number of psychologists, psychiatrists and psychotherapists argue that psychology's collusion with consumerism is symptomatic of its wider collusion with capitalist/ neoliberal economics (e.g. Cushman, 1995; Moscovici, 1972; Parker, 2007; Sloan, 1997).

6 Although pure behaviourism has now been consigned to psychology's history books, its ontology and epistemology continues to exert a significant influence over social psychological theory. A good example of this can be seen in the emerging movement of positive psychology, which employs theories of behaviourism, claiming they are superior to alternative interpretative approaches to psychology. Positive psychologists, chief among them Martin Seligmann, argue that interpretative approaches are based on inferior ontologies and epistemologies such as phenomenology and hermeneutics (e.g. Peterson and Seligman, 2004: 4; Seligman, 2003: 275; Seligman and Csikszentmihalyi, 2000: 7).

7 Lifestyle is defined in our inquiry as the choice of clothes, speech, leisure pursuits, eating and drinking preferences, home, car and holidays that individuals make in a self-conscious manner (Featherstone, 2007: 81). Choice of lifestyle is a means of communicating to ourselves and others our skills, attitudes, values, interests and beliefs.

8 The element of safety has been identified as being particularly important for women (Rappaport, 2000).

9 A good example of this is the luxury cruise liner the *Oasis of the Seas*, which has become the world's largest floating simulation. At the centre of its eighteen decks

is a park, aptly named Central Park, which contains over 12,000 trees and shrubs. Also on board are a chapel, ice rink, 37 bars, 10 whirlpools, scores of shops, a fitness centre and a 380-seat theatre. The ship itself has five times the tonnage of the *Titanic* and is longer than any aircraft carrier in the US fleet. Docked at its home port in Fort Lauderdale, Florida, its identical rows of curved glass balconies make it indistinguishable from the apartments and office blocks that dot the Miami skyline in the distance. On board it looks and feels like anything but a ship, which is all part of its heightened illusion. The liner is sold as an 'urban experience', a city on water which is what most of its passengers enjoy: getting a cappuccino in one of the ships seven distinct 'neighbourhoods' and indulging in serious consumption (Adams, 2009).

10 The terms 'consumer culture' and 'consumer society' are used interchangeably throughout our inquiry. However, we use the term consumer culture in the majority of cases.

11 We take our definition of ideology from Steger and Roy (2010: 11) who note: 'ideologies are systems of widely shared ideas and patterned beliefs that are accepted as truth by significant groups in society . . . ideologies organize their core ideas into fairly simple truth games that encourage people to act in certain ways. These claims are assembled by codifiers of ideologies to legitimize certain political interests and to defend and challenge dominant power structures.'

12 Former and current heads of government who have now questioned neoliberalism include former Australian Prime Minister Kevin Rudd (2009), former British Prime Minister Gordon Brown (Painter, 2009), and the US President Barack Obama (Obama, 2009).

2 Theories of consumer culture

1 The *Oxford English Dictionary* (online version) (2011) defines commodification as the 'action of turning something into, or treating something as, a (mere) commodity; commercialization of an activity, etc., that is not by nature commercial'.

2 'Marx himself never used the phrase false consciousness' (Eagleton, 1991: 89), instead it was his chief collaborator Friedrich Engels whose ideas stemmed from Marx's writings on ideology (Bottomore, 1991: 247–52).

3 Marx made a similar observation when he wrote that money must be constantly on the move if it is to retain its value.

4 Guy Debord (1967/1994) in his book *Society of the Spectacle* makes a similar claim arguing the mass-mediated image of the commodity has supplanted genuine human interaction in advanced capitalist society.

5 The transition or otherwise to a postmodern society has been an ongoing debate within the humanities and social sciences now for a number of years. However, these debates have been largely muted in the social psychology literature, except for a handful of journal articles and two edited collections *Postmodernism and Psychology* (Kvale, 1992b) and *Postmodern Psychologies* (Holzman and Morss, 2000). The absence of this debate has been detrimental to the subdiscipline. While the majority of social psychologists are either bewildered, indifferent, or opposed to postmodern interpretations of social life, it is an area of social scientific inquiry that points to various trends in contemporary society that have important implications for the ways in which individuals and groups think, feel, and behave. Bocock (1993: 80) puts this argument most succinctly when he notes: 'The issue is not to find out if the analytical model of post-modernity is "true" or "false", but, as with any model, to use it to highlight certain features of social, cultural and psychological change'.

6 See Kvale (2003) for an analysis of how this shift in the culture at large, based on the motif of the shopping mall, has influenced contemporary styles of psychological research and professional practice.

3 Self-identity in consumer culture

1 Maintaining a successful career for most people has now become problematic given the highly insecure nature of employment in the West (Sennett, 1998).

2 For a more indepth analysis of the commodification of self-identity in relation to romance see Illouz's (1997) *Consuming the Romantic Utopia.*

3 The success of Facebook is also evidence of the culture of narcissism that has infected contemporary Western society, which will be discussed in more detail in the next section.

4 A characteristic feature of consumer cultures is the number of products and services now devoted to 'bodily and psychic improvement' (Giddens, 1991: 171). These include cosmetics, cosmetic surgery, fashion apparel, personal training, yoga, courses in wine appreciation, social networking, leadership, motivation, emotional intelligence, assertiveness training, and impression management, to name just a few.

5 The 'citizen as consumer' is most often invoked by political leaders during periods of crisis and economic recession. A striking example of this occurred in the wake of the 9/11 World Trade Center and Pentagon bombings where for a period of time the United States economy risked falling into recession. In response, President George W. Bush asked the American people to continue spending money in order to stabilise the economy, sending a clear message to the terrorists that the resolve of the United States would not be broken.

6 There are some rare exceptions to this. For example, Roberts and Helson (1997) inquired into the often cited claim that American culture is becoming increasingly individualistic, leading to the individualisation of people's personalities. However, the basic problem with a study like this and so many others like it that are regularly published in personality and social psychology journals, is that the authors tested their claim by administering a series of personality and other inventories to a group of students from a single US college (see Arnett, 2008). It therefore tells us very little about whether US society is actually becoming more individualistic, and how this shift in culture and personality has come about. It also seems that the emphasis in studies of this nature is to prove the author's prowess in selecting and administering appropriate personality inventories and statistical tests with which to analyse the resultant data, than it is about actually inquiring into the topic at hand. This of course is not the fault of the authors, but the editors and reviewers of these particular journals whose notions of first-rate social science are narrowly conceived (see Cialdini, 2009). It is argued that an analysis of this type (a cultural analysis) can really only effectively shed light on a phenomenon like 'increasing levels of individualism' by systematically investigating changes in cultural practices over a selected historical time frame, and by analysing the dominant discourses and ideologies communicated in the mass media, through political rhetoric, governments and their agencies, and educational institutions.

7 Nevertheless, Lasch's (1979) analysis has been criticised on a number of fronts. The most commonly cited is that it lacks empirical support. Also, others such as Giddens (1991: 179) argue that, despite Lasch's insightful understanding of the powerful forces inherent in capitalist modes of social organisation, the effects on the population are scarcely received in an uncritical way.

8 Scanlon (2000a) points out that other feminist interpreters of consumer culture, those writing from a cultural studies perspective, argue that women may also play with the images thrust at them, subverting the dominant ideologies and notions of femininity they represent.

9 The linking of feminine self-identity with knowledge of consumer products and services began to emerge with the opening of the world's first department stores (Rappaport, 2000). Because department stores were the first public spaces other than churches that were considered respectable for women to visit without a male companion (Bowlby,

1987: 189), developing knowledge of the products that department stores sold became an important form of cultural capital for upper class women of the era.

10 As have homosexual (Faderman, 2000) and certain racial self-identities (Coltrane and Messineo, 2000; McClintock, 2000; Steele, 2000).

11 Just some of the TV programmes devoted to real estate themes include: *The Block* (Australia), *Hot Property* (UK), *Better Homes and Gardens* (Australia), *Ground Force* (UK), *My Celebrity Homes* (US), *Renovation Realities* (US), *Restoration Home* (UK), *How Clean Is Your House?* (UK), *Grand Designs* (UK), *Location, Location, Location* (Australia and UK), *Homes Under the Hammer* (UK), *Changing Rooms* (UK and Australia), and *Extreme Makeover: Home Edition* (US).

12 In his study on the personal consequences of work under the new conditions of 'flexible capitalism' (neoliberalism), Sennett (1998) argues that downsizing, short-term contracts, casualisation, and contingent project work have corroded people's characters. The reason for this is that people have come to mistrust the very institutions which once provided mutual and long-term commitment, reciprocity and loyalty. All of which once formed the basis for building and developing character.

4 Emotional and behavioural problems in consumer culture

1 In their painstakingly researched book *Manufacturing Consent*, Herman and Chomsky (1994: 14–18) found the majority of mass media in the US is reliant on advertising to ensure its existence. Television programming is essentially paid for by advertisers who want to see content that encourages consumerist lifestyles, or at least content that avoids 'serious complexities and disturbing controversies that interfere with the "buying mood"' (p. 17). In a similar vein David Simon, the writer/producer of the critically acclaimed television series *The Wire,* had this to say about the links between television content and advertising: 'Until recently, all of television has been about selling. Not selling a story, of course, but selling the intermissions to that story. And therefore little programming that might interfere with the mission of reassuring viewers as their God-given status as indebted consumers has ever been broadcast – and certainly nothing in the form of a continuing series. For half a century, network television wrapped its programs around the advertising – not the other way around, as it may have seemed to some' (Simon, 2010: 2). See also Hertz (2001: 7 and 175) for other examples of the links between mass media content and advertising.

2 Brinkmann (2008) argues that the transition from an industrial society to a consumer society coincided with a change in psychologies from psychoanalysis and behaviourism – industrial society – to humanistic psychology (the pioneer of self-actualisation studies) and social constructionism – consumer society. Other studies that have made similar claims include Buss (1979), Carrette (2003) and Kvale (2003).

3 A similar study conducted in Australia found that 70 per cent of respondents considered themselves fully disengaged from the national agenda, while their interests and aspirations reflected a desire for material abundance (Mackay, 2004).

4 O'Malley and Kroupp (2006) conducted a study on children's leisure, finding they are 'increasingly drawn to leisure activities that are solitary – such as computer games and television – instead of group activities (such as Boy Scouts) . . . . In our opinion, our society in particular, a society rich with technology, is directed, though unintentionally, to indifference and to introvertedness.'

5 A classic example of the link between global consumer culture and narcissism, aggression and violence can be seen nightly on so-called 'reality television' programmes where contestants hoping to gain some degree of celebrity, willingly submit themselves to a set of contrived and humiliating rituals. Viewers of these programmes delight in the 'cut-throat scorn for the weaknesses of others and a sadistic affirmation of ruthlessness and steroidal power. Getting voted off the island or being

told "You're fired!" now renders real life despair and misfortune entertaining, even pleasurable' (Giroux, 2008: 595; see also Couldry, 2008).

6 There are myriad statistics that attest to the growing gap between rich and poor. Here are just some examples: (1) The richest 1 per cent of US citizens own 22 per cent of all income and approximately 40 per cent of all wealth in that country. In 2005, average CEO pay was 369 times that of the average worker, compared with 131 times in 1993 and 36 times in 1976 (Dreier, 2007, cited in Giroux, 2008: 597). (2) Across OECD countries average incomes of the richest tenth of the population is now approximately nine times that of the poorest tenth of the population (OECD, 2011b). (3) In the UK the bottom tenth of earners saw their pay increase by 0.1 per cent between 2010 and 2011, while the top tenth saw their pay grow 18 times faster (Allen and Ball, 2011). (4) In Australia the average net worth for the wealthiest households jumped 15 per cent in the four years to June 2010, compared with 4 per cent for the poorest households (Bloomberg, 2011).

7 This problem is exacerbated by the mass media as the following quote illustrates. 'What is hard to deny is that when the poor see wealth from which they are excluded they have confirmed reason to feel anger and much else. In Dickens day the poor in East London, lacking television or radio, even telephones, had little direct knowledge of the rich in Kensington' (Elliott and Lemert, 2009: 175).

8 Some examples of this include wearing T-shirts printed with Che Guevara's image, sporting clothes and accessories promoted by US rap groups, the clothing brand FCUK, and playing violent sexist video games such as *Grand Theft Auto, 50 Cent: Bulletproof* and *Call of Duty: Modern Warfare*.

9 Clothing manufacturers and merchants as far back as the 1930s have been targeting children in their marketing and advertising. Advertising was initially aimed at parents through women's magazines. These advertisements advised mothers to stimulate their children's consumer desires and that children should be allowed to choose their own clothing to assist them in learning 'good taste', which would help to develop their personalities (Cook, 2004; see also Schor, 2004).

10 It is easy to forget just how targeted these solutions have become when we consider that there are products and services for hair (shampoo, conditioner, hair dressing, hair removal, hair gel), the mouth (mouth wash, tooth paste, dental floss), skin (moisturisers, sun screens, cleaning agents, antiperspirant, perfumes, fake tan), nails (nail clippers, nail varnish, nail boards) and eyes (eye liner, eye lashes, eye drops), to name just a few. You can also have cosmetic surgery on your eyes, cheeks, mouth, ears, neck, legs, thighs, teeth, stomach, genitals, breasts (for women), and pectorals (for men).

5 Consumer culture and space

1 The concept 'sense of place' is an outgrowth of humanistic approaches to geography and is defined as 'the particular ways in which human beings invest their surroundings with meaning' (Hubbard *et al.*, 2004: 351).

2 Evidence for this can be seen in the deindustrialisation of many cities in the West where spaces once set aside for production such as harbour-side wharfs, factories, industrial estates, and large railway stations have been transformed by developers into spaces for consumption such as casinos, water-front shopping centres, museums, entertainment venues and open-air market places (Harvey, 2001; Miles, 2010; Zukin, 1991).

3 Like Ritzer, Augé (1995) argues that non-places cannot be defined as relational, historical or concerned with identity.

4 The most highly commodified forms of labour are those referred to as 'McJobs'. McJobs are defined as 'low-pay, low-prestige, low-dignity, low benefit, no-future jobs in the service sector. Frequently considered a satisfying career choice by people who have never held one' (Coupland, 1991: 5). Jobs where people are more likely to be

treated as non-people are characterised by their interchangeability, where interactions with customers are scripted, and where there is a frequent turnover in staff (Ritzer, 2007: 78–82).

5 See Ritzer (2007: 162–91), for a discussion on the global spread of consumer values.

6 See also Arnett (2002) who states that one of the main psychological effects of globalisation is the transformation of identity.

7 A good case in point is the worldwide bidding process for the rights to host the Olympic Games or Football World Cup.

8 Since the deinstitutionalisation of the mentally ill in the late 1960s and 1970s in most Western countries, their appearance on the street has become a common feature of most cities. For many people the mentally ill cause fear, alarm, and embarrassment, so their exclusion from spaces of consumption is designed to avoid any disruption to economic exchange.

9 The term 'community' is a misnomer in this respect as research published by the University of Glasgow in 2003 titled *Gated Communities in England* found that residents of these spaces have no desire to come into contact with anyone inside (and certainly not outside) the gated or walled area, so that a sense of community is actually lower inside gated environments (Bauman, 2011: 66).

10 Residential houses are not the only city buildings to be fortified. The Maryland Science Center in Baltimore was purposefully designed without windows, in order to 'guard the southern approach to the Inner Harbour from potential rioting by neighbourhood residents' (Harvey, 2001: 150).

6 Conclusion

1 Sweden and Norway have gone even further by prohibiting the advertising of unhealthy foods to children (Obesity Policy Coalition, 2011).

2 Lyotard (1984: 4–5) argues that knowledge in the West is now produced and packaged in order to be sold and that it has ceased to be an end in itself. The consequence of this is that the purpose of universities is no longer the transmission of knowledge; instead it is to improve the economic system by preparing young people to enter the workforce (Lyotard, 1984: 49). For a more recent analysis of the corporatisation and commodification of higher education see Hil (2012).

3 Nafstad and Blakar (2012) argue that a greater commitment to researching ideology would make social psychology more relevant. In their paper they provide an example of their method for assessing ideological changes in society by identifying shifts in language usage in media discourse.

References

Aarts, H., and Dijksterhuis, A. (2003) The silence of the library: Environment, situational norm, and social behaviour. *Journal of Personality and Social Psychology*, 84(1), 18–28.

Adams, T. (2009) Big, bigger, biggest: Giant of the sea is making waves. *Sydney Morning Herald* (27 Nov.), p. 13.

Aiello, J., Thompson, D. E., and Baum, A. (1981) The symbiotic relationship between social psychology and environmental psychology: Implications from crowding, personal space, and intimacy regulation research. In J. H. Harvey (ed.), *Cognition, Social Behavior, and the Environment* (pp. 423–38), Hillsdale, NJ: Lawrence Erlbaum.

Aldridge, A. (2001) The paradigm contingent career: Women in regional newspaper journalism. *Sociological Research Online*, 6(3). Retrieved May 2006 from http://www. socresonline.org.uk/6/3/aldridge.html

Aldridge, A. (2003) *Consumption,* Cambridge: Polity Press.

Allen, J. (2000) On Georg Simmel: Proximity, distance and movement. In M. Crang and N. Thrift (eds), *Thinking Space* (pp. 54–70), London: Routledge.

Allen, K., and Ball, J. (2011) Pay gap widens between rich and poor. *Guardian* (23 Nov.), retrieved Jan. 2012 from http://www.guardian.co.uk/society/2011/nov/23/pay-gap-rich-poor-widens.

Allport, G. W. (1954) The historical background of modern social psychology. In G. Lindzey (ed.), *Handbook of Social Psychology* (vol. 1, pp. 3–56), Reading, MA: Addison-Wesley.

Allport, G. W. (1958) *The Nature of Prejudice,* Garden City, NY: Doubleday.

Altman, I. (1976) Environmental psychology and social psychology. *Personality and Social Psychology Bulletin*, 2(2), 96–113.

American Academy of Paediatrics (2001) *Television and the Family,* Elk Grove Village, IL: American Academy of Paediatrics.

American Psychiatric Association (2000) *Diagnostic and Statistical Manual of Mental Disorders-IV-TR* (4th edn), Washington, DC: American Psychiatric Association.

Anderson, C. A., and Huesmann, L. R. (2007) Human aggression: A social-cognitive view. In M. A. Hogg and J. Cooper (eds), *The Sage Handbook of Social Psychology* (pp. 259–87), London: Sage.

Anderson-Connolly, R., Grunberg, L., Greenberg, E. S., and Moore, S. (2002) Is lean mean? Workplace transformation and employee wellbeing. *Work, Employment and Society*, 16(3), 389–413.

Andrews, B., and Brown, G. W. (1993) Self-esteem and vulnerability to depression: The concurrent validity of interview and questionnaire measures. *Journal of Abnormal Psychology*, 102, 565–72.

Angermeyer, M. C., and Schulze, B. (2001) Reinforcing stereotypes: How the focus on forensic cases in news reporting may influence public attitudes towards the mentally ill. *International Journal of Law and Psychiatry*, 24(4–5), 469–86.

Argyle, M. (1992) *The Social Psychology of Everyday Life*, London: Routledge.

Argyle, M., Furnham, A., and Graham, J. A. (1981) *Social Situations*, Cambridge: Cambridge University Press.

Armistead, N. (1974) *Reconstructing Social Psychology,* Harmondsworth: Penguin.

Arnett, J. J. (2002) The psychology of globalization. *American Psychologist*, 57(10), 774–83.

Arnett, J. J. (2008) The neglected 95%: Why American psychology needs to become less American. *American Psychologist*, 63(7), 602–614.

Aron, A., and Corne, S. (1994) *Writings for a Liberation Psychology: Ignacio Martin-Baro*, Cambridge, MA: Harvard University Press.

Aronson, E., Wilson, T. D., and Akert, R. M. (1999) *Social Psychology* (3rd edn), New York: Addison-Wesley.

Association of Teachers and Lecturers (2008) *Poll: Brand Bullying*, London: Association of Teachers and Lecturers.

Augé, M. (1995) *Non-Places: Introduction to an Anthropology of Supermodernity,* tr. J. Howe, London: Verso.

Augoustinos, M. (1999) Ideology, false consciousness and psychology. *Theory and Psychology*, 9(3), 295–312.

Bandura, A. (1977) *Social Learning Theory* (2nd edn), Englewood Cliffs, NJ: Prentice Hall.

Barber, B. R. (2007) *Consumed: How Markets Corrupt Children, Infantilize Adults and Swallow Citizens Whole*, New York: W. W. Norton.

Baritz, L. (1960) *The Servants of Power: A History of the Use of Social Science in American Industry,* New York: Wiley.

Baudrillard, J. (1968/1996) *The System of Objects,* tr. J. Benedict, London: Verso.

Baudrillard, J. (1970/1998) *The Consumer Society: Myths and Structures,* tr. C. Turner, Thousand Oaks, CA: Sage.

Baum, A., Gatchel, R., Aiello, J., and Thompson, D. (1981) Cognitive mediation of environmental stress. In J. H. Harvey (ed.), *Cognition, Social Behavior, and the Environment* (pp. 513–33), Hillsdale, NJ: Erlbaum.

Bauman, Z. (1983) Industrialism, consumerism and power. *Theory, Culture and Society,* 1(3), 32–43.

Bauman, Z. (1988) *Freedom,* Milton Keynes: Open University Press.

Bauman, Z. (1989) *Legislators and Interpreters*, Cambridge: Polity.

Bauman, Z. (1992) *Intimations of Postmodernity*, London: Routledge.

Bauman, Z. (1996) From pilgrim to tourist: A short history of identity. In S. Hall and P. du Gay (eds), *Questions of Cultural Identity* (pp. 18–36), London: Sage.

Bauman, Z. (2000) *Liquid Modernity*. Cambridge: Polity Press.

Bauman, Z. (2001a) Consuming life. *Journal of Consumer Culture*, 1(1), 9–29.

Bauman, Z. (2001b) *The Individualized Society*. Cambridge: Polity Press.

Bauman, Z. (2004) The consumerist syndrome in contemporary society. *Journal of Consumer Culture*, 4(3), 291–312.

Bauman, Z. (2005) *Work, Consumerism and the New Poor* (2nd edn), Buckingham: Open University Press.

Bauman, Z. (2007) *Consuming Life,* Cambridge: Polity Press.

Bauman, Z. (2011) *Collateral Damage: Social Inequalities in a Global Age,* Cambridge: Polity Press.

Baumeister, R. F., Bushman, B. J., and Campbell, W. K. (2000) Self-esteem, narcissism, and aggression: Does violence result from low self-esteem or from threatened egotism? *Current Directions in Psychological Science*, 9(1), 26–9.

Beck, A. T., and Weishaar, M. E. (2005) Cognitive therapy. In R. J. Corsini and D. Wedding (eds), *Current Psychotherapies* (7th edn, pp. 238–68), Belmont, CA: Brooks/Cole.

Beck, U. (1992) *Risk Society: Towards a New Modernity,* London: Sage.

Beck, U. (2001) Interview with Ulrich Beck. *Journal of Consumer Culture*, 1(2), 261–77.

Beck, U., Giddens, A., and Lash, S. (1994) *Reflexive Modernization: Politics, Tradition and Aesthetics in the Modern Social Order,* Stanford, CA: Stanford University Press.

Beder, S. (2001) *Selling the Work Ethic: From Puritan Pulpit to Corporate PR,* London: Zed Books.

Bem, D. J. (1972) Self-perception theory. In L. Berkowitz (ed.), *Advances in Experimental Social Psychology* (vol. 6, pp. 1–62), New York: Academic Press.

Bem, S. L. (1981) Gender schema theory: A cognitive account of sex typing. *Psychological Review*, 88, 354–64.

Berkowitz, L. (1972) Frustrations, comparisons, and other sources of emotion arousal as contributors to social unrest. *Journal of Social Issues*, 28, 77–91.

Bertman, S. (1998) *Hyperculture: The Human Cost of Speed,* Westport, CT: Praeger.

Birch, C., and Paul, D. (2003) *Life and Work,* Sydney: University of New South Wales Press.

Bloomberg (2011) Gap between rich and poor widens. *Sydney Morning Herald* (Business, 14 Oct.)*,* p. 4.

Bocock, R. (1992) Consumption and lifestyles. In S. Hall and R. Bocock (eds), *The Social and Cultural Forms of Modernity* (pp. 119–68), Cambridge: Polity Press.

Bocock, R. (1993) *Consumption,* London: Routledge.

Boddy, T. (1992) Underground and overhead: Building the analogous city. In M. Sorkin (ed.), *Variations on a Theme Park: The New American City and the End of Public Space* (pp. 123–53), New York: Noonday Press.

Boltanski, L., and Chiapello, S. (2006) *The New Spirit of Capitalism,* London: Verso.

Bonner, F., and Du Gay, P. (1992) Representing the enterprising self: Thirtysomething and contemporary consumer culture. *Theory, Culture and Society*, 9, 67–92.

Bordo, S. (1993) *Unbearable Weight: Feminism, Western Culture, and the Body,* Berkeley, CA: University of California Press.

Bordo, S. (2000) *The Male Body: A New Look at Men in Public and Private,* New York: Farrar, Straus & Giroux.

Bottomore, T. B. (ed.) (1991) *A Dictionary of Marxist Thought* (2nd edn), Oxford: Blackwell.

Bourdieu, P. (1982) *Distinction: A Social Critique of the Judgement of Taste,* tr. R. Nice, Cambridge, MA: Harvard University Press.

Bourdieu, P. (1990) *The Logic of Practice,* tr. R. Nice, Cambridge: Polity Press.

Bourdieu, P. (1998) The essence of neoliberalism. *Le Monde Diplomatique* (English edn), December, pp. 4–5.

Bourdieu, P., and Wacquant, L. (1992) *An Invitation to Reflexive Sociology,* Chicago, IL: University of Chicago Press.

Bourgeois, J. J., Hall, M. J., Crosby, R. M., and Drexler, K. G. (1993) An examination of narcissistic personality traits as seen in a military population, *Military Medicine*, 158(3), 170–4.

Bowlby, R. (1987) Modes of shopping: Mallarme at the Bon Marche. In N. Armstrong and L. Tennenhouse (eds), *The Ideology of Conduct* (pp. 185–205), New York: Methuen.

Bowlby, R. (1993) *Shopping with Freud*, London: Routledge.

Braverman, H. (1974) *Labor Monopoly Capital: The Degradation of Work in the Twentieth Century,* New York: Monthly Review Press.

Brewster-Smith, M. (1983) The shaping of American social psychology: A personal perspective from the periphery. *Personality and Social Psychology Bulletin,* 9(2), 165–80.

Brinkmann, S. (2008) Changing psychologies in the transition from industrial society to consumer society. *History of the Human Sciences*, 21(2), 85–110.

Brown, J. D., and Gallagher, F. M. (1992) Coming to terms with failure: Private self-enhancement and public self-effacement. *Journal of Experimental Social Psychology*, 28(1), 3–22.

Brown, M. B., and Lohr, M. J. (1987) Peer group affiliation and adolescent self-esteem: An integration of ego-identity and symbolic-interaction theories. *Journal of Personality and Social Psychology*, 52(1), 47–55.

Buffardi, L. E., and Campbell, W. K. (2008) Narcissism and social networking web sites. *Personality and Social Psychology Bulletin*, 34(10), 1303–14.

Bunting, M. (2005) *Willing Slaves: How the Overwork Culture is Ruling our Lives,* London: HarperCollins.

Burr, V. (1995) *An Introduction to Social Construction,* London: Routledge.

Bushman, B. J., and Baumeister, R. F. (1998) Threatened egotism, narcissism, self-esteem, and direct displaced aggression: Does self-love or self-hate lead to violence. *Journal of Personality and Social Psychology*, 75, 219–29.

Buss, A. (1979) Humanistic psychology as liberal ideology: The sociohistorical roots of Maslow's theory of self-actualization. *Journal of Humanistic Psychology*, 19(3), 43–55.

Buunk, A. P. (2006) Social psychology deserves better: Marketing the pivotal social science. In P. Van Lange (ed.), *Bridging Social Psychology: Benefits of Transdisciplinary Approaches* (pp. 83–8), Hillsdale, NJ: Lawrence Erlbaum.

Buunk, A. P., and Dijkstra, P. (2008) Social psychology and mental health. In L. Steg, A. P. Buunk and T. Rothengatter (eds), *Applied Social Psychology: Understanding and Managing Social Problems* (pp. 249–70), Cambridge: Cambridge University Press.

Camp, M. E., Webster, C. R., Coverdale, T. R., Coverdale, J. H., and Nairn, R. (2010) The Joker: A dark night for depictions of mental illness. *Academic Psychiatry,* 34(2), 145–9.

Campbell, I. (2001) *Cross-National Comparisons: Work Time around the World,* Sydney: Australian Council of Trade Unions.

Campbell, J. (2004) *Margaret Thatcher: The Iron Lady,* London: Jonathan Cape.

Carlisle, S., Hanlon, P., and Hannah, M. (2008) Status, taste and distinction in consumer culture: Acknowledging the symbolic dimensions of inequality. *Public Health,* 122(6), 631–7.

Carrette, J. (2003) Psychology, spirituality and capitalism: The case of Abraham Maslow. *Critical Psychology*, 8, 73–95.

Casey, C. (2002) New age religion and identity at work. In M. Dent and S. Whitehead (eds), *Managing Professional Identities: Knowledge, Performativity and the 'New' Professional* (pp. 201–216), London: Routledge.

Castells, M. (2000) *The Information Age: Economy, Society and Culture. The Rise of the Network Society* (2nd edn, vol. 1), Malden, MA: Blackwell Publishing.

Castells, M. (2004) *The Information Age: Economy, Society and Culture. The Power of Identity* (2nd edn, vol. 2), Malden, MA: Blackwell Publishing.

Chalke, D. (2004) *Adultescents: The New Youth,* Melbourne: Quantum Market Research.

Chaney, D. (1996) *Lifestyles,* London: Routledge.

Chartered Society of Physiotherapists (2004) *Employment Relations and Union Services: Health and Safety – Workplace Stress*, London: Chartered Society of Physiotherapists.

Chiu, C.-Y., and Cheng, S. Y. Y. (2007) Toward a social psychology of culture and globalization: Some social cognitive consequences of activating two cultures simultaneously. *Social and Personality Psychology Compass*, 1(1), 84–100.

Chomsky, N. (1999) *Profits over People: Neoliberalism and the Global Order*, New York: Seven Stories Press.

Chong, D., Citrin, J., and Conley, P. (2001) When self-interest matters. *Political Psychology*, 22(3), 541–70.

Christopherson, S. (1994) The fortress city: Privatized spaces, consumer citizenship. In A. Amin (ed.), *Post-Fordism: A Reader* (pp. 409–27), Oxford: Blackwell.

Cialdini, R. B. (2009) We have to break up. *Perspectives on Psychological Science*, 4, 5–6.

Clarke, S. (2005) The neoliberal theory of society. In A. Saad-Filho and D. Johnston (eds), *Neoliberalism: A Critical Reader* (pp. 50–9), London: Pluto Press.

Clarke, V. (2007) Man not included? A critical psychology analysis of lesbian families and male influence in child rearing. *Journal of GLBT Family Studies: Innovations in Theory, Research and Practice*, 3(4), 309–49.

Cohen, L. (2003) *A Consumers' Republic: The Politics of Mass Consumption in Postwar America*, New York: Knopf Publishers.

Coleman, P. (2004) *Shopping Environments: Evolution, Planning and Design*, London: Architectural Press.

Colman, A. M. (2009) *Oxford Dictionary of Psychology* (3rd edn), Oxford: Oxford University Press.

Coltrane, S., and Messineo, M. (2000) The perpetuation of subtle prejudice: Race and gender imagery in 1990s television advertising. *Sex Roles*, 42(5–6), 363–89.

Comaroff, J., and Comaroff, J. L. (eds) (2001) *Millennial Capitalism and the Culture of Neoliberalism*, Durham, NC: Duke University Press.

Connell, R. (2010) Understanding neoliberalism. In S. Braedley and M. Luxton (eds), *Neoliberalism and Everyday Life* (pp. 22–36), Montreal: McGill-Queens University Press.

Cook, D. T. (2004) *The Commodification of Childhood: The Children's Clothing Industry and the Rise of the Child Consumer*, Durham, NC: Duke University Press.

Cook, D. T. (2007) Leisure and consumption. In C. Rojek, A. J. Veal and S. M. Shaw (eds), *A Handbook of Leisure Studies* (pp. 304–16), Basingstoke: Palgrave Macmillan.

Corrigan, P. (1997) *The Sociology of Consumption*, London: Sage.

Couch, C. (2011) *The Strange Non-Death of Neoliberalism*, Cambridge: Polity.

Couldry, N. (2008) Reality TV, or the secret theater of neoliberalism. *Review of Education, Pedagogy, and Cultural Studies*, 30, 3–13.

Coupland, D. (1991) *Generation X: Tales for an Accelerated Culture*, New York: St Martin's Press.

Cowan, R. S. (1983) *More Work for Mother: The Ironies of Household Technology from the Open Hearth to the Microwave*, New York: Basic Books.

Credit Action Group. (2007) Debt facts and figures. Retrieved Oct. 2007, from http://www.creditaction.org.uk/documents/DebtStatisticsApril2007.pdf.

Croker, J., and Major, B. (1989) Social stigma and self-esteem: The self-protective properties of stigma. *Psychological Review*, 96(4), 608–30.

Cross, G. (1993) *Time and Money: The Making of Consumer Culture*, London: Routledge.

Crossely, N. (2005) *Key Concepts in Critical Social Theory*. London: Sage.

Cruikshank, B. (1996) Revolutions within: Self-government and self-esteem. In A. Barry, T. Osbourne and N. Rose (eds), *Foucault and Political Reason: Liberalism, Neoliberalism and Rationalities of Government* (pp. 231–51), London: University College Press.

Curtis, A. (writer) (2002) *The Century of the Self* [DVD], London: BBC Four.

Cushman, P. (1990) Why the self is empty: Toward a historically situated psychology. *American Psychologist*, 45(5), 599–611.

Cushman, P. (1995) *Constructing the Self, Constructing America: A Cultural History of Psychotherapy,* Cambridge, MA: Da Capo Press.

Cushman, P. (2002) How psychology erodes personhood. *Journal of Theoretical and Philosophical Psychology*, 22(2), 103–13.

Dale, K. L., and Baumeister, R. F. (2000) Self-regulation and psychopathology. In R. M. Kowalski and M. R. Leary (eds), *The Social Psychology of Emotional and Behavioral Problems: Interfaces of Social and Clinical Psychology* (pp. 139–66), Washington, DC: American Psychological Association.

Danziger, K. (2000) Making social psychology experimental: A conceptual history. *Journal of the History of the Behavioural Sciences*, 36(4), 329–47.

Darley, J. M., and Gilbert, D. T. (1985) Social psychological aspects of environmental psychology. In G. Lindzey and E. Aronson (eds), *Handbook of Social Psychology* (vol. 2, pp. 949–91), New York: Knopf.

Das, S. (interviewee) (2011) The year in review. *Late Night Live*. Australia: ABC Radio National: http://www.abc.net.au/radionational/programs/latenightlive/the-year-in-review/3715680.

Daunton, M., and Hilton, M. (eds) (2001) *The Politics of Consumption: Material Culture and Citizenship in Europe and America,* Oxford: Berg.

Davis, M., and Monk, D. B. (eds) (2007) *Evil Paradises: Dreamworlds of Neoliberalism,* New York: New Press.

Davis, S. (1998) *Blur: The Speed of Change in the Global Economy,* New York: Perseus Books.

Dean, M. (2010) *Governmentality: Power and Rule in Modern Society* (2nd edn), London: Sage.

Debord, G. (1967/1994) *Society of the Spectacle,* tr. D. Nicholson-Smith, New York: Zone Books.

Deery, S., and Walsh, J. (1999) The decline of collectivism? A comparative study of white collar employees in Britain and Australia. *British Journal of Industrial Relations*, 37, 245–69.

de Graaf, J., Wann, D., and Naylor, T. H. (2005) *Affluenza: The All-Consuming Epidemic* (2nd edn), San Francisco, CA: Berrett-Koehler.

de Grazia, V. (1996) Introduction. In V. de Grazia and E. Furlough (eds), *The Sex of Things: Gender and Consumption in Historical Perspective* (pp. 1–10), Berkeley, CA: University of California Press.

Diener, E., Larsen, R. J., and Emmons, R. A. (1984) Person × Situation interactions: Choice of situations and congruence response models. *Journal of Personality and Social Psychology*, 47(3), 580–92.

Diener, E., Suh, E. M., Lucas, R. E., and Smith, H. L. (1999) Subjective wellbeing: Three decades of progress. *Psychological Bulletin*, 125, 276–302.

Dijkstra, P., Gibbons, F. X., and Buunk, A. P. (2010) Social comparison theory. In J. E. Maddux and J. P. Tangney (eds), *Social Psychological Foundations of Clinical Psychology* (pp. 195–210), New York: Guilford Press.

Dixon, J., and Levine, M. (2012) Introduction. In J. Dixon and M. Levine (eds), *Beyond Prejudice: Extending the Social Psychology of Conflict, Inequality and Social Change* (pp. 1–23), Cambridge: Cambridge University Press.

Doerr, C. E., and Baumeister, R. F. (2010) Self-regulatory strength and psychological adjustment: Implications of the limited resource model of self-regulation. In J. E. Maddux and J. P. Tangney (eds), *Social Psychological Foundations of Clinical Psychology* (pp. 71–82), New York: Guilford Press.

Dollard, J., Doob, L. W., Miller, N. E., Mowrer, O. H., and Sears, R. R. (1939) *Frustration and Aggression,* New Haven, CT: Yale University Press.

Donnellan, M. B., Trzesniewski, K. H., Robins, R. W., Moffitt, T. E., and Caspi, A. (2005) Low self-esteem is related to aggression, antisocial behavior, and delinquency. *Psychological Science*, 16(4), 328–35.

Douglas, M., and Isherwood, B. (1982) *The World of Goods,* New York: Norton.

Douglas, S. (2000) Narcissism as liberation. In J. Scanlon (ed.), *The Gender and Consumer Culture Reader* (pp. 267–82), New York: New York University Press.

Dowd, J. J. (1991) Social psychology in a postmodern age: A discipline without a subject. *The American Sociologist*, 22(3–4), 188–209.

D'Souza, R. M., Strazdins, L., Lim, L. L.-Y., Broom, D. H., and Rodgers, B. (2003) Work and health in a contemporary society: Demands, control, and insecurity. *Journal of Epidemiology and Community Health*, 57, 849–54.

Durning, A. (1992) *How Much is Enough? The Consumer Society and the Future of the Earth,* New York: W. W. Norton.

Durrer, V., and Miles, S. (2009) New perspectives on the role of cultural intermediaries in social inclusion in the UK. *Consumption, Markets and Culture*, 12(3), 225–41.

Dworkin, S., and Wachs, F. L. (2009) *Body Panic: Gender, Health, and the Selling of Fitness,* New York: New York University Press.

Eagleton, T. (1991) *Ideology: An Introduction,* London: Verso.

Edensor, T. (1998) *Tourists at the Taj: Performance and Meaning at a Symbolic Site,* London: Routledge.

Edwards, J. R., Caplan, R. D., and Harrison, R. V. (1998) Person-environment fit theory: Conceptual foundations, empirical evidence, and directions for future research. In C. L. Cooper (ed.), *Theories of Organizational Stress* (pp. 28–67), Oxford: Oxford University Press.

Ehrlich, P., and Ehrlich, P. (2004) *One with Nineveh: Politics, Consumption, and the Human Future,* Washington, DC: Island Press.

Elden, S. (2001) *Mapping the Present: Heidegger, Foucault and the Project of a Spatial History,* London: Continuum.

Elliott, A. (2008) *Concepts of the Self* (2nd edn), Cambridge: Polity Press.

Elliott, A., and Lemert, C. (2009) *The New Individualism: The Emotional Costs of Globalization* (2nd edn), London: Routledge.

Elliott, R., and Ritson, M. (1997) Post-structuralism and the dialectics of advertising: Discourse, ideology, resistance. In S. Brown and D. Turley (eds), *Consumer Research: Postcards from the Edge* (pp. 190–219), London: Routledge.

Evans, G. W., and Lepore, S. J. (1993) Household crowding and social support: A quasi-experimental analysis. *Journal of Personality and Social Psychology*, 65, 308–16.

Evans, G. W., Lepore, S. J., and Schroeder, A. (1996) The role of interior design elements in human responses to crowding. *Journal of Personality and Social Psychology*, 70(1), 41–6.

Evans, G. W., Palsane, M. N., Lepore, S. J., and Martin, J. (1989) Residential density and psychological health: The mediating effects of social support. *Journal of Personality and Social Psychology*, 57(6), 994–9.

Ewen, E., and Ewen, S. (2006) *Typecasting: On the Arts and Sciences of Human Inequality,* New York: Seven Stories Press.

Ewen, S. (1976/2001) *Captains of Consciousness: Advertising and the Social Roots of Consumer Culture* (rev edn), New York: Basic Books.

Ewen, S. (1988) *All Consuming Images: The Politics of Style in Contemporary Culture,* New York: Basic Books.

Ewen, S. (1996) *PR: A Social History of Spin,* New York: Basic Books.

Ewen, S., and Ewen, E. (1992) *Channels of Desire: Mass Images and the Shaping of American Consciousness,* Minneapolis, MN: University of Minnesota Press.

Faderman, L. (2000) Lesbian chic: Experimentation and repression in the 1920s. In J. Scanlon (ed.), *The Gender and Consumer Culture Reader* (pp. 153–65), New York: New York University Press.

Fear, J., and Denniss, R. (2009) *Something for Nothing: Unpaid Overtime in Australia* (Policy Briefing, no. 7), Canberra: Australia Institute.

Featherstone, M. (1983) Consumer culture: An introduction. *Theory, Culture and Society*, 1(3), 4–9.

Featherstone, M. (1987) Lifestyle and consumer culture. *Theory, Culture and Society,* 4(1), 55–70.

Featherstone, M. (1991) The body in consumer culture. In M. Featherstone, M. Hepworth and B. S. Turner (eds), *The Body: Social Process and Cultural Theory* (pp. 170–96), London: Sage.

Featherstone, M. (2001) Consumer culture. In N. J. Smelser and P. B. Baltes (eds), *International Encyclopaedia of the Social and Behavioral Sciences* (pp. 2662–9), Amsterdam: Elsevier.

Featherstone, M. (2007) *Consumer Culture and Postmodernism* (2nd edn), London: Sage.

Featherstone, M. (2010) Body, image and affect in consumer culture. *Body and Society,* 16(1), 193–221.

Federal Reserve (2007) Consumer credit – G.19. Retrieved Oct. 2007, from http://www.federalreserve.gov/releases/g19.

Feminist Lesbians Group (2005) Exploring new ways of insubmission in social representation. *Annual Review of Critical Psychology*, 5, 107–14.

Ferraro, F., Pfeffer, J., and Sutton, R. I. (2005) Economics, language and assumptions: How theories can become self-fulfilling. *Academy of Management Review,* 30(1), 9–24.

Festinger, L. (1954) A theory of social comparison. *Human Relations*, 7(2), 117–40.

Fischer, E., and Arnold, S. (1990) More than a labor of love: Gender roles and Christmas gift shopping. *Journal of Consumer Research*, 17, 333–45.

Fitzgerald, M., Stockdale, J., and Hale, C. (2003) *Young People and Street Crime,* London: Youth Justice Board for England and Wales.

Florance, I., Mullensiefen, D., and Carter, S. (2011) How to get ahead in the psychology of advertising. *The Psychologist*, 24(6), 462–5.

Folger, R., and Konovsky, M. A. (1989) Effects of procedural and distributive justice on reactions to pay raise decisions. *Academy of Management Journal,* 32(1), 115–30.

Foucault, M. (1961) *Madness and Civilization: A History of Insanity in the Age of Reason,* tr. R. Howard, London: Routledge.

Foucault, M. (1969) *The Archaeology of Knowledge,* tr. A. Sheridan, London: Routledge.

Foucault, M. (1975) *Discipline and Punish: The Birth of the Prison,* tr. A. Sheridan, London: Penguin.

Foucault, M. (1981) *Power/Knowledge: Selected Interviews and Other Writings, 1972–77,* London: Harvester Press.

Foucault, M. (1983) The subject and power. In H. L. Dreyfus and P. Rabinow (eds), *Michel Foucault: Beyond Structuralism and Hermeneutics* (2nd edn, pp. 208–26), Chicago, IL: Chicago University Press.

Foucault, M. (1986) Of other spaces. *Diacritics,* 16(1), 22–7.

Foucault, M. (1991) Politics and the study of discourse. In G. Burchell, C. Gordon and P. Miller (eds), *The Foucault Effect: Studies in Governmentality* (pp. 53–86), Chicago, IL: University of Chicago Press.

Fox, D., Prilleltensky, I., and Austin, S. (2009) Critical psychology for social justice: Concerns and dilemmas. In D. Fox, I. Prilleltensky and S. Austin (eds), *Critical Psychology: An Introduction* (2nd edn, pp. 3–19), London: Sage.

Frank, T. (2000) *One Market under God: Extreme Capitalism, Market Populism and the End of Economic Democracy,* New York: Doubleday Press.

Fredrickson, B. L., Roberts, T. A., Noll, S. M., Quinn, D. M., and Twenge, J. M. (1998) That swimsuit becomes you: Sex differences in self-objectification, restrained eating, and math performance. *Journal of Personality and Social Psychology,* 75, 269–84.

Freeden, M. (2003) *Ideology: A Very Short Introduction,* Oxford: Oxford University Press.

Freud, S. (1957) On the history of the psycho-analytic movement: Papers on metapsychology and other works. In *The Standard Edition of the Complete Psychological Works of Sigmund Freud* (vol. 14), London: Hogarth Press.

Fromm, E. (1947/2003) *Man for Himself: An Inquiry into the Psychology of Ethics,* London: Routledge.

Fromm, E. (1956/1991) *The Sane Society,* London: Routledge.

Fromm, E. (1961/2004) *Marx's Concept of Man,* tr. T. B. Bottomore, London: Continuum.

Fromm, E. (1962/2009) *Beyond the Chains of Illusion: My Encounter with Marx and Freud,* New York: Continuum.

Garhammer, M. (1998) Time pressure in modern Germany. *Loisir et Société (Society and Leisure),* 21(2), 327–50.

Geertz, C. (1975) *The Interpretation of Cultures,* New York: Basic Books.

Gelber, S. M. (2000) Do it yourself: Constructing, repairing, and maintaining domestic masculinity. In J. Scanlon (ed.), *The Gender and Consumer Culture Reader* (pp. 70–93), New York: New York University Press.

Genosko, G. (2005) Baudrillard, Jean. In G. Ritzer (ed.), *Encyclopaedia of Social Theory* (vol. 1, pp. 29–35), Thousand Oaks, CA: Sage.

Gergen, K. J. (1991) *The Saturated Self: Dilemmas of Identity in Contemporary Life,* New York: Basic Books.

Gergen, K. J. (2012) The social dimension of social psychology: A historical analysis. In A. W. Kruglanski and W. Stroebe (eds), *Handbook of the History of Social Psychology* (pp. 137–57), Hove: Psychology Press.

Giddens, A. (1990) *The Consequences of Modernity,* Stanford, CA: Stanford University Press.

Giddens, A. (1991) *Modernity and Self-Identity: Self and Society in the Late Modern Age,* Stanford, CA: Stanford University Press.

Giddens, A. (1992) *The Transformation of Intimacy: Sexuality, Love and Eroticism in Modern Societies,* Stanford, CA: Stanford University Press.

Giddens, A. (2003) An interview with Anthony Giddens. *Journal of Consumer Culture,* 3(3), 387–99.

Giddens, A. (2006) *Sociology* (5th ed.), Cambridge: Polity.

Gifford, R. (2005) Applying social psychology to the environment. In F. W. Schneider, J. A. Gruman and L. M. Coutts (eds), *Applied Social Psychology: Understanding and Addressing Social and Practical Problems* (pp. 307–30), Thousand Oaks, CA: Sage.

Gill, R. (2008) Culture and subjectivity in neoliberal and postfeminist times. *Subjectivity*, 25, 432–45.

Giroux, H. A. (2008) Beyond the biopolitics of disposability: Rethinking neoliberalism in the New Gilded Age. *Social Identities*, 14(5), 587–620.

Gleick, J. (1999) *Faster: The Acceleration of Just About Everything,* London: Little Brown & Co.

Goffman, E. (1959) *The Presentation of Self in Everyday Life,* Harmondsworth: Pelican Books.

Goldberg, M. E., Gorn, G. J., Peracchio, L. A., and Bamossy, G. (2003) Materialism among youth. *Journal of Consumer Behaviour*, 13, 278–88.

Goodman, S. (2008) Justifying harsh treatment of asylum seekers through the support of social cohesion. *Annual Review of Critical Psychology*, 6, 110–24.

Gorz, A. (1989) *Critique of Economic Reason,* New York: Verso.

Gough, B. (2002) 'I've always tolerated it but . . .': Heterosexual masculinity and the discursive reproduction of homophobia. In A. Coyle and C. Kitzinger (eds), *Lesbian and Gay Psychology: New Perspectives* (pp. 219–38), Malden, MA: Blackwell Publishing.

Gough, B., and McFadden, M. (2001) *Critical Social Psychology: An Introduction,* Basingstoke: Palgrave Macmillan.

Gram-Hanssena, K., and Bech-Danielsenb, C. (2004) House, home and identity from a consumption perspective. *Housing, Theory and Society*, 21(1), 17–26.

Gramsci, A. (1971) *Selections from the Prison Notebooks of Antonio Gramsci,* tr. Q. Hoare and G. Nowell Smith, London: Lawrence & Wishart.

Graumann, C. F. (2001) Introducing social psychology historically. In M. Hewstone and W. Stroebe (eds), *Introduction to Social Psychology* (3rd edn, pp. 3–22), Malden, MA: Blackwell.

Greenwood, J. D. (2004a) *The Disappearance of the Social in American Social Psychology,* Cambridge: Cambridge University Press.

Greenwood, J. D. (2004b) What happened to the 'social' in social psychology? *Journal for the Theory of Social Behaviour*, 34(1), 19–34.

Gregory, G. D., and Di Leo, M. (2003) Repeated behavior and environmental psychology: The role of personal involvement and habit formation in explaining water consumption. *Journal of Applied Social Psychology*, 33(6), 1261–96.

Griffiths, D. (2005) *Adolescent Angst,* London: Priory Group.

Griffiths, M., and Renwick, B. (2003) *Misfortune or Mismanagement: A Study of Consumer Debt Issues,* Newcastle: University of Newcastle and Financial Counsellors of NSW.

Gronow, J. (1997) *The Sociology of Taste,* Cambridge: Polity Press.

Gunter, B., and Furnham, A. (1998) *Children as Consumers,* London: Routledge.

Guthman, J., and Du Puis, M. (2006) Embodying neoliberalism: Economy, culture, and the politics of fat. *Environment and Planning D: Society and Space*, 24(3), 427–48.

Hackley, C. (2002) The panoptic role of advertising agencies in the production of consumer culture. *Consumption, Markets and Culture,* 5(3), 211–29.

Hahnel, R. (2002) The *ABC's of Political Economy: A Modern Approach,* London: Pluto Press.

Halimi, S. (1998) Myopic and cheapskate journalism. *Le Monde Diplomatique* (Sept.), pp. 2–3.

Hall, S., Winlow, S., and Ancrum, C. (2008) *Criminal Identities and Consumer Culture: Crime, Exclusion and the New Culture of Narcissism,* Abingdon: Willan.

Halweil, B., Mastny, L., French, H., Gardner, G. et al. (2004) *State of the World 2004: Progress towards a Sustainable Society,* New York: Worldwatch Institute and Earthscan.

Hamilton, C. (2002) *Overconsumption in Australia: The Rise of the Middle-Class Battler* (no. 49), Canberra: Australia Institute.

Hamilton, C. (2003a) *Growth Fetish,* Sydney: Allen & Unwin.

Hamilton, C. (2003b) *Overconsumption in Britain: A Culture of Middle-Class Complaint* (no. 57), Canberra: Australia Institute.

Hamilton, C., and Denniss, R. (2005) *Affluenza: When Too Much is Never Enough,* Sydney: Allen & Unwin.

Hanley, N., Shogren, J. F., and White, B. (2001) *Introduction to Environmental Economics,* Oxford: Oxford University Press.

Hansen, S., McHoul, A., and Rapley, M. (2003) *Beyond Help: A Consumers' Guide to Psychology,* Ross-on-Wye: PCCS Books.

Hare-Mustin, R. T., and Marecek, J. (2009) Clinical psychology: The politics of madness. In D. Fox, I. Prilleltensky and S. Austin (eds), *Critical Psychology: An Introduction* (2nd edn, pp. 75–92), Thousand Oaks, CA: Sage.

Harker, R., Mahar, C., and Wilkes, C. (1990) *An Introduction to the work of Pierre Bourdieu: The Practice of Theory,* Basingstoke: Palgrave Macmillan.

Harms, P. D., Roberts, B. W., and Winter, D. (2006) Becoming the Harvard man: Person-environment fit, personality development, and academic success. *Personality and Social Psychology Bulletin,* 32(7), 851–65.

Harsch, B. A. (1999) Consumerism and environmental policy: Moving past consumer culture. *Law Ecology Quarterly,* 26, 543–610.

Harter, S. (1993) Causes and consequences of low self-esteem in children and adolescents. In R. F. Baumeister (ed.), *Self-Esteem: The Puzzle of Low Self-Regard* (pp. 87–116), New York: Plenum.

Harvey, D. (1973) *Social Justice and the City,* London: Edward Arnold.

Harvey, D. (1985) *The Urbanisation of Capital,* Oxford: Blackwell.

Harvey, D. (1989) *The Condition of Postmodernity: An Enquiry into the Origins of Cultural Change,* Oxford: Blackwell.

Harvey, D. (2001) *Spaces of Capital: Towards a Critical Geography,* Edinburgh: Edinburgh University Press.

Harvey, D. (2005) *A Brief History of Neoliberalism,* Oxford: Oxford University Press.

Hayes, G. (2003) Walking the streets: Psychology and the flaneur. *Annual Review of Critical Psychology,* 3, 50–66.

Hayes, N. (1993) *Principles of Social Psychology,* Hove: Psychology Press.

Haynes, A., Devereux, E., and Breen, M. J. (2005) Fear, framing and foreigners: The othering of immigrants in the Irish print media. *Critical Psychology,* 16, 100–21.

Hearn, A. (2008) Meat, mask, burden: Probing the contours of the branded self. *Journal of Consumer Culture,* 8(2), 197–217.

Henriques, J. (1984) Social psychology and the politics of racism. In J. Henriques, W. Hollway, C. Urwin, C. Venn and V. Walkerdine (eds), *Changing the Subject: Psychology, Social Regulation and Subjectivity* (pp. 60–89), New York: Methuen.

Henriques, J., Hollway, W., Urwin, C., Venn, C., and Walkerdine, V. (eds) (1984) *Changing the Subject: Psychology, Social Regulation and Subjectivity,* New York: Methuen.

Henry, M. (1999) Marx. In S. Critchley and W. Schroeder (eds), *A Companion to Continental Philosophy* (pp. 118–27), Oxford: Blackwell.

Hepburn, A. (2003) *An Introduction to Critical Social Psychology*. London: Sage.

Herman, E. S., and Chomsky, N. (1994) *Manufacturing Consent: The Political Economy of the Mass Media,* London: Vintage.

Hertz, N. (2001) *The Silent Takeover: Global Capitalism and the Death Democracy,* London: Arrow Books.

Heyes, C. (2009) Diagnosing culture: Body dysmorphic disorder and cosmetic surgery. *Body and Society*, 15(4), 73–93.

Higgins, E. T. (1987) Self-discrepancy: A theory relating self and affect. *Psychological Review*, 94, 319–40.

Hil, R. (2012) *Whackademia: An Insider's Account of the Troubled University,* Sydney: NewSouth Publishing.

Hill, D. B. (2006) Theory in applied social psychology: Past mistakes and future hopes. *Theory and Psychology*, 16(5), 613–40.

Hochschild, A. R. (1989) *The Second Shift: Working Parents and the Revolution at Home,* New York: Penguin Viking.

Hochschild, A. R. (2003) *The Commercialization of Intimate Life,* Berkeley, CA: University of California Press.

Hogg, M. A. (2000) Social identity and social comparison. In J. Suls and L. Wheeler (eds), *Handbook of Comparison: Theory and Research* (pp. 56–85), New York: Kluwer/ Plenum.

Hogg, M. A. (2003) Social identity. In M. R. Leary and J. P. Tangney (eds), *Handbook of Self and Identity* (pp. 462–79), New York: Guildford.

Hogg, M. A., and Abrams, D. (2003) Intergroup behaviour and social identity. In M. A. Hogg and J. Cooper (eds), *The Sage Handbook of Social Psychology* (pp. 335–60), London: Sage.

Hogg, M. A., and Vaughan, G. M. (2005) *Social Psychology* (4th edn), Harlow: Pearson.

Hogg, M. A., Terry, D. J., and White, K. M. (1995) A tale of two theories: A critical comparison of identity theory with social identity theory. *Social Psychology Quarterly*, 58(4), 255–69.

Hollway, W. (2007) Social psychology: Past and present. In W. Hollway, H. Lucey and A. Phoenix (eds), *Social Psychology Matters* (pp. 1–32), Maidenhead: Open University Press.

Holmes, J. (2001) *Narcissism,* Cambridge: Icon Books.

Holt, D. B. (1998) Does cultural capital structure American consumption? *Journal of Consumer Research*, 25(1), 1–25.

Holzman, L., and Morss, J. (eds) (2000) *Postmodern Psychologies, Societal Practice, and Political Life,* New York: Routledge.

Hook, D. (2011) *A Critical Psychology of the Postcolonial: The Mind of Apartheid,* Hove: Psychology Press.

Howard, A. (2004) *Counselling and Identity: Self Realisation in a Therapy Culture,* Basingstoke: Palgrave.

Howard, J. A. (2000) Social psychology of identities. *Annual Review of Sociology*, 26, 367–93.

Howell, D. R., and Mamadou, D. (2007) *Charting U.S. Economic Performance with Alternative Labor Market Indicators: The Importance of Accounting for Job Quality*, New York: Schwartz Center for Economic Policy Analysis.

Hubbard, P., Kitchin, R., and Valentine, G. (eds) (2004) *Key Thinkers on Space and Place,* London: Sage.

Hughes, J. (2005) Bringing emotions to work: Emotional intelligence, employee resistance and the reinvention of character. *Work, Employment and Society,* 19(3), 603–25.

Humphery, K. (2010) *Excess: Anti-Consumerism in the West,* Cambridge: Polity.

Hyler, S. E., Gabbard, G. O., and Schneider, I. (1991) Homicidal maniacs and narcissistic parasites: Stigmatization of mentally ill persons in the movies. *Hospital Community Psychiatry*, 42, 1044–8.

Ibanez, T., and Iniguez, L. (eds) (1997) *Critical Social Psychology,* London: Sage.

Ingleby, D. (1991/2002) Introduction to the second edition. In E. Fromm (ed.), *The Sane Society* (pp. xiv–lv). London: Routledge.

Illouz, E. (1997) *Consuming the Romantic Utopia: Love and the Cultural Contradictions of Capitalism,* Berkeley, CA: University of California Press.

Jackson, T. (2008) What politicians are afraid to say. *New Scientist* (18 Oct.), pp. 42–3.

Jacoby, J. (2001) Consumer psychology. In N. J. Smelser and P. B. Baltes (eds), *International Encyclopaedia of the Social and Behavioral Sciences* (pp. 2674–8), Amsterdam: Elsevier.

Jager, M. (1986) Class definition and the aesthetics of gentrification: Victoriana in Melbourne. In N. Smith and P. Williams (eds), *Gentrification of the City* (pp. 78–91), Boston, MA: Allen & Unwin.

Jagger, E. (2001) Marketing Molly and Melville: Dating in a postmodern, consumer society. *Sociology*, 35(1), 39–57.

James, O. (2007) *Affluenza: How to be Successful and Stay Sane,* London: Vermilion.

Jameson, F. (1991) *Postmodernism, or, the Cultural Logic of Late Capitalism,* Durham, NC: Duke University Press.

Jantzen, C., Ostergaard, P., and Vieira, C. M. (2006) Becoming a 'woman to the backbone': Lingerie consumption and the experience of feminine identity. *Journal of Consumer Culture*, 6(2), 177–202.

Jenkins, R. (2008) *Social Identity* (3rd edn), London: Routledge.

Jones, A. M., and Buckingham, J. T. (2005) Self-esteem as a moderator of the effect of social comparison on women's body image. *Journal of Social and Clinical Psychology*, 24(8), 1164–87.

Jorgensen, B. S., and Stedman, R. C. (2001) Sense of place as an attitude: Lakeshore owner's attitudes towards their properties. *Journal of Environmental Psychology*, 21(3), 233–48.

Joseph, R. A., Larrick, R. P., Steele, C. M., and Nisbett, R. E. (1992) Protecting the self from negative consequences of risky decisions. *Journal of Personality and Social Psychology*, 62(1), 26–37.

Jost, J. T. (1995) Negative illusions: Conceptual clarification and psychological evidence concerning false consciousness. *Political Psychology,* 16, 397–424.

Jost, J. T., and Banaji, M. R. (1994) The role of stereotyping in system-justification and the production of false consciousness. *British Journal of Social Psychology,* 33, 1–27.

Kadet, A. (2011) Extreme multitasking: Surviving the superjob. *Smart Money.* Retrieved March 2011 from, http://www.smartmoney.com/plan/employment/surviving-the-superjob-1304556743727

Kasser, T. (2003) *The High Price of Materialism,* Cambridge MA: MIT Press.

Kasser, T., and Ahuvia, A. (2002) Materialistic values and well-being in business students. *European Journal of Social Psychology*, 32(1), 137–46.

Kasser, T., and Kanner, A. D. (2004) Where is the psychology of consumer culture? In T. Kasser and A. D. Kanner (eds), *Psychology and Consumer Culture: The Struggle for a Good Life in a Materialistic World* (pp. 3–7), Washington, DC: American Psychological Association.

Kasser, T., and Kasser, V. (2001) The dreams of people high and low in materialism. *Journal of Economic Psychology*, 22(6), 693–719.

Kasser, T., and Ryan, R. M. (1993) A dark side of the American dream: Correlates of financial success as a central life aspiration. *Journal of Personality and Social Psychology*, 65(2), 410–22.

Kasser, T., and Ryan, R. M. (1996) Further examining the American dream: Differential correlates of intrinsic and extrinsic goals. *Personality and Social Psychology Bulletin*, 22(3), 280–7.

Kasser, T., Ryan, R. M., Couchman, C. E., and Sheldon, K. M. (2004) Materialistic values: Their causes and consequences. In T. Kasser and A. D. Kanner (eds), *Psychology and Consumer Culture: The Struggle for the Good Life in a Materialistic World* (pp. 11–28), Washington, DC: American Psychological Society.

Kaye, J. D. (2008) Thinking thoughtfully about cognitive behaviour therapy. In R. House and D. Loewenthal (eds), *Against and for CBT: Toward a Constructive Dialogue* (pp. 169–78), Ross-on-Wye: PCCS.

Kellner, D. (1992) Popular culture and the construction of postmodern identities. In S. Lash and J. Friedman (eds), *Modernity and Identity* (pp. 141–77), Oxford: Blackwell Publishing.

Kidner, S. W. (2007) Depression and the natural world: Towards a critical ecology of psychological distress. *Critical Psychology*, 19, 123–48.

Kivimaki, M., Vahtera, J., Penetti, J., and Ferrie, J. E. (2000) Factors underlying the effect of organizational downsizing on the health of employees: Longitudinal cohort study. *British Medical Journal*, 320, 971–5.

Kivimaki, M., Honkonen, T., Wahlbeck, K., Elovainio, M., Pentti, J., Klaukka, T., *et al.* (2007) Organisational downsizing and increased use of psychotropic drugs among employees who remain in employment. *Journal of Epidemiology and Community Health*, 61, 154–8.

Konig, A. (2008) Which clothes suit me? The presentation of the juvenile self. *Childhood*, 15(2), 225–37.

Kotz, D. M. (2002) Globalization and neoliberalism. *Rethinking Marxism*, 14(2), 64–79.

Kouvonen, A., Kivimaki, M., Virtanen, M., Pentti, J., and Vahtera, J. (2005) Work stress, smoking status, and smoking intensity: an observational study of 46190 employees. *Journal of Epidemiology and Community Health*, 59, 63–9.

Kowalski, R. M., and Leary, M. R. (2000) Interfaces of social and clinical psychology: Where we have been, where we are. In R. M. Kowalski and M. R. Leary (eds), *The Social Psychology of Emotional and Behavioral Problems: Interfaces of Social and Clinical Psychology* (pp. 7–33), Washington, DC: American Psychological Association.

Kowinski, W. S. (1985) *The Malling of America: An Inside Look at the Great Consumer Paradise,* New York: William Morrow.

Kruegar, J. (1998) Enhancement bias in descriptions of self and others. *Personality and Social Psychology Bulletin*, 24(5), 505–16.

Kurz, T., Donaghue, N., and Walker, I. (2005) Utilizing a social-ecological framework to promote water and energy conservation. *Journal of Applied Social Psychology*, 35(6), 1281–1300.

Kvale, S. (1992a) Postmodern psychology: A contradiction in terms? In S. Kvale (ed.), *Psychology and Postmodernism* (pp. 31–57), London: Sage.

Kvale, S. (ed.) (1992b) *Psychology and Postmodernism,* London: Sage.

Kvale, S. (2003) The church, the factory and the market: Scenarios for psychology in a postmodern age. *Theory and Psychology*, 13(5), 579–603.

Lachance-Grzela, M., and Bouchard, G. (2010) Why do women do the lion's share of housework? A decade of research. *Sex Roles,* 63(11–12), 767–80.

Laermans, R. (1993) Learning to consume: Early department stores and the shaping of the modern consumer culture, 1896–1914. *Theory, Culture and Society*, 10(4), 79–102.

Lair, D. J., Sullivan, K., and Cheney, G. (2005) Marketization and the recasting of the professional self: The rhetoric and ethics of personal branding. *Management Communication Quarterly*, 18(3), 307–43.

Lamont, M., and Molnar, V. (2001) How blacks use consumption to shape their collective identity. *Journal of Consumer Culture*, 1(1), 31–45.

Lane, R. E. (2001) Self-reliance and empathy: The enemies of poverty and the poor. *Political Psychology*, 22(3), 473–92.

Lasch, C. (1977) The narcissistic personality of our time. *Partisan Review*, 44(1), 9–19.

Lasch, C. (1979) *The Culture of Narcissism: American Life in an Age of Diminishing Expectations,* New York: W. W. Norton & Co.

Lasch, C. (1991) Liberalism and civic virtue. *Telos*, 88(2), 57–68.

Leary, M. R. (1995) *Self-Presentation: Impression Management and Interpersonal Behavior,* Madison, WI: Brown & Benchmark.

Leary, M. R. (2006) The bridge between social and clinical psychology: Wide but sparsely travelled. In P. Van Lange (ed.), *Bridging Social Psychology: Benefits of Transdisciplinary Approaches* (pp. 307–11), Hillsdale, NJ: Lawrence Erlbaum.

Leary, M. R., Schreindorfer, L. S., and Haupt, A. L. (1995) The role of low self-esteem in emotional and behavioral problems: Why is low self-esteem dysfunctional? *Journal of Social and Clinical Psychology,* 14(3), 297–314.

Lechner, F. J. (1991) Simmel on social space. *Theory, Culture and Society*, 8, 195–201.

Lees, L., Slater, T., and Wyly, E. (2007) *Gentrification,* London: Routledge.

Lefebvre, H. (1939/1968) *Dialectical Materialism,* tr. J. Sturrock, London: Cape.

Lefebvre, H. (1974/1991a) *The Production of Space,* tr. D. Nicholson-Smith, Oxford: Blackwell.

Lefebvre, H. (1947/1991b) *The Critique of Everyday Life,* tr. J. Moore (vol. 1), London: Verso.

Lefebvre, H. (1976a) *The Survival of Capitalism: Reproduction of the Relations of Production,* London: Allison & Busby.

Lefebvre, H. (1976b) *Reflections on the Politics of Space,* tr. M. Enders, *Antipode*, 8, 30–7.

Lefebvre, H. (1987) An interview with Henri Lefebvre. *Environment and Planning D: Society and Space*, 5, 27–38.

Lemke, T. (2001) The birth of bio-politics: Michael Foucault's lectures at the College de France on neoliberal governmentality. *Economy and Society*, 30(2), 190–207.

Leonard, P. (1984) *Personality and Ideology: Towards a Materialist Understanding of the Individual,* London: Macmillan.

Levine, M. P., and Murnen, S. K. (2009) Everybody knows that mass media are/are not (pick one) a cause of eating disorders: A critical review of evidence for a causal link between media, negative body image, and disordered eating in females. *Journal of Social and Clinical Psychology*, 28(1), 9–42.

Linn, N., Vining, J., and Feeley, P. A. (1994) Toward a sustainable society: Waste minimization through environmentally conscious consuming. *Journal of Applied Social Psychology*, 24(17), 1550–72.

Linley, P. A., and Joseph, S. (eds) (2004) *Positive Psychology in Practice,* New York: John Wiley & Sons.

Lippman, W. (1922/1965) *Public Opinion: An Important Work on the Theory of Public Opinion in Relation to Traditional Democratic Theory,* New York: Free Press.

Lizardo, O. (2008) The question of culture, consumption and stratification revisited. *Sociologica: Italian Journal of Sociology Online*, 2(2), 1–32.

Loader, I. (1999) Consumer culture and the commodification of policing and security. *Sociology*, 33(2), 373–92.

Lubit, R. (2002) The long-term impact of destructively narcissistic managers. *Academy of Management Review*, 16(1), 127–38.

Lunt, P. (1995) Psychological approaches to consumption: Varieties of research – past, present and future. In D. Miller (ed.), *Acknowledging Consumption: A Review of New Studies* (pp. 238–63), London: Routledge.

Lunt, P., and Livingstone, S. M. (1992) *Mass Consumption and Personal Identity*, Buckingham: Open University Press.

Lury, C. (1996) *Consumer Culture*, Cambridge: Polity Press.

Lynch, E. C. (1968) Walter Dill Scott: Pioneer industrial psychologist. *Business History Review*, 42(2), 149–70.

Lyotard, J.-F. (1984) *The Postmodern Condition: A Report on Knowledge*, tr. G. Bennington and B. Massumi, Manchester: Manchester University Press.

McCann, J. T., and Biaggio, M. K. (1989) Narcissistic personality features and self-reported anger. *Psychological Reports*, 1, 55–8.

MacCannell, D. (1992) *Empty Meeting Grounds: The Tourist Papers*, London: Routledge.

McClintock, A. (2000) Soft soap empire: Commodity racism and imperial advertising. In J. Scanlon (ed.), *The Gender and Consumer Culture Reader* (pp. 129–52), New York: New York University Press.

McCormick, B. (1992) *Hayek and the Keynesian Avalanche*, New York: Harvester Wheatsheaf.

McCracken, G. (1988) *Culture and Consumption: New Approaches to the Symbolic Character of Consumer Goods and Activities*, Bloomington, IN: Indiana University Press.

McCreanor, T., Barnes, H. M., Mandi, G., Kaiwai, H., and Borell, S. (2005) Consuming identities: Alcohol marketing and the commodification of youth experience. *Addiction Research and Theory*, 13(6), 579–90.

McDonald, M., Wearing, S., and Ponting, J. (2008) Narcissism and neoliberalism: Work, leisure and alienation in an era of consumption. *Loisir et Société (Society and Leisure)*, 30(1), 489–510.

MacEwan, A. (1999) *Neoliberalism or Democracy? Economic Strategy, Markets, and Alternatives for the 21st Century*, London: Zed Books.

McHoul, A., and Grace, W. (1993) *A Foucault Primer: Discourse, Power and Subject*, New York: New York University Press.

Mackay, H. (1997) Introduction. In H. Mackay (ed.), *Consumption and Everyday Life* (pp. 1–12), London: Sage.

Mackay, H. (2004) *Aspirations: The Ipsos Mackay Report*, Sydney: Ipsos.

Mackay, S., Antonopoulos, N., Martin, J., and Swinburn, B. A. (2011) *A Comprehensive Approach to Protecting Children from Unhealthy Food Advertising*, Melbourne: Obesity Policy Coalition.

McKendrick, N., Brewer, J., and Plumb, J. H. (1983) *The Birth of Consumer Society: The Commercialization of Eighteenth Century England*, London: Hutchison.

McKenna, K. Y. A., and Bargh, J. A. (2000) Plan 9 from cyberspace: The implications of the internet for personality and social psychology. *Personality and Social Psychology Review*, 4(1), 57–75.

Maddux, J. E. (2010) Social psychological foundations of clinical psychology: History and orienting principles. In J. E. Maddux and J. P. Tangney (eds), *Social Psychological Foundations of Clinical Psychology* (pp. 3–14), New York: Guilford Press.

Magnusson, E., and Marecek, J. (2010) Sociocultural means to feminist ends: Discursive and constructionist psychologies of gender. In S. R. Kirschner and J. Martin (eds), *The Sociocultural Turn in Psychology: The Contextual Emergence of Mind and Society* (pp. 88–110), New York: Columbia University Press.

Malson, H. (1998) *The Thin Woman: Feminism, Post-Structuralism and the Social Psychology of Anorexia Nervosa,* London: Routledge.

Malson, H. (2009) Appearing to disappear: Postmodern femininities and self-starved subjectivities. In H. Malson and M. Burns (eds), *Critical Feminist Approaches to Eating Dis/orders* (pp. 135–45), London: Routledge.

Mandel, E., and Novack, G. (1970) *The Marxist Theory of Alienation,* New York: Pathfinder.

Marcuse, H. (1964/2002) *One Dimensional Man: Studies in the Ideology of Advanced Industrial Society,* London: Routledge.

Markus, H. (1977) Self-schemata and processing information about the self. *Journal of Personality and Social Psychology*, 35, 63–78.

Markus, H., and Nurius, P. (1986) Possible selves. *American Psychologist*, 41, 954–69.

Marshall, G. (1998) *Oxford Dictionary of Sociology* (2nd edn), Oxford: Oxford University Press.

Martin, C. L., and Ruble, D. (2004) Children's search for gender cues: Cognitive perspectives on gender development. *Current Directions in Psychological Science*, 13(2), 67–70.

Marx, K. (1844/1973) *The Economic and Philosophic Manuscripts of 1844,* tr. M. Milligan, London: Lawrence & Wishart.

Marx, K. (1857/1973) *The Grundrisse: Foundations of the Critique of Political Economy,* tr. M. Nicolaus, Harmondsworth: Penguin.

Marx, K. (1867/2004) *Capital: Critique of Political Economy,* tr. B. Fowkes (vol. 1), Harmondsworth: Penguin.

Matthews, G. (1987) *'Just a Housewife': The Rise and Fall of Domesticity in America,* New York: Oxford University Press.

Mayo, E. (2005) *Shopping Generation,* London: National Consumer Council of the UK.

Mazzeo, S. E., Trace, S. E., Mitchell, K. S., and Gow, R. W. (2007) Effects of a reality TV cosmetic surgery makeover programs on eating disordered attitudes and behaviors. *Eating Behaviors*, 8(3), 390–7.

Meadows, D. H., Meadows, D. L., Randers, J., and Behrens, W. W. (1972) *The Limits to Growth,* New York: Universe Books.

Meyers, D. G. (2000) *The American Paradox: Spiritual Hunger in an Age of Plenty,* New Haven, CT: Yale University Press.

Miles, S. (1998) *Consumerism: As a Way of Life,* London: Sage.

Miles, S. (2000) *Youth Lifestyles in a Changing World,* Buckingham: Open University Press.

Miles, S. (2010) *Spaces for Consumption,* London: Sage.

Miller, D. (1987) *Material Culture and Mass Consumption,* Oxford: Blackwell.

Miller, P., and Rose, N. (1997) Mobilizing the consumer: Assembling the subject of consumption. *Theory, Culture and Society*, 14(1), 1–36.

Milner, M. (2005) *Freaks, Geeks, and Cool Kids: American Teenagers, Schools, and the Culture of Consumption,* New York: Routledge.

Minam, H., and Tanaka, K. (1995) Social and environmental psychology: Transaction between physical space and group dynamic processes. *Environment and Behavior*, 27(1), 43–55.

Mirowsky, J., and Ross, C. E. (2003) *Social Causes of Psychological Distress* (2nd edn), Hawthorne, NY: Aldine De Gruyter.

Mischel, W. (1974) Processes in delay of gratification. *Advances in Experimental Social Psychology*, 7, 249–92.

Moloney, P., and Kelly, P. (2008) Beck never lived in Birmingham: Why cognitive behaviour therapy may be a less helpful treatment for psychological distress than is often supposed. In R. House and D. Loewenthal (eds), *Against and for CBT: Toward a Constructive Dialogue* (pp. 278–88), Ross-on-Wye: PCCS.

Moos, R. H., Harris, R., and Schonborn, K. (1981) Psychiatric patients and staff reaction to their physical environment. In A. Furnham and M. Argyle (eds), *The Psychology of Social Situations: Selected Readings* (pp. 314–18), Oxford: Pergamon.

Morf, C. C., and Rhodewalt, F. (2001) Unravelling the paradoxes of narcissism: A dynamic self-regulatory processing model. *Psychological Inquiry*, 12(4), 177–96.

Moscovici, S. (1972) Society and theory in social psychology. In J. Israel and H. Tajfel (eds), *The Context of Social Psychology* (pp. 17–68), London: Academic Press.

Mummendey, A., and Otten, S. (2001) Aggressive behaviour. In M. Hewstone and W. Stroebe (eds), *Introduction to Social Psychology* (pp. 315–40), Malden, MA: Blackwell.

Munck, R. (2005) Neoliberalism and politics, and the politics of neoliberalism. In A. Saad-Filho and D. Johnston (eds), *Neoliberalism: A Critical Reader* (pp. 60–9), London: Pluto Press.

Mutz, D. C., and Goldman, S. K. (2010) Mass media. In J. F. Dovidio, M. Hewstone, P. Peter Glick and V. M. Esses (eds), *The Sage Handbook of Prejudice, Stereotyping and Discrimination* (pp. 241–57), Thousand Oaks, CA: Sage.

Nafstad, H. E. (2002) The neo-liberal ideology and self-interest paradigm as resistance to change. *Radical Psychology*, 3(2), 3–15.

Nafstad, H. E., Blakar, R. M., Carlquist, E., Phelps, J. M., and Rand-Hendriksen, K. (2007) Ideology and power: The influence of current neo-liberalism in society. *Journal of Community and Applied Social Psychology*, 17(4), 313–27.

Nafstad, H. E., and Blakar, R. M. (2012) Ideology and social psychology *Social and Personality Psychology Compass*, 6(4), 282–94.

Neumark, D. (ed.) (2000) *On the Job: Is Long-Term Employment a Thing of the Past?,* New York: Russell Sage Foundation.

Nicholson, I. A. M. (2002) *Inventing Personality: Gordon Allport and the Science of Selfhood,* Washington, DC: American Psychological Association.

Obama, B. (2009) President Barack Obama inauguration speech. Retrieved Oct. 2009 from http://www.nytimes.com/2009/01/20/us/politics/20text-obama.html.

Obesity Policy Coalition (2011) Policy brief: International laws restricting food advertising. Retrieved Dec. 2011 from http://www.opc.org.au/paper.aspx?ID=intfoodadv_polbrief&Type=policydocuments.

O'Brien, D. T., and Wilson, D. S. (2011) Community perception: The ability to assess the safety of unfamiliar neighbourhoods and respond adaptively. *Journal of Personality and Social Psychology*, 100(4), 606–20.

O'Dea, J. A., and Abrahams, S. (2000) Improving the body image, eating attitudes, and behaviors of young male and female adolescents: A new educational approach that focuses on self-esteem. *International Journal of Eating Disorders*, 28(1), 43–57.

Office of National Statistics (2010) Time use survey [electronic version]. Retrieved March 2010 from http://www.statistics.gov.uk/glance/#society.

Oishi, S., Kesebir, S., and Snyder, B. H. (2009) Sociology: A lost connection in social psychology. *Personality and Social Psychology Review,* 13(4), 334–53.

O'Malley, N., and Kroupp, R. (2006) Kids leisure time becoming more solitary, artwork shows. Retrieved July 2011 from http://oregonstate.edu/ua/ncs/archives/2006/feb/kids-leisure-time-becoming-more-solitary-artwork-shows.

Organisation for Economic Co-operation and Development (OECD) (2011a) Average annual hours actually worked per worker. Retrieved Dec. 2011, from http://stats.oecd.org/index.aspx?DatasetCode=ANHRS.

Organisation for Economic Co-operation and Development (OECD) (2011b) *Divided We Stand: Why Inequality Keeps Rising,* Paris: Organisation for Economic Co-Operation and Development.

Ostrove, J. M., and Cole., E. R. (2003) Privileging class: Toward a critical psychology of social class in the context of education. *Journal of Social Issues*, 59(4), 677–692.

Owens, T. J. (2003) Self and identity. In J. Delamater (ed.), *Handbook of Social Psychology* (pp. 205–32), New York: Kluwer Academic.

Oxford English Dictionary (online version) (2011) Commodification. Retrieved Jan. 2012 from http://www.oed.com/Entry/37198.

Painter, A. (2009) The Washington consensus is dead. *Guardian* (9 April) Retrieved April 2011 from http://www.guardian.co.uk/commentisfree/cifamerica/2009/apr/09/obama-g20-nato-foreign-policy.

Pakulski, J., and Waters, M. (1996) *The Death of Class,* London: Sage.

Pancer, S. M. (1997) Social psychology: The crisis continues. In D. Fox and I. Prilleltensky (eds), *Critical Psychology: An Introduction* (pp. 150–65), Thousand Oaks CA: Sage.

Parker, I. (1989) *The Crisis in Modern Social Psychology – and How to End it,* London: Routledge.

Parker, I. (2007) *Revolution in Psychology: Alienation to Emancipation,* Ann Arbor, MI: Pluto Press.

Parker, I., Georgaca, E., Harper, D., McLaughlin, T., and Stowell-Smith, M. (1995) *Deconstructing Psychopathology,* London: Sage.

Paterson, M. (2006) *Consumption and Everyday Life,* London: Routledge.

Pavia, R. (1998) The constitution of self: The imperatives of interpretation and the loss of sense. *Tempo Social: Revista de Sociologia da USP,* 10(1), 83–104.

Pearce, D., Turner, K., and Bateman, I. (1992) *Environmental Economics: An Elementary Introduction,* London: Financial Times/Prentice Hall.

Pepitone, A. (1981) Lessons from the history of social psychology. *American Psychologist*, 36(9), 972–85.

Perelman, M. (2005) *Manufacturing Discontent: The Trap of Individualism in Corporate Society,* London: Pluto Press.

Peterson, C., and Seligman, M. E. P. (2004) *Character Strengths and Virtues: A Handbook and Classification,* Washington, DC: American Psychological Association.

Pettigrew, T. F. (1981) Extending the stereotype concept. In D. L. Hamilton (ed.), *Cognitive Processes in Stereotyping and Intergroup Behavior* (pp. 303–32), Hillsdale, NJ: Erlbaum.

Pickering, M. (2001) *Stereotyping: The Politics of Representation,* Basingstoke: Palgrave.

Pocock, B., van Wanrooy, B., Strazzari, S., and Bridge, K. (2001) *Fifty Families: What Unreasonable Hours are Doing to Australians, their Families and their Communities*, Sydney: Australian Council of Trade Unions.

Polivy, J., and Herman, C. P. (2004) Sociocultural idealization of thin female body shapes: An introduction to the special issue on body image and eating disorders. *Journal of Social and Clinical Psychology*, 23(1), 1–16.

Ponting, J. (2009) *Consuming Nirvana: The Social Construction of Surfing Tourist Space,* Saarbrucken, Germany: VDM Verlag.

Post, D. (1980) Floyd H Allport and the launching of modern social psychology. *Journal of the History of the Behavioural Sciences*, 16(4), 369–76.

Proshansky, H. M. (1976) Comment on environmental and social psychology. *Personality and Social Psychological Bulletin,* 2(4), 359–63.

Proshansky, H. M. (1981) An environmental psychologist's perspective on the interdisciplinary approach in psychology. In J. H. Harvey (ed.), *Cognition, Social Behavior, and the Environment* (pp. 3–20), Hillsdale, NJ: Lawrence Erlbaum.

Proshansky, H. M., Fabian, A. K., and Kaminoff, R. (1983) Place-identity: Physical world socialization of the self. *Journal of Environmental Psychology,* 3(1), 57–83.

Pugh, A. J. (2004) Windfall child rearing: Low income care and consumption. *Journal of Consumer Culture*, 4(2), 229–49.

Pugh, A. J. (2009) *Longing and Belonging: Parents, Children, and Consumer Culture,* Berkeley, CA: University of California Press.

Putnam, R. D. (1995) Bowling alone: America's declining social capital. *Journal of Democracy*, 6(1), 65–78.

Putnam, R. D. (2001) *Bowling Alone: The Collapse and Revival of American Community,* New York: Simon & Schuster/Touchstone.

Quinn, J. (2008) The shallowest generation. Retrieved Dec. 2008 from http://www.financialsensearchive.com/editorials/quinn/2008/1103.html.

Radner, H. (1997) Producing the body: Jane Fonda and the new public feminine. In P. Sulkunen, J. Holwood, H. Radner and G. Schulze (eds), *Constructing the New Consumer Society* (pp. 108–33), London: Macmillan.

Rappaport, E. D. (2000) 'A new era of shopping': The promotion of women's pleasure in London's west end, 1909–1914. In J. Scanlon (ed.), *The Gender and Consumer Culture Reader* (pp. 30–48), New York: New York University Press.

Read, J. (2009) A genealogy of homo-economicus: Neoliberalism and the production of subjectivity. In S. Binkley and J. Capetillo (eds), *A Foucault for the 21st Century: Governmentality, Biopolitics and Discipline in the New Millennium* (pp. 2–15), Newcastle: Cambridge Scholars Publishing.

Reeves, R. (2003, 29 June) ICM Research-Observer Time Poll, *The Observer*, p. 5.

Reicher, S., and Wetherell, M. (1999) Editorial. *British Journal of Social Psychology,* 38(2), 113–14.

Renner, M. (2006) *State of the World 2005: A Worldwatch Institute Report on Progress toward a Sustainable Society,* New York: W. W. Norton.

Reserve Bank of Australia (2007) Credit and charge card statistics – C1. Retrieved Oct. 2007, http://www.rba.gov.au/Statistics/Bulletin/CO1hist.xls.

Richins, M. (1991) Social comparison and the idealized images of advertising. *Journal of Consumer Research,* 18(1), 71–83.

Richins, M. (1995) Social comparison, advertising, and consumer discontent. *American Behavioral Scientist*, 38(4), 593–607.

Richins, M., and Dawson, S. (1992) Materialism as a consumer value: Measure development and validation. *Journal of Consumer Research*, 19, 303–16.

Riesman, D. (1961a) *The Lonely Crowd: A Study of the Changing American Character,* New Haven, CT: Yale University Press.

Riesman, D. (1961b) The lonely crowd: A reconsideration in 1960. In S. M. Lipset and D. Riesman (eds), *Culture and Social Character: The Work of David Riesman Reviewed* (pp. 419–58), New York: Free Press.

Ring, K. (1967) Some sober questions about frivolous values. *Journal of Experimental Social Psychology*, 3, 113–23.

Riso, L. P., and McBride, C. (2007) Introduction: A return to focus on cognitive schemas. In L. P. Riso, P. L. du Toit, D. J. Stein and J. E. Young (eds), *Cognitive Schemas and Core Beliefs in Psychological Problems: A Scientist-Practitioner Guide* (pp. 3–9), Washington, DC: American Psychological Association.

Ritzer, G. (1995) *Expressing America: A Critique of the Global Credit Card Society,* Newbury Park, CA: Pine Forge.

Ritzer, G. (1998a) Introduction. In J. Baudrillard (ed.), *The Consumer Society* (pp. 1–24), Thousand Oaks, CA: Sage.

Ritzer, G. (1998b) *The McDonaldization Thesis: Explorations and Extensions,* Thousand Oaks, CA: Sage.

Ritzer, G. (2000) *The Mcdonaldization of Society* (5th edn), Thousand Oaks, CA: Pine Forge Press.

Ritzer, G. (2007) *The Globalization of Nothing* (2nd edn), Thousand Oaks, CA: Pine Forge Press.

Ritzer, G. (2009) *Enchanting a Disenchanted World: Continuity and Change in the Cathedrals of Consumption* (3rd edn), Thousand Oaks, CA: Pine Forge Press.

Ritzer, G., and Slater, D. (2001) Editorial. *Journal of Consumer Culture,* 1(1), 5–8.

Ritzer, G., Goodman, D., and Wiedenhoft, W. (2001) Theories of consumption. In G. Ritzer and B. Smart (eds), *Handbook of Social Theory* (pp. 410–26), Thousand Oaks, CA: Sage.

Ritzer, G., Ryan, M., and Stepnisky, J. (2005) Transformations in consumer settings. In S. Ratneshwar and D. G. Mick (eds), *Inside Consumption: Consumer Motives, Goals and Desires* (pp. 292–308), London: Routledge.

Roberts, B. W., and Helson, R. (1997) Changes in culture, changes in personality: The influence of individualism in a longitudinal study of women. *Journal of Personality and Social Psychology*, 72(3), 641–51.

Roberts, M. L. (1998) Gender, consumption and commodity culture. *American Historical Review*, 103(3), 817–44.

Rodaway, P. (1995) Exploring the subject in hyper-reality. In S. Pile and N. Thrift (eds), *Mapping the Subject: Geographies of Cultural Transformation* (pp. 241–66), London: Routledge.

Rogers, M. L. (1999) *Barbie Culture,* London: Sage.

Rogers, S. (2011) Recession blamed for rise in divorce rates. *Guardian Weekly* (16–29 Dec.), p. 17.

Rogers, T. B., Kuiper, N. A., and Kirker, W. S. (1977) Self-reference and the encoding of personal information. *Journal of Personality and Social Psychology*, 35, 677–88.

Rojek, C. (2000) Leisure and the rich today: Veblen's thesis after a century. *Leisure Studies*, 19(1), 1–15.

Rose, N. (1996) *Inventing Our Selves: Psychology, Power, and Personhood,* Cambridge: Cambridge University Press.

Rose, N. (1999) *Governing the Soul: The Shaping of the Private Self* (2nd edn), London: Free Association Books.

Rose, N. (2008) Psychology as a social science. *Subjectivity*, 25(4), 446–62.

Rose, N., and Miller, P. (1990) Governing economic life. *Economy and Society*, 19(1), 1–31.

Rose, N., and Miller, P. (1992) Political power beyond the State: Problematics of government. *British Journal of Sociology*, 43(2), 173–205.

Rosenfeld, P., Giacalone, R. A., and Riordan, C. (1995) *Impression Management in Organizations: Theory, Measurement, Practice,* London: Routledge.

Rouse, J. (2003) Power/knowledge. In G. Gutting (ed.), *The Cambridge Companion to Foucault* (2nd edn, pp. 95–122), Cambridge: Cambridge University Press.

Rudd, K. (2009) The global financial crisis. *The Monthly: Australian Politics, Society and Culture* (Feb.), pp. 20–9.

Sampson, E. E. (1989) The challenge of social change for psychology: Globalization and psychology's theory of the person. *American Psychologist*, 44(6), 914–21.

Sassatelli, R. (2007) *Consumer Culture: History, Theory and Politics,* London: Sage.

Sassatelli, R. (2010) *Fitness Culture: Gyms and the Commercialization of Discipline and Fun,* Basingstoke: Palgrave.

Saukko, P. (2009) A critical discussion of normativity in discourses on eating disorders. In H. Malson and M. Burns (eds), *Critical Feminist Approaches to Eating Dis/Orders* (pp. 63–72), London: Routledge.

Scanlon, J. (2000a) Introduction. In J. Scanlon (ed.), *The Gender and Consumer Culture Reader* (pp. 1–12), New York: New York University Press.

Scanlon, J. (Ed.) (2000b) *The Gender and Consumer Culture Reader,* New York: New York University Press.

Schlosser, E. (2002) *Fast Food Nation: What the All American Meal is Doing to the World,* London: Penguin.

Schmitt, R. (2003) *Alienation and Freedom,* Boulder, CO: Westview Press.

Schor, J. (1991) *The Overworked American: The Unexpected Decline of Leisure,* New York: Basic Books.

Schor, J. (1999) *The Overspent American: Upscaling, Downshifting, and the New Consumer,* New York: Basic Books.

Schor, J. (2004) *Born to Buy: The Commercialised Child and the New Consumer Culture,* New York: Simon & Schuster.

Schor, J. (2007) In defence of consumer critique: Revisiting the consumption debate of the twentieth century. *Annals of the American Academy*, 611, 16–30.

Schor, J. (2008) Sustainable consumption and worktime reduction. *Journal of Industrial Ecology*, 9(1–2), 37–50.

Schwartz, B. (2005) *The Paradox of Choice: Why More is Less,* New York: Harper Perennial.

Sedikides, C., and Gregg, A. P. (2003) Portraits of the self. In M. A. Hogg and J. Cooper (eds), *The Sage Handbook of Social Psychology* (pp. 93–122), London: Sage.

Sedikides, C., and Strube, M. J. (1995) The multiply motivated self. *Personality and Social Psychology Bulletin*, 21(12), 1330–5.

Seiter, E. (1993) *Sold Separately: Children and Parents in Consumer Culture,* New Brunswick, NJ: Rutgers University Press.

Seligman, M. E. P. (2003) *Authentic Happiness: Using the New Positive Psychology to Realize your Potential for Lasting Fulfilment,* Sydney: Random House.

Seligman, M. E. P., and Csikszentmihalyi, M. (2000) Positive psychology: An introduction. *American Psychologist*, 55(1), 5–14.

Sennett, R. (1977) *The Fall of Public Man: On the Social Psychology of Capitalism,* New York: Norton.

Sennett, R. (1998) *The Corrosion of Character: The Personal Consequences of Work in the New Capitalism,* New York: Norton.

Sennett, R. (2006) *The Culture of the New Capitalism,* New Haven, CT: Yale University Press.

Shaikh, A. (2005) The economic mythology of neoliberalism. In A. Saad-Filho and D. Johnston (eds), *Neoliberalism: A Critical Reader* (pp. 41–9), London: Pluto Press.

Shankar, A., Cherrier, H., and Canniford, R. (2006) Consumer empowerment: A Foucauldian interpretation. *European Journal of Marketing*, 40(9/10), 1013–30.

Sherif, M., and Sherif, C. W. (1953) *Groups in Harmony and Tension: An Integration of Studies of Intergroup Relations,* Oxford: Harper & Brothers.

Shields, R. (1992) The individual, consumption cultures and the fate of community. In R. Shields (ed.), *Lifestyle Shopping: The Subject of Consumption* (pp. 99–113), London: Routledge.

Shields, R. (2004) Henri Lefebvre. In P. Hubbard, R. Kitchin and G. Valentine (eds), *Key Thinkers on Space and Place* (pp. 208–13), London: Sage.

Shilling, C. (2003) *The Body and Social Theory* (2nd edn), London: Sage.

Sieff, E. M. (2003) Media frames on mental illnesses: The potential impact of negative frames. *Journal of Mental Health*, 12(3), 259–69.

Silveria, P. (1990) Narcissism: A social symptom. *Tempo Social: Revista de Sociologia da USP*, 2(2), 129–44.

Silverman, I. (1977) Why social psychology fails. *Canadian Psychological Review*, 18, 353–8.

Sim, S. (2004) *Fundamentalist World: The New Dark Age of Dogma,* Duxford: Icon Books.

Simmel, G. (1907/1990) *The Philosophy of Money,* tr. T. Bottomore and D. Frisby, London: Routledge.

Simmel, G. (1950a) The stranger. In K. H. Wolff (ed.), *The Sociology of Georg Simmel* (pp. 402–8), Glen Coe, IL: Free Press.

Simmel, G. (1950b) The metropolis and mental life. In K. H. Wolff (ed.), *The Sociology of Georg Simmel* (pp. 409–24) Glen Coe, IL: Free Press.

Simmel, G. (1991a) Money in modern culture. *Theory, Culture and Society*, 8(3), 17–31.

Simmel, G. (1991b) The problem of style. *Theory, Culture and Society*, 8(3), 63–71.

Simon, D. (2010) Introduction. In R. Alverez (ed.), *The Wire: Truth Be Told* (pp. 1–32), New York: Grove Press.

Sipiora, M. P. (2000) Alienation, the self, and television: Psychological life in mass culture. *The Humanistic Psychologist*, 28(1–3), 181–93.

Slater, D. (1997) *Consumer Culture and Modernity,* Cambridge: Polity Press.

Slater, D. (2005) Consumer culture. In G. Ritzer (ed.), *Encyclopaedia of Social Theory* (vol. 1, pp. 139–45), Thousand Oaks, CA: Sage.

Slater, D., and Tonkiss, F. (2001) *Market Society: Markets and Modern Social Theory,* Cambridge: Polity Press.

Sloan, T. (1997) Theories of personality: Ideology and beyond. In D. Fox and I. Prilleltensky (eds), *Critical Psychology: An Introduction* (pp. 87–103), Thousand Oaks, CA: Sage.

Sloan, T. (ed.) (2000) *Critical Psychology: Voices for Change,* Basingstoke: Palgrave Macmillan.

Sloan, T. (2001) Ideology criticism in theory and practice. *Critical Psychology*, 1, 163–8.

Smail, D. (2001) *The Nature of Unhappiness,* London: Robinson.

Smail, D. (2005) *Power Interest and Psychology: Elements of a Social Materialist Understanding of Distress,* Ross-on-Wye: PCCS.

Smart, B. (2003) *Economy, Culture and Society: A Sociological Critique of Neoliberalism,* Madienhead: Open University Press.

Smart, B. (2010) *Consumer Society: Critical Issues and Environmental Consequences,* London: Sage.

Smith, H. J., and Ortiz, D. J. (2002) Is it just me? The different consequences of personal and group relative deprivation. In I. Walker and H. J. Smith (eds), *Relative Deprivation: Specification, Development, and Integration* (pp. 91–115), Cambridge: Cambridge University Press.

Smith, N. (1992) New city, new frontier: The lower east side as wild wild west. In M. Sorkin (ed.), *Variations on a Theme Park: The New American City and the End of Public Space* (pp. 61–93), New York: Noonday Press.

Smith, N., and Williams, P. (1986) *Gentrification of the City,* Boston, MA: Allen & Unwin.

Snooks, G. D. (2000) *The Global Crisis Makers: An End to Progress and Liberty?,* London: Macmillan.

Snyder, M. (1974) Self-monitoring of expressive behaviour. *Journal of Personality and Social PsychoFlogy*, 30(4), 525–37.

Stedman, R. C. (2002) Toward a social psychology of place: Predicting behavior from place-based cognitions, attitude, and identity. *Environment and Behavior*, 34(5), 561–81.

Steele, C. M. (1988) The psychology of self-affirmation: Sustaining the integrity of the self. In L. Berkowitz (ed.), *Advances in Experimental Social Psychology* (vol. 21, pp. 261–302), New York: Academic Press.

Steele, J. (2000) Reduced to images: American Indians in nineteenth-century advertising. In J. Scanlon (ed.), *The Gender and Consumer Culture Reader* (pp. 109–28), New York: New York University Press.

Steg, L., and Gifford, R. (2008) Social psychology and environmental problems. In L. Steg, A. P. Buunk and T. Rothengatter (eds), *Applied Social Psychology: Understanding and Managing Social Problems* (pp. 184–205), Cambridge: Cambridge University Press.

Steg, L., and Rothengatter, T. (2008) Introduction to applied social psychology. In L. Steg, A. P. Buunk and T. Rothengatter (eds), *Applied Social Psychology: Understanding and Managing Social Problems* (pp. 1–27), Cambridge: Cambridge University Press.

Steger, M. B., and Roy, R. K. (2010) *Neoliberalism: A Very Short Introduction,* New York: Oxford University Press.

Stevenson, N. (2002) Consumer culture, ecology and the possibility of cosmopolitan citizenship *Consumption, Markets and Culture*, 5(4), 305–19.

Stole, I. (2003) Televised consumption: Women, advertisers and the early daytime television industry. *Consumption, Markets and Culture*, 6(1), 65–80.

Storper, M. (2001) Lived effects of the contemporary economy: Globalization, inequality, and consumer society. In J. Comaroff and J. L. Comaroff (eds), *Millennial Capitalism and the Culture of Neoliberalism* (pp. 88–124), Durham NC: Duke University Press.

Strauman, T. J., Costanzo, P. R., Jones, N. P., McLean, A. N., and Merrill, K. A. (2007) Contributions of social psychology to clinical psychology: Three views of a research frontier. In A. W. E. H. Kruglanski and E. Tory (eds), *Social Psychology: Handbook of Basic Principles* (2nd edn, pp. 850–68), New York: Guilford Press.

Strauman, T. J., McCrudden, M. C., and Jones, N. P. (2010) Self-regulation and psychopathology: Toward an integrative perspective. In J. E. Maddux and J. P. Tangney (eds), *Social Psychological Foundations of Clinical Psychology* (pp. 84–113), New York: Guilford Press.

Strazdins, L., D'Souza, R. M., Lim, L. Y., Broom, D. H., and Rodgers, B. (2004) Job strain, job insecurity, and health: Rethinking the relationship. *Journal of Occupational Health Psychology*, 9(4), 296–305.

Stryker, S., and Burke, P. J. (2000) The past, present, and future of identity theory. *Social Psychology Quarterly*, 63(4), 284–97.

Sulkunen, P. (1997) Introduction: The new consumer society – rethinking the social bond. In P. Sulkunen, J. Holwood, H. Radner and G. Schulze (eds), *Constructing the New Consumer Society* (pp. 1–18) London: Macmillan.

Sulkunen, P. (2009) *The Saturated Society: Governing Risk and Lifestyles in Consumer Culture,* London: Sage.

Sulkunen, P., Holwood, J., Radner, H., and Schulze, G. (eds) (1997) *Constructing the New Consumer Society,* London: Macmillan.

Suls, J., Martin, R., and David, J. P. (1998) Person–environment fit and its limits: Agreeableness, neuroticism, and emotional reactivity to interpersonal conflict. *Personality and Social Psychology Bulletin*, 24(1), 88–98.

Suls, J., Martin, R., and Wheeler, L. (2002) Social comparison: Why, with whom and with what effect? *Current Directions in Psychological Science*, 11(5), 159–63.

Sussman, W. I. (1984) *Culture as History: The Transformation of American Society in the Twentieth Century*, New York: Random House.

Suzuki, D. (2003) Consumer culture no accident. Posted in *Science Matters*, retrieved Dec. 2011 from http://www.davidsuzuki.org.

Tafjel, H. (1969) Cognitive aspects of prejudice. *Journal of Social Issues*, 25(4), 79–97.

Tajfel, H. (1970) Experiments in intergroup discrimination. *Scientific American*, 223, 96–102.

Tajfel, H. (1974) Social identity and intergroup behaviour. *Social Science Information*, 13, 65–93.

Tafjel, H., and Turner, J. C. (1986) The social identity theory of inter-group behaviour. In S. Worchel and L. W. Austin (eds), *Psychology of Intergroup Relations* (pp. 7–24), Monterey, CA: Brooks/Cole.

Tafjel, H., Billig, M., Bundy, R., and Flament, C. (1971) Social categorization and intergroup behaviour. *European Journal of Social Psychology*, 1, 149–78.

Talwar, J. P. (2002) *Fast Food, Fast Track: Immigrants, Big Business and the American Dream,* Boulder, CO: Westview.

Tangney, J. P., and Salovey, P. (2010) Emotions of the imperilled ego: Shame, guilt, jealousy, and envy. In J. E. Maddux and J. P. Tangney (eds), *Social Psychological Foundations of Clinical Psychology* (pp. 245–71), New York: Guilford Press.

Taylor, C. R., Lee, J. Y., and Stern, B. B. (1995) Portrayals of African, Hispanic, and Asian Americans in magazine advertising. *American Behavioral Scientist*, 38(4), 608–21.

Tennen, H., and Affleck, G. (1993) The puzzles of self-esteem: A clinical perspective. In R. F. Baumeister (ed.), *Self-Esteem: The Puzzle of Low Self-Regard* (pp. 241–62), New York: Plenum.

Teo, T. (2009) Philosophical concerns in critical psychology. In D. Fox, I. Prilleltensky and S. Austin (eds), *Critical Psychology: An Introduction* (pp. 36–53), London: Sage.

Terkenli, T. S. (2002) Landscapes of tourism: Towards a global cultural economy of space. *Tourism Geographies*, 4(3), 227–54.

Thoits, P. A. (1991) On merging identity theory and stress research. *Social Psychology Quarterly*, 54(2), 101–12.

Thompson, C. J., and Hirschman, E. C. (1995) Understanding the socialized body: A poststructuralist analysis of consumers' self-conceptions, body images, and self-care practices. *Journal of Consumer Research*, 22(2), 139–53.

Thompson, J. K., Coovert, M. D., and Stormer, S. M. (1999) Body image, social comparison, and eating disturbance: A covariance structure modelling investigation. *International Journal of Eating Disorders*, 26(1), 43–51.

Thomson, A. (2009) *Erich Fromm,* Basingstoke: Palgrave Macmillan.

Thorne, B. M., and Henley, T. B. (2005) *Connections in the History and Systems of Psychology* (3rd edn), Boston, MA: Houghton Mifflin.

Tomlinson, J. (1990) *Hayek and the Market,* Sydney: Pluto Press.

Trentmann, F. (2007) Citizenship and consumption. *Journal of Consumer Culture*, 7(2), 147–58.

Trifonas, P., and Balomenos, E. (2003) *Good Taste: How What You Choose Defines Who You Are,* Duxford: Icon Books.

Tuffin, K. (2004) *Understanding Critical Social Psychology,* London: Sage.

Tuffin, K., Morgan, M., Frewin, K., and Jardine, A. (2000) Economic rationalism in action. *New Zealand Journal of Psychology*, 29(1), 30–6.

Turner, J. C., Hogg, M. A., Oakes, P. J., Reicher, S. D., and Wetherell, M. S. (1987) *Rediscovering the Social Group: A Self-Categorization Theory,* Oxford: Blackwell.

Twenge, J. M., and Campbell, W. K. (2010) *The Narcissism Epidemic: Living in the Age of Entitlement,* New York: Free Press.

Tyler, T. R., and Lind, E. A. (2002) Understanding the nature of fraternalistic deprivation. In I. Walker and H. J. Smith (eds), *Relative Deprivation: Specification, Development, and Integration* (pp. 44–68), Cambridge: Cambridge University Press.

Tyler, T. R., and Smith, H. J. (1998) Social justice and social movements. In D. T. Gilbert, S. T. Fiske and G. Lindzey (eds), *Handbook of Social Psychology* (4th edn, vol. 2, pp. 595–629), New York: McGraw-Hill.

Urry, J. (1995) *Consuming Places,* London: Routledge.

Urry, J. (2010) Consuming the planet to excess. *Theory, Culture and Society*, 27(2–3), 191–212.

US Department of Justice. (2011) *Correctional Population in the United States, 2010*, Washington, DC: US Department of Justice.

Ussher, J. M. (1989) *The Psychology of the Female Body,* London: Routledge.

Uusitalo, L. (1998) Consumption in postmodernity: Social structuration and the construction of the self. In M. Bianchi (ed.), *The Active Consumer: Novelty and Surprise in Consumer Choice* (pp. 215–35), London: Routledge.

Uzzell, D. (2010) Collective solutions to a global problem. *The Psychologist,* 23(11), 880–3.

van der Pilgt, J. (1996) Social psychology and environmental issues. In G. R. Semin and K. Fiedler (eds), *Applied Social Psychology* (pp. 173–97), London: Sage.

van Horn, J. E., Schaufeli, W. B., and Tarvis, T. W. (2001) Lack of reciprocity among Dutch teachers: Validation of reciprocity and the relation to stress and well-being. *Work and Stress*, 15(3), 199–213.

Varman, R., and Vikas, R. M. (2007) Freedom and consumption: Toward conceptualizing systemic constraints for subaltern consumers in a capitalist society *Consumption, Markets and Culture*, 10(2), 117–31.

Vazire, S., and Funder, D. C. (2006) Impulsivity and the self-defeating behavior of narcissists. *Personality and Social Psychology Review,* 10(2), 154–65.

Veblen, T. (1899/1994) *The Theory of the Leisure Class: An Economic Study of Institutions,* New York: Penguin Classics.

Voyce, M. (2006) Shopping malls in Australia: The end of public space and the rise of 'consumerist citizenship'? *Journal of Sociology*, 42(3), 269–86.

Waerdahl, R. (2005) May be I'll need a pair of Levi's before junior high? Child youth trajectories and anticipatory socialization. *Childhood*, 12(2), 201–19.

Wahl, O. F. (1992) Mass media images of mental illness: A review of the literature. *Journal of Community Psychology*, 20(4), 343–52.

Wahl, O. F. (1995) *Medic Madness: Public Images of Mental Illness,* New Brunswick, NJ: Rutgers University Press.

Wang, J. (2005) Work stress as a risk factor for major depressive episode. *Psychological Medicine*, 35(6), 865–71.

Warde, A. (1997) *Consumption, Food and Taste: Culinary Antinomies and Commodity Culture,* London: Sage.

Warde, I. (2011) Higher finance. *Le Monde Diplomatique* (English edn, Sept.), pp. 4–5.

Wearing, B., and Wearing, S. (1992) Identity and the commodification of leisure. *Leisure Studies,* 11, 3–18.

Wearing, S., and McDonald, M. (2004) Commodification. In J. Jenkins and J. Pigram (eds), *The Encyclopaedia of Leisure and Outdoor Recreation* (pp. 60–1), London: Routledge.

Wearing, S., and Wearing, B. (2000) Smoking as a fashion accessory in the 1990s: Conspicuous consumer, identity and adolescent women's leisure choices. *Leisure Studies,* 19, 45–58.

Wearing, S., McDonald, M., and Wearing, M. (in press) Consumer culture, the mobilisation of the narcissistic self, and adolescent deviant leisure. *Leisure Studies.*

Wheeler, L. (2000) Individual differences in social comparison. In J. Suls and L. Wheeler (eds), *Handbook of Social Comparison: Theory and Research* (pp. 141–58), New York: Kluwer/Plenum.

Wheelock, J. (1999a) Fear or opportunity? Insecurity in employment. In M. Hill, J. Vail and J. Wheelock (eds), *Insecure Times. Living with Insecurity in Modern Society* (pp. 77–90), London: Routledge.

Wheelock, J. (1999b) Who dreams of failure? Insecurity in modern capitalism. In M. Hill, J. Vail and J. Wheelock (eds), *Insecure Times: Living with Insecurity in Modern Society* (pp. 23–40), London: Routledge.

White, G. D. (2004) Political apathy disorder: Proposal for a new DSM diagnostic category. *Journal of Humanistic Psychology,* 44(1), 47–57.

Wickham, G. (1997) Governance of consumption. In P. Sulkunen, J. Holwood, H. Radner and G. Schulze (eds), *Constructing the New Consumer Society* (pp. 277–92), London: Macmillan.

Wilkinson, R. G. (2005) *The Impact of Inequality: How to Make Sick Societies Healthier,* New York: New Press.

Williams, R. (1970) *American Society,* New York: Knopf.

Williams, S. J., and Bendelow, G. (1998) *The Lived Body: Sociological Themes, Embodied Issues,* London: Routledge.

Wilson, N. (2003) *Britain's Rising Personal Debt,* Leeds: Credit Management Research Centre, Leeds University Business School.

Wolsko, C. (2012) Transcribing and transcending the ego: Reflections on the phenomenology of chronic social comparison. *Journal of Humanistic Psychology,* 52(3), 321–49.

Wood, J. V., and Lockwood, P. (2000) Social comparisons in dysphoric and low self-esteem people. In R. M. Kowalski and M. R. Leary (eds), *The Social Psychology of Emotional and Behavioral Problems: Interfaces of Social and Clinical Psychology* (pp. 97–135), Washington, DC: American Psychological Association.

Wykes, M., and Gunter, B. (2005) *The Media and Body Image: If Looks Could Kill,* Thousand Oaks, CA: Sage.

Yergin, D., and Stanislaw, J. (2002) *The Commanding Heights: The Battle for the World Economy,* New York: Simon & Schuster.

Zieleniec, A. (2007) *Space and Social Theory,* London: Sage.

Zukin, S. (1991) *Landscapes of Power: From Detroit to Disney World,* Berkeley, CA: University of California Press.

Index

public space 101; and social control
31
person–environmental interaction 98–100;
person–environment fit theory 98, 100,
112, 124–5
persuasion 4, 65, 114 *see also* advertising
Pickering, M. 76, 84–5, 122
political cynicism 54
political economy 2 *see also* economics;
economy; capitalist *see* capitalism;
consumer led recoveries 7; free market
12–18; neoliberal *see* neoliberalism
pollution 11, 77, 114, 115, 119
possible selves 44–5
postindustrial society 34, 40
postmodern society 34, 129n5
poststructural theories of consumer culture
28–33, 120
post-traumatic stress disorder 70
poverty 17, 52, 56, 66, 88–9, 116; rich–
poor gap 87, 89, 132nn6–7
power *see also* disempowerment:
exercised through seduction 36, 40;
power/knowledge (Foucault) 28, 29,
35, 36, 66; relations 37, 39, 60, 91
predisposition, inherent/genetic 49, 57,
75, 122, 126
prejudice 38, 50, 65, 74–5, 84, 95, 111,
112, 113 *see also* exclusion
private security firms 111, 126
privatisation: of council housing 110; of
public space 102, 111, 112
producer society 36, 85
production: in capitalism 38; mechanisms
11, 36; social change to consumption
from 10–11, 21–4, 31, 36, 55, 97;
social psychology's focus on 1; spaces
101
Protestant work ethic 10, 79; view of
consumption and leisure 1
psychoanalysis 4, 26, 42, 121
psychological pauperisation 56
psychology: abnormal 5, 69–70, 94–5,
123; ambivalence towards social
policy/criticism 5–6; clinical 5, 69–70,
94–5; cognitive 43, 70; collusion with
consumerism and advertising 3–5;
community 5, 118; consumer 1–2,
3; critical 5, 85, 118 *see also* critical
social psychology; discursive 5, 118;
humanistic 5, 118, 131n2; social *see*
social psychology; and social change
5, 98
psychopathology 5, 70, 71, 95

public policy/legislation 2, 17–18, 82,
116, 117–18, 127; social policy 2, 5–6,
16, 118, 119
public relations 4, 18, 77, 119
public space *see* space
Pugh, A. J. 58
Putnam, R. D. 86, 102

rationality 8, 11, 14, 15, 16, 65–6,
82, 83, 84, 87, 117; neoliberal *see*
neoliberalism; rational self-regulation
see self-regulation
Read, J. 29, 56
Reagan, R. 14, 120
'reality television' 131–2n5
Reeves, R. 79
reflexivity: institutional 83; and self-
identity 34, 35–6, 40, 48, 53, 65, 121,
122
relative deprivation 72, 75, 89–90
Richins, M. L. 78
rich–poor gap 87, 89, 132nn6–7
risk 17, 66, 82, 94, 110, 121
Ritzer, G. 8, 9, 31, 33, 52, 83, 85, 102–3,
104–5, 106, 108, 109; *et al.* 8, 10, 119;
and Slater, D. 15
Robbers Cave State Park experiments 75
Roberts, B. W. and Helson, R. 130n6
Roberts, M. L. 39
Rodaway, P. 104
Rogers, T. B. *et al.* 44
Rojek, C. 26
Rose, N. 66
Rudd, K. 129n12

Sahlins, M. 56
Sampson, E. E. 106
Sandel, M. 106
Sane Society, The (Ingleby) 26
Sassatelli, R. 91, 110
Scanlon, J. 61, 130n8
schemas 44–5, 70; body schemas 93
Schor, J. 9, 79
Scott, W. D. 3–4, 77, 119
security firms 111, 126
Sedikides, C. and Strube, M. J. 46
seduction 36, 66, 104, 109, 125; power
exercised through 36, 40
self-actualisation 77
self-affirmation 46, 51
self-categorisation 65
self-comparison *see* social comparison
self-concept 44, 45, 46, 65, 70, 74;
fragmentation 107